BY ANDREW YANG

Forward

The War on Normal People

Smart People Should Build Things

FORWARD

FORWARD

*Notes on the Future
of Our Democracy*

ANDREW YANG

CROWN
NEW YORK

Published in the United States by Crown, an imprint of Random House,
a division of Penguin Random House LLC, New York.

CROWN and the Crown colophon are registered trademarks of
Penguin Random House LLC.

Photograph on page 191 is courtesy of the
Barack Obama Presidential Library.

Library of Congress Cataloging-in-Publication Data
Names: Yang, Andrew, author.
Title: Forward / Andrew Yang.
Description: First edition. | New York: Crown, [2021] |
Includes bibliographical references and index.
Identifiers: LCCN 2021029712 (print) | LCCN 2021029713 (ebook) |
ISBN 9780593238653 (hardcover) | ISBN 9780593238660 (ebook)
Subjects: LCSH: Yang, Andrew, 1975- | Politicians—United States—
Biography. | Asian American businesspeople—Biography. |
Taiwanese Americans—Biography. | Presidents—United States—
Election—2020. | Political campaigns—United States—History—
21st century. | United States—Politics and government—2017-2021. |
United States—Economic conditions—2009-
Classification: LCC E901.1.Y36 A3 2021 (print) |
LCC E901.1.Y36 (ebook) | DDC 324.2092 [B]—dc23
LC record available at lccn.loc.gov/2021029712
LC ebook record available at lccn.loc.gov/2021029713

PRINTED IN THE UNITED STATES OF AMERICA ON ACID-FREE PAPER

crownpublishing.com

2 4 6 8 9 7 5 3 1

First Edition

To everyone who supported my presidential and mayoral campaigns, thank you. I see you and appreciate you. I aspire to live up to your support every single day. We are only getting started.

CONTENTS

PART III: FORWARD

DEMOCRACY BY A THREAD

*W*hy isn't it working?

That's a question millions of Americans have been asking about our country. For some time now, many of us have had this growing sense that our way of life and the shared beliefs and expectations that underpin our democracy have become endangered.

We sense that, somewhere along the way, the machinery of our democracy started faltering—and now it is failing.

Politicians tell us to vote and volunteer and endlessly beg us for donations. Many of us do these things. But it's not doing the trick.

Despite doing all the "right things," many of us are struggling more than our parents or grandparents did to gain a foothold in the middle class. The digital gadgets in our pockets keep becoming more sophisticated, but our basic ability to distinguish truth from fiction is eroding. We can no longer assume that fundamental functions of American democracy, like the smooth counting of votes on Election Day or the ability of Congress to pass laws, will occur. Some of us have stopped believing in science, while others have simply come to doubt the possibility that brighter days lie ahead. The unprecedented disruption of the COVID-19 pandemic laid our anxieties bare. Unity and consensus seem like fading dreams.

Many of us were surprised and horrified at the ascent of Donald Trump, and yet we sense, on some level, that the aggrieved mistrust and political anger he tapped into were real and will continue to exist long after he's gone. As I write this, there is a Democratic majority in D.C. with the slimmest conceivable margins, with Vice President Kamala Harris's tie-breaking vote in the Senate necessary to get anything done. Democracy hangs by a thread.

How did it come to this?

What happened to our belief in the future?

And, most important, what can we do about it?

I WROTE THE initial drafts of the chapters that became this book in a feverish stretch in the months following the end of my presidential campaign. I wanted to capture my experiences and what I learned while it was fresh in my mind, and I poured thousands of words a week onto my computer. Even with my presidential campaign over, my sense of urgency remained about the problems we face. Some of these were specific lessons from the campaign trail, like the perverse dance between presidential candidates and the media. Others reflect beliefs I've come to hold based on reading, interviews, and working with activists who have spent years trying to sustain our democracy. These initial bits of writing were like a series of mini-essays about the cascading, interrelated set of problems that are growing within our political process and way of governing. Over several drafts, which I completed in early 2021, I shaped these raw writings into proper chapters, stitching them together to form the tapestry of arguments you see here. I hope this book will inspire the same kind of deep reflection in you as my experiences over the past few years inspired in me.

My last book, *The War on Normal People,* was about the ongoing dehumanization of our economy and the need to adopt universal basic income (UBI) and how it offers us the best chance to evolve to the next stage of capitalism. That is probably how you first heard about me: as the 2020 presidential candidate who wanted to give everyone money.

The War on Normal People had a powerful but narrow goal: to address the crisis in our economy by promoting universal basic income. That book was published in the spring of 2018, just as I was beginning to campaign for the 2020 Democratic nomination. Three and a half years later, I still have the same vision and concerns. If anything, the intervening years have reinforced my convictions about the perilous state of our economy and our democracy. But my perspective on what ails us and my vision for the future have also deepened and advanced based on what I've learned running for office. I now have a better sense of the challenges to our democratic process. Some of the warning signs of the health of our democracy are flashing red, while others lie hidden, like a bit of faulty wiring, waiting to blow.

This book reflects these advances in my thinking. Compared with *The War on Normal People,* the scope here is broader, the insights (I hope) are more nuanced, and yet the ultimate theme remains much the same: our economic and political order is facing unprecedented dangers, many of them brought on by new technologies, and only bold new leadership and policies have a chance to overcome decades of political dysfunction and leaders who are rewarded regardless of whether they rise to the challenge.

I've spent the lion's share of the past four years on the move— talking to Americans, listening to their problems, and, through my organization, Humanity Forward, promoting cash relief and experimenting with it at the local level.

In addition to free money, the other thing you might have heard about me is that I'm a solutions guy. And after thousands of hours spent talking to my fellow citizens and thinking of the future, I have a sense of how we can put ourselves back on the path to prosperity.

This book is the road map. It's about how to make that vision— and, by extension, any actual lasting change on a national scale—a reality. Not in the abstract, but for real. I've found the necessary lever, and I'm eager to share it with you.

. . .

IN WRITING, I had three primary goals, which are reflected in the book's three-part structure. The first is to share my story of running for president, and not because I'm interested in recent history. I'm sharing it because I learned some useful lessons from it, particularly about the media and the way information spreads today, as well as the misaligned system of incentives underlying how we campaign for elected positions in this country. When I started my campaign for president, no one had any idea who I was. When I announced my run, I was regarded as more of an anonymous oddity or novelty than a viable contender. I eventually found myself onstage in front of tens of millions of viewers debating politicians who had been in the public eye for decades, grooming themselves for their moment for a generation or more.

Somehow, it worked—at least for a while. Hundreds of thousands of Americans got behind me and donated to my campaign—thank you—and thousands dropped everything to campaign or volunteer in Iowa and New Hampshire and around the country. My organization, Humanity Forward, grew to a mailing list of more than a million Americans who support a movement to humanize our economy. How did this happen? I believe my experiences can inform how we can better activate people, grow movements, and improve our own lives.

There are millions of good ideas out there that never make it into the real world. I ran for president on more than 180 policies, from improving mental health to modernizing economic measures to fighting for data rights. My campaign wasn't successful—I'm not the president obviously—but most people agree that we succeeded in putting universal basic income, once considered a quixotic idea, onto the national political radar. Today 55 percent of Americans agree that we should pass universal basic income. It is more mainstream and popular than ever. Dozens of mayors, everywhere from Los Angeles to St. Paul to Atlanta to Newark, are adopting it.

So now the majority of Americans are for it, problem solved, right? Unfortunately, no.

My second goal with this book is to lay out some of the forces that are holding us back. These forces go far beyond the broken economy I highlighted in my last book. We are witnessing a cascade of crises, from a pandemic to a punitive economy to police brutality to the selling of our attention and digital data to the highest bidders. Our democratic institutions are faltering right and left, and our systems are not designed for speed or significant change. Trust is fading. Democracy itself is losing legitimacy. Our political system is a fixed duopoly that will want to move slowly, if at all. Our leaders are rewarded based not on solving problems but on accruing resources and retaining office. Media companies have their own set of incentives that lead them to operate on a different wavelength from most of the American people. Local news is dying. And social media is driving our everyday discourse and our mental health to volatile extremes. These are all crises, and they are all linked in ways we will unpack in the pages ahead.

My third goal in writing is to present a set of key structural reforms that will give us a fighting chance of coming back from the brink. Thinkers I admire like Katherine Gehl, Michael Porter, and Ezra Klein have made this observation: those who believe that our politics are broken are wrong. Politics is functioning exactly as our structural incentives demand. The problem is that those demands have nothing to do with improving our lives; more often than not, people get rewarded more for keeping a problem around than for solving it.

Klein, who spent fifteen years in Washington, D.C., as a political reporter, powerfully summarized this tendency in his book *Why We're Polarized:*

> We collapse systemic problems into personalized narratives . . .
> We try to fix the system by changing the people who run it, only
> to find that they become part of the system, too . . . Every few
> years, a new crop of politicians emerges promising . . . to govern
> on behalf of the people . . . And then the clock ticks forward, the

insurgents become the establishment, public disillusionment sets in, . . . and we start again. This cycle is a tributary feeding into the country's political rage—it is maddening to keep trying to fix a problem that only seems to get worse.

He is right. Putting people—however well-intentioned—into a corruptive system of personal and political incentives produces nothing but dysfunction and disillusionment.

How do we change that? The key is to change legislative incentives and accountability to align with how the vast majority of us are doing, and reward legislators for doing the right thing by voters. Right now, members of Congress have a reelection rate of about 90 percent, while Congress's approval rating hovers around 21 percent. Their incentives rest on placating the most extreme 20 percent of their constituents who actually vote in party primaries, which makes it easier to blame the other side. This is an enormous reason why polarization is rising and little good is happening.

I really like and admire a lot of the people in Congress I have met. The best of them are sick and tired of not getting enough done.

Whereas my last book focused on one central policy proposal, universal basic income, this book will present a small menu of important structural solutions, and we should push for all of them. One of them, electoral reform that establishes ranked-choice voting and open primaries across the country, I consider paramount. These electoral reforms are the skeleton key that will realign our leaders' political incentives and make so much else possible.

With ranked-choice voting, candidates would need to achieve majority support from all the voters in their district and not just the party primary voters. The duopoly would diminish in both power and intensity. Voters could express their preferences without fear of "wasting" their vote. Negative campaigning would be discouraged. Real third parties would emerge. This change along with public campaign financing would give us a chance at real reform and make our politics much more dynamic, responsive, and accountable. Then—and only then—will sustained change be possible.

A TRAIT THAT the proposals in this book share is that, at the end of the day, none of them is so complex or difficult to understand. They will help things work better. But they aren't in the interest of many politicians who have become accustomed to succeeding within the current system, and so they aren't solutions that you tend to hear much about from current elected officials or the media. There isn't an interest group fighting for them aside from the American people ourselves. The same was true for universal basic income.

I know, the plumbing of democracy is not sexy. But fixing things is sexy. I'm a problem solver pursuing solutions, and I now believe that no long-term solutions will happen with our current political structures and incentives. Innovation is required. The same way that my name is now associated with universal basic income, it will soon be associated with ranked-choice voting and open primaries around the country as the lever that will enable dramatic new approaches. Ranked-choice voting will be the crucial change that unlocks us from stasis and polarization.

Imagine being able to vote for whomever you like and having real choices, and then being able to rank a second or third candidate whom you also find appealing. This simple and fundamental change would be transformative for both the types of people elected and their incentives once they are in office. It's a modernization of our voting process that is long overdue.

The lights may be flickering, but the power isn't out—yet. There is no reason for us to accept a future that we don't want. We still have the capacity to build one to be excited about for ourselves and our families. But it is only possible if we have a clear vision as to what the obstacles are and then fight like mad to clear them.

I'm going to begin by unpacking what it's actually like to run for president. Let's get started.

PART I

TRYING TO CHANGE THE WORLD

CHAPTER 1

A WINDING PATH TO CENTER STAGE

O n July 31, 2019, I was backstage in the Fox Theatre in Detroit for the second presidential debate of the Democratic primaries. It was a hot summer day outside, but the theater was thoroughly air-conditioned and cool.

"Candidates, take your places," a producer instructed. We lined up at opposite ends of the stage, five candidates on each side. I was right behind Kamala Harris, who had shot to the top of the field thanks to her confrontation with Joe Biden in the previous debate. I was glad to be second from the front as opposed to being consigned to the edge of the stage, like New York's mayor, Bill de Blasio, whose six-foot-five frame was like a bookend to the row of candidates. There was a hierarchy to the line that got reinforced in various ways.

As we waited, Kamala turned to me and smiled. "Hey, Andrew. Can you do me a favor and hold this handkerchief for me? I don't have any pockets."

"Sure thing," I responded. It felt good to be useful. It also felt good to have a normal conversation right before going onstage, where our statements and gestures would be picked apart by millions of viewers around the country. I took the handkerchief from Kamala and slipped it in my left jacket pocket.

"Okay, it's starting. Go out when you hear your name called," said the producer, an efficient woman with a headset. "Good luck out there."

A booming voice filled the theater, over a soundtrack of intro music. "An enthusiastic audience at the historic Fox Theatre in downtown Detroit, Michigan. Welcome to our viewers in the United States and around the world . . . this is the CNN Democratic presidential debate." There was a whoosh of red, white, and blue graphics on the video screen at the back of the stage. "Please welcome, from Delaware, former Vice President Joe Biden." Joe came walking out onstage from the opposite side to loud applause.

"From California, Senator Kamala Harris." I watched as Kamala strode out onstage, waving and smiling, before greeting Joe. Next up was Senator Cory Booker, and then my name was called. "Businessman Andrew Yang." Always *businessman*. I made my way quickly across the stage, to relatively modest applause, shaking Kamala's hand, and then Joe's, and then Cory's before settling in my spot.

I was the fourth candidate out of ten to come onstage, so there was a bit of a wait. Through the blinding stage lights, I gazed out into the crowd and tried to make out any familiar faces. I had been told where my cheering section would be sitting but didn't recognize anyone. I waved to no one in particular. Two dozen photographers came out and took pictures, while we ignored them, smiling at the sea of blurred faces.

As soon as the photographers started to disperse, we all turned and assumed our places at our assigned lecterns. I took big steps, taking care not to trip on the elevated stage. I looked at the notepad on my lectern and the glass of water on a hidden shelf behind it. I tore the first page off the notepad so I would have at least two visible sheets of surface area. I wrote the first few words of my prepared sixty-second closing on the first sheet as a reminder, as well as some talking points and notes from my team. "Smile. Pause. Pivot." The second sheet I would use to take notes on other people's answers as new subjects came up.

I reached into my jacket pocket and took out the handkerchief and gave it back to Kamala, who was to my immediate right.

She took it gratefully. "Thank you, pal." She began writing notes on her own notepad.

One of the three moderators, Jake Tapper, started to read instructions. I knew the chances of my getting the first question were zero. I took a breath to calm myself. I was back on the debate stage, thanks to thousands of Americans getting behind me. Would it be for the final time? I wondered. My poll numbers would need to rise for me to qualify for the next one. I was determined to make the most of the opportunity to speak to the country and state my case for humanizing the economy. If it was my last chance, I'd make it count.

FAST-FORWARD TO September 30, 2019. It's been more than eight weeks since the debate in Detroit, and defying the prognostications of just about everyone, I was still in the race.

Since the Detroit debate, our rallies had gotten bigger and bigger. A few days later, I would announce that the campaign had raised more than $10 million in the third quarter, more than triple what I'd brought in for the previous one. Now I found myself backstage in a very different setting—getting ready for a rally in MacArthur Park in downtown Los Angeles. This time the greenroom was a concrete room in the park's facilities. As I waited for the rally to begin, I was picking at some snacks that the team laid out for me—SkinnyPop, Honest Tea, barkTHINS with almonds, and fruit. A crowd of thousands was outside cheering and chanting, getting fired up by the opening act, my friend the rapper MC Jin.

There were plenty of things to feel good about. We had just raised $10 million in the third quarter in increments of just $35. New supporters joined the campaign every day. Anytime I went out in public, I got recognized and people would yell, "Go get 'em!" The energy around the campaign was palpable.

My campaign manager, Zach Graumann, briefed me about the

event as a camera crew looked on, projecting a combination of efficiency and encouragement. "Okay, you're on after Brian Yang, the actor and producer who is going to introduce you after speeches from local supporters. We had four thousand RSVPs on Facebook and anticipate close to double that in turnout . . . You're allowed to curse tonight, but don't go too crazy, as national media outlets are here to cover you. After the event you've got to give two minutes to the *L.A. Times* reporter writing a profile on you, and give some time for the local news in a press gaggle. You don't have time for selfies or we'll miss our flight to Iowa, so just sign autographs and shake hands from the stage down to the crowd and we'll pull you out when it's time."

I nodded, listening while stretching and starting to hop up and down. I could hear the crowd shouting just a couple dozen feet away.

"You ready?" Zach said. "Game time. You were born for this." He punched my chest. I headed out into the night, with a pair of burly security guards flanking me as I exited the holding room.

Outside the door, I looked up, marveling at the clear sky overhead. It was a beautiful night in Los Angeles. For a split second, I allowed myself to pause and imagine the lives of the people who came to see me who were gathered outside. What inspired them to take a night away from their jobs, or relaxing on the couch after a long day, to come here? What does it take to bring someone out—to give them renewed hope for a better future? I tried to put myself in their shoes, to get myself both balanced and pumped up.

I had a couple rules for these events: be true to myself and try to have fun. I wanted people who came to feel that I was really there, that I wasn't giving a stump speech that they could just watch online. In the best cases, I would feed off their energy and channel it back to them, and there was a real sense of communion. I felt like a rock star or pro wrestler waiting to get out in front of thousands of fans. It charged me up and gave me a sense of joy.

From the stage, I heard my cue. "Ladies and gentlemen, it is my

Yang campaign rally in Los Angeles, September 30, 2019

pleasure to introduce . . . the next president of the United States, ANNN-DREEEW YAAAANGG!"

Mark Morrison's "Return of the Mack," my campaign theme song that captured the tone and energy of the campaign, started blasting from the towering rock-concert-quality speakers mounted on both sides of the stage. I strode onstage. Fireworks and pyrotechnics blasted to my left and right. As far as the eye could see, thousands of people stood and cheered; the official count later would peg the turnout at seven thousand. Close to the stage I could see "MATH" signs, legions of blue "MATH" caps, banners reading "YANG GANG," and oversized pictures of my face rendered as a bitmoji and cardboard $1,000 bills.

"Helloooo, Los Angeles!" I yelled to the crowd. "How beautiful are you? You don't look like the internet to me!" Every statement brought a roar from the crowd.

Then I launched into my routine, giving a thirty-minute speech about how Trump was not the cause but the symptom of a disease that had been building up for years. How jobs were getting automated away in massive numbers. How the Washington establishment's halfhearted attempts to retrain America's workforce weren't working and no one cared. How gross domestic product (GDP), the measure around which so many decisions were made, was useless and didn't measure the kind of work my wife did every day. How a freedom dividend of $1,000 a month would be the best thing we could do for our families. How I was going to be the first president to use PowerPoint at the State of the Union.

"POWER-POINT! POWER-POINT!" they chanted. They knew me well.

I called out the fact that I was one of the only candidates in the field that 10 percent or more of Donald Trump voters said they would vote for in the general election. "They're looking around the field and asking, 'Who can beat Donald Trump?' 'Who can beat Donald Trump?'"

The crowd started chanting, "YANG BEATS TRUMP! YANG BEATS TRUMP!"

I laughed. "That's right, Yang does beat Trump! It's like a game of rock-paper-scissors. And if Donald Trump is the scissors, then I'm the fucking rock!"

The crowd erupted.

I WAS THE last person anyone expected to be on either of these stages. I wasn't a governor or mayor or member of Congress. I grew up the son of Taiwanese immigrants who met in Berkeley, California, as students in the 1960s. My father got his PhD in physics and became an engineer for General Electric and IBM. My mom got her master's in math and statistics and led the computer services department at a local university. I grew up in upstate New York playing Dungeons & Dragons and video games and reading comic books and science fiction.

My parents worked full-time, so when we were young, my brother and I went home with another family after school. Thanks to the Ingrahams and their neighbors the Plunketts, Larry and I learned how to play sports and poker and climb trees. We played "stick fighting"—fighting each other with sticks—and "dirt-bomb fighting," which involved going to a construction site and throwing clods of dirt at each other. Dirt-bomb fighting always ended with someone saying, "There was a rock in that one!" which was against the rules.

I skipped a grade—kindergarten—so as I went through school, I was always smaller and scrawnier than the other kids in my class. As one of the only Asian kids in the school, I took a lot of abuse. I got called "Gook" and "Chink" and "Long Duck Dong," which I didn't understand until I saw *Sixteen Candles.* All I wanted to do was fit in, but that seemed like wishful thinking. I was grateful that my parents had named me Andrew; at least my *name* was half-normal. Gym class was the worst. In softball, the gym teacher stuck me in the outfield with other kids deemed uncoordinated. Of course, the ball was hit to me anyway. I remember standing there, awkwardly fumbling with the ball while everyone screamed at me to throw it as the batter rounded the bases. My own turns at the plate didn't go much better: I once fouled the ball off so many times that the gym teacher just called me out so the game could go on.

One day when I was about thirteen, my father came home from the lab spitting mad. When I asked him what was wrong, he said, "When you're at IBM and you can't invent anything anymore, they make you a manager. So at the lab it's all Chinese engineers doing the work while the white managers boss us around." He then cursed at me for leaving comic books on the ground. His frustration at having his career limited based on what his superiors thought about him stuck with me: it was something that later made me want to be an entrepreneur.

I spent a lot of my childhood shy, angry, and trying to do anything possible to avoid being a nerd. When challenged, I would fight, generally on the losing side. I felt like the outsider in most any situation. In eighth grade, one of my classmates, Dan Miller, came back after the summer dressed in all black with eyeliner, combat boots, and a thick mane of hair. We used to go to the local arcade together to play *Street Fighter II*. Dan got me and some other friends into the Cure, the Smiths, Nine Inch Nails, and other bands. We found a sixteen-and-over club a few towns away—the Boardwalk—where we would go on Friday nights to listen to alternative rock and see the occasional band. My first concert was Depeche Mode in 1989, and I wore my *Violator* T-shirt around until it became tattered.

Still, I wasn't entirely a disaffected teenager. I took piano lessons every week and went to Chinese-language school on Saturdays, where I got left back every other year. I would get bigger, and the kids around me stayed small. My parents also sent me to tennis camp to help me look well-rounded for college applications. It turned out I was actually interested in sports, despite my struggles on the baseball diamond. In high school I became a big fan of the Ewing-era Knicks. I thought it would be pathetic if I was an Asian kid who watched basketball but didn't play, so I vowed to learn. At first it was miserable, and at pickup games after school, when I would miss a layup, other kids would say, "I guess that was a Chinese layup," and laugh mercilessly. I went out for the junior varsity team and got cut after the first couple days. But I kept on playing.

My brother was two and a half years older, so he started driving me around when I was thirteen. When he was set to head to college at UC Berkeley, that taste of freedom appeared to be over. I was going on fifteen and stuck at home with my parents, relying upon friends for rides. I asked my parents if I could go away to prep school, and to my surprise they just about jumped for joy. "Boarding school" was TV language for "your parents hate you," but in my case it was my idea. I went away for the last two years of high school in New Hampshire, which was itself a culture shock. I met kids who had been bred from birth to be the leadership class. Their sense of confidence and entitlement was foreign to me; as the son of immigrants, I was told that I should expect nothing to come easily. Some of my classmates at Exeter had gotten a very different message.

I was a good student at Exeter and tested well. I got into Brown and Stanford and decided to go to Brown to be closer to family. Also, the photo that adorned Stanford's acceptance packet was a crowd at a football game, which wasn't really my style. I spent my college years in the gym working out, practicing Tae Kwon Do, and playing video games. I spent a semester in Hong Kong, where I had some family who lived in the suburbs. On Friday nights I would take a bus out to visit them in Repulse Bay and spend the weekend playing my uncle in chess or racquetball. That time in Hong Kong made me aware of both my family in Asia and just how American I was.

After college I went to law school and became an unhappy lawyer in New York City for five months. I left to become a failed dot-com entrepreneur. After that I worked for a wireless software start-up that ran out of money—you know things are bad when your co-workers start moving into the conference room and showering in the office—and then a health-care software company. I had a knack for taking jobs with companies that ran out of money. I started hustling on the side as a test prep instructor and curriculum developer and a nightclub promoter. A bunch of people I didn't know showed up to my twenty-seventh birthday party at a lounge and bought a lot of drinks. I thought, "Huh, maybe there's a business there," so I started throwing parties under the name "Ignition NYC" with the technologist Gunny Scarfo and Amy Engelhardt, a woman I'd met back at the Boardwalk when we were teenagers.

My side gig teaching the GMAT and developing curricula eventually became an executive role when the founder of the company, Zeke Vanderhoek, asked me to take over as the CEO. I led the company for several years until it became number one in the country and was bought by a public company in 2009. During those years I also met my wife, Evelyn, and we got married. I was thirty-four and a millionaire.

In 2011, I left my job as the president of a division of *The Washington Post* to start a nonprofit. Venture for America was my attempt to give young people some of the lessons I'd learned as a failed entrepreneur. The organization channels enterprising recent college graduates to start-ups in Detroit, New Orleans, Baltimore, Cleveland, and other cities around the country. As I used to say, "If you're a directionless college grad and you say you want to go to law school, your parents will think it's great, and the government will give you a $100,000 loan, no questions asked. If you say you want to start a business, your parents will think it's a terrible idea, and no one will give you $100,000 to try anything. That's why we have thousands of unhappy, indebted law school grads and are short thousands of entrepreneurs."

Venture for America became a vibrant community of hundreds of idealistic young people who have helped create thousands of jobs in cities around the country, many in places not known as hubs of entrepreneurism. It also brought me to Michigan, Ohio, Missouri, Alabama, Louisiana, and other places I hadn't spent much—or any—time in. Over six years I saw the sweep of economic changes and the aftermath of automation waves that had crushed various communities. Many people who could leave left these places a long time ago, and those who were left behind were increasingly despondent.

I had been trained to think that the economy and the market

could improve people's lives if you could get people the right re-sources and instill in them certain skills. But that approach had started to feel hollow after traveling the Midwest and the South for six years. Walking through some of those towns opened my eyes.

It hit me hard. I dug more into the economic numbers. Four million manufacturing jobs had been eliminated in recent years, and I realized that what I saw in the Midwest and the South was the new normal. And even that normal was going to get ground to dust by future and impending waves of automation and technology that were going to overrun communities until there was nothing left. What happened to those millions of manufacturing jobs would soon happen to retail jobs, call center jobs, trucking jobs, and on and on through the economy. Both my time in these communities and the data were saying the same thing. The tide was coming in, and more and more people were going to get swept away. And then Trump won.

Imagine being someone who had spent six years helping create hundreds of jobs in the Midwest and the South—and getting awards for it—and realizing that your work was like pouring water in a bathtub that had a giant hole ripped in the bottom of it and the water rushing out had helped elect Donald Trump.

We were in deep trouble, and I felt like I had stared at the problems for six years. Venture for America was doing important work, but the economic system it was operating in had gone haywire and turned on millions of people.

It was time for me to do something to fix that broken system.

CHAPTER 2

DECIDING TO DO THE
UNREASONABLE THING

When I declared my run for the presidency in February 2018, it got a little write-up in *The New York Times*. The headline for the piece was "His 2020 Campaign Message: The Robots Are Coming." The article ran in the Business section, not the main news section that covered politics. I was called a "longer-than-long-shot" candidate by a friendly journalist, Kevin Roose, whom I knew from Brown.

The truth is that I was lucky to even get my announcement noticed in the *Times*. When the newspaper asked to take pictures to go with the story, I had to rent an office for a couple hours for the shoot because my campaign headquarters at that time was operating out of my mom's apartment with a handful of young staffers. Our real office would have looked utterly ridiculous. Instead, we picked a nice-looking loft with hardwood floors and big windows and had an extra person or two show up for the photo shoot to make the place look busy. It was pretty obvious we weren't really working out of this loft full-time. One of the photographers looked around and said, "Nice choice."

I originally filed the paperwork to run for president several months earlier, in November 2017. No one noticed, unsurprisingly. Every four years hundreds of Americans fill out an online form with the Federal Election Commission (FEC) to run for president. You hear about only a handful in the media, but the actual declared candidates are legion. The form is free and the FEC doesn't ask for much. Real-life presidential candidates for 2020 included Vermin Supreme, Jo 753, Kurios I, President Caesar, and Sexy Vegan, and committee names included Black Label Empire (House of Lords) Darth Cyber Units, Heart Doc Andrew Stops the Oligarchy, and the Committee to Put Backbone in the White House. So Andrew Yang filing for president was not exactly headline news.

Article II, Section 1, Clause 5 of the Constitution sets only three qualifications for holding the presidency:

1. You must be a natural-born U.S. citizen.
2. You must be at least thirty-five years old.
3. You must have been a resident in the United States for at least fourteen years.

This likely describes you. Literally anyone who meets these criteria can run.

The next step after filing with the FEC is to get an Employer Identification Number and open a bank account. The FEC requires that you file records of your campaign committee contributions and expenditures if you spend more than $5,000. After I filed the initial form, I went to my local Citibank branch in the Hell's Kitchen neighborhood of Manhattan and opened up a checking account. The Citibank clerk didn't think much of it. She asked, "What is this account for?"

"A political campaign," I responded.

"What are you running for?"

"President."

She looked confused, because she didn't want to seem rude. "Should I know who you are?"

"No." I shrugged.

"Okay. Well, I wish you a lot of success."

. . .

I LOOK BACK fondly on the early days of the campaign—the time before we announced. The earliest days were all about imagining what the campaign could be. When you have a debit card in your hand with "Friends of Andrew Yang" stamped on it, it's a fun step.

I had decided to run almost a year earlier, in March 2017. Donald Trump had won in November, and I thought, "Wow, things are coming apart quickly." At the time I was still the head of Venture for America, training entrepreneurs and helping grow companies in places like Detroit, Cleveland, New Orleans, and Baltimore. I had walked the streets of towns in Ohio and Michigan and Pennsylvania that had been decimated by the loss of manufacturing jobs and knew that the same future was in store for countless more communities.

I saw Trump's victory as a red flag—a country crying out for help. The problems had become worse and were accelerating quickly. The feedback mechanism between the people and our government had largely broken down. No one seemed to understand or care that our economy was being reshaped in ways that left far too many behind.

The solution would be an enormous lift, an unprecedented shift in the way Americans viewed jobs and opportunity. What was required was a recasting of our economy to serve human needs instead of capital efficiency. The rules of the economy would need to be rewritten. And the only way to do that would be through the federal government, the only entity with the power to reconfigure a $22 trillion economy that had turned its back on millions of Americans.

That required running for president.

I sometimes joked on the trail that I wasn't someone who grew up fantasizing about being president, because I am not insane. I was told to get good grades and get a good job like many other first-generation kids. Politics were not discussed in our house. No one

in the Yang household was saying, "You could be president some-
day." It was more like, "You're terrible, go clean your room." I think
my dad's turn of phrase was "Try not to be a burden on society."

Fast-forward twenty-five years and I was running for president.
It seemed like a highly irrational decision, but I was driven by a
number of things.

I had worked in technology and entrepreneurship for years by
this point and had many friends in those fields. These well-informed
friends, almost without exception, shared the view that an automation wave was coming that was going to displace millions. Said one
friend who runs an AI company, "We are getting better and better
at things that will make a large number of workers extraneous." My
friend predicted "a lost generation of workers." An investor friend
in Boston said that 70 percent of the companies he invested in were
looking to eliminate jobs as part of their business plans. In December 2016, in Barack Obama's last full month in office, his administration published a study projecting that 83 percent of jobs that paid
less than $20 per hour will be subject to automation and that more
than 2.2 million car-, bus-, and truck-driving jobs would be replaced by self-driving vehicles. Millions of retail jobs were certain
to be wiped out by Amazon, as it devised ever-more-efficient ways
to absorb business lines and deliver goods to people at costs that
other retailers couldn't match.

I was sure that a freight train was coming and that we were
idling, oblivious, on the tracks. Despite the coming cataclysm, I
was beginning to realize something else: either politicians didn't
understand the gravity of what was coming, or they simply saw no
incentive to rock the boat by pointing the problem out or proposing meaningful solutions.

That left it to the rest of us. In entrepreneurship there are two
main approaches. One is to say, "Well, someone else will take care
of that." That approach seldom works. The other is to do it yourself. I called friends in technology to see if anyone else was going to
make this case, and the answer was no.

Becoming the Paul Revere of automation—and figuring out what to do about the problem—were daunting challenges, but I had been part of unlikely successes before. My education company had transformed from employing a single tutor to being the industry leader. Venture for America had gone from a PowerPoint deck on my computer to a multimillion-dollar nonprofit organization operating in more than a dozen cities. As further proof, Evelyn had agreed to marry me. I knew that great things were possible from humble beginnings if you had the right people involved.

After spending six years running a nonprofit to help develop young entrepreneurs and create jobs, I found it impossible to sit back and pretend to be the champion of job creation when I thought that the opposite was about to happen society-wide. Entrepreneurship was dying by the numbers around the country, and hundreds of thousands of jobs were about to be eliminated due to AI and automation. Fighting against this tide felt like the right thing to do and an extension of my work.

As CEO of Venture for America, I had met Presidents Obama, Bill Clinton, George W. Bush, and a multitude of governors, senators, mayors, and members of Congress. Meeting them had a couple effects on me. First, it convinced me that nothing significant was likely to change. Our political class is generally not made up of people who are looking to head in a new direction. They are often stuck in a web of meet and greets and fundraisers designed to perpetuate the status quo. Second, it impressed on me that our political leaders were not otherworldly beings with capacities beyond yours and mine. Most of them were pretty ordinary, or at least no more capable than people I knew and worked with.

I also had an instinct that there was something missing from the political marketplace. Democrats and Republicans were having the same arguments, passing the leadership torch back and forth, while communities around the country were sinking into the mud. If you're an entrepreneur, you sense when the market is missing something and you try to offer it. When I surveyed the political landscape, I sensed that there was both a need and an appetite for a different approach. Surely, I figured, there were people who would feel the same way I did.

I think of myself as an operator, in the sense that I'm quite practical and numbers-driven. So, I looked at the things that I would need to do to run for president: present a vision, make an argument, raise money, build a team, write a book, get press, grow an organization, give rise to a movement, go a couple years without a salary. I figured I had done or could do most all of those things. But, if elected, what would I actually do to fix the problems I had identified?

I had first discovered universal basic income a few years earlier through thinkers like Andy Stern, Martin Ford, and Rutger Bregman. It struck me as inevitable that we would adopt universal basic income eventually, but it was still a marginal idea that most people had never heard of. I thought I could bring it to the mainstream and that my campaign could accelerate the end of poverty and begin a movement toward a better and more sustainable way of life for tens of millions of people. Imagine thinking you might be able to advance human civilization. It was the biggest opportunity one could imagine.

Evelyn approached my notion of running for president as she would an interesting project her spouse had taken on. Perhaps for the best, she didn't take it that seriously at first. "I'll believe it when I see it" was her initial take. Talking to her about it initially required some reassurance on my part that I was still very lucid and rational. She's a very good sport and the rock of the family. Like me, she had become a big universal basic income advocate but, like most reasonable people, didn't think my campaign would go that far. "I believe in you and everything you do, honey."

I looked at our downsides: time away from my family, money, my reputation, a loss of privacy, and possible total humiliation. It could be that no one would listen to the magical Asian man who wanted to give everyone money. I could live with that. At least I'd be able to look at myself in the mirror and say that I stood up for what I believed was right and fought for a vision of the future I would actually be proud to leave to our children.

When I began to confide to people I knew that I was running for president in the summer of 2017 as I stepped down as CEO of Venture for America, the reactions were not uniformly positive. I got "President of what, your co-op board?" and many similar responses. People I asked for help were likely to listen politely—or even impolitely—and then decline to help. There were some awkward, even painful conversations. "I just don't like to get involved in politics" was something I heard several times. Other friends of mine would tell me later, "I have to be honest, I thought you were crazy." And those were the good ones. Occasionally I would call a friend I knew would be supportive just to balance it out. One of my particularly kind friends actually cried tears of joy, out of respect (I think) for my level of commitment.

Most politicians spend years fine-tuning a Rolodex of potential donors. My initial "email list" was simply my Gmail address book. Here is the email I sent to my friends and contacts telling them I was running for president:

————————Forwarded message————————

From: Andrew Yang <andrew@ubi2020.org>
Date: Sun, Nov 26, 2017 at 1:48 PM
Subject: The starting gun
Cc: hq@ubi2020.org

Hello all,

You are the best people I know—and some of the best people anywhere. THANK YOU for believing that we can have a positive impact on the trajectory of the country. It's an honor and privilege to consider you friends and supporters. I hope you have the chance to meet each other in the days to come.

I'm running for President as a Democrat in 2020 because I

believe we must start having honest conversations about and formulate real solutions to the growing impact of technological unemployment/automation that has already displaced millions of Americans and will soon affect millions more. The elimination of 4 million manufacturing jobs in Ohio, Michigan, Pennsylvania, Wisconsin and other midwestern states gave us Donald Trump. The displacement of retail workers, truck drivers, fast food workers, call center workers, etc. will strain our society beyond repair. The simple truth is that our technology is advancing faster than our labor market can adapt.

The most immediate and vital step is to implement a Universal Basic Income ("the Freedom Dividend") of $12k/year for all adults. This will serve as an economic and social support for the transition and preserve our consumer market while we shift to a new economy. It will be paid for largely by a new VAT at half the European level. Over time a VAT will be crucial to capture some of the gains of automation which typically accrue to sophisticated private firms.

My platform revolves around 3 key proposals:

1. Universal Basic Income ("the Freedom Dividend")
2. Evolution to the next stage of capitalism, "Human Capitalism," geared toward optimizing around human wellbeing in addition to GDP
3. Single-payer health care—necessary in the aftermath of job reduction

You may not agree with me on every front. But I hope that you agree that we need to elevate meaningful solutions. I also hope that you're excited to have me as a spokesperson for new approaches.

The campaign is coming together beautifully; I've found the best sign that you're going to succeed is when amazing people want to come work with you. By that metric, we're going to accomplish great things.

Thank you again for your support and belief. With your help, we can Build a Future our children will be proud of. See you on the path to the White House in 2020. Your grateful friend,

—Andrew

Imagine getting that from one of your friends in 2017.

One thing you might notice is that the name of the campaign was originally "UBI2020." I wanted to build the entire campaign around universal basic income. My natural inclination is to let ideas lead. Universal basic income was an idea whose time had come. And I confess I struggled with naming the campaign after myself because I wanted the campaign to be less about me and more about the ideas and the problems I was setting out to solve.

But when I asked my team which would work better, "UBI2020" or "Yang2020," they all thought "Yang2020." They believed that the movement needed a figurehead, and they wanted me to avoid being seen as simply a one-issue candidate. Over time I've learned that they were right. People don't listen to ideas. People listen to other people.

We tested the appeal of universal basic income through a polling firm. We tried out different names for it: "universal basic income," "Social Security for all," "prosperity dividend," "income for all." We found that every term tested around the same level for self-described Democrats; around 30 percent of people liked "universal basic income," with minor variation. But one name stuck out as getting the same appeal among self-described conservatives: "freedom dividend." That's what we went with; the data had spoken.

We did similar testing for various taglines for the campaign. "Fight for the Future," "Invest in People," "Prosperity for All," "A Better Life." The one that did the best was easily "Humanity First." That appealed to me because it spoke to multiple meanings. It's funny; it felt somewhat revolutionary, but what else would you put first? Money? Machines?

The initial incarnation of my "team" consisted of zero political professionals. Instead, it was a handful of young people crazy enough to join the presidential campaign of an anonymous entrepreneur. Muhan Zhang was a coder who had completed Venture for America. Andrew Frawley was a young marketer who believed in universal basic income. Carly Reilly had just moved to New York to work in media. Matt Shinners was a Harvard Law grad and policy genius from my education company. And Zach Graumann, my campaign manager, had worked on Wall Street at UBS while starting a nonprofit for underprivileged kids.

In those early days, the idea that our little ragtag campaign would go on to raise tens of millions of dollars from hundreds of thousands of donors, outcompete the campaigns of five senators, four governors, six members of Congress, and the mayor of New York City, and get hundreds of thousands of votes nationwide was beyond what anyone would regard as remotely plausible.

We set to work.

CHAPTER 3

THE WING DING IS STACKED AGAINST ME; OR, HOW WE LEARN ABOUT CANDIDATES

"Okay, so now I'm running for president," I thought in early 2018. I was still quite anonymous, so this decision led to any number of awkward conversations. For example, I would be at a kid's birthday party and another dad, clutching a beer and making small talk, might ask me, "What do you do for work?" If I answered, "I'm running for president," it would seem positively bizarre. In theory I should have been working it every waking moment, but the last thing I wanted to do was try to persuade every dad at the birthday party to support me. So I'd answer with something vague like "I'm an author" or "I work in policy" and then change the subject.

My hesitancy seemed justified by what happened when I did actually try to inform people. Every conversation took half an hour. And most people weren't exactly pumped up afterward. It was more often a confused "Good luck," like the Citibank teller.

The operator in me continued to tell my brain that the inputs my campaign needed were pretty straightforward. I needed to raise enough money to not just keep the organization running but to grow it. I needed to generate publicity and get press. And I needed to get voters on board, particularly in the first states that would vote. Later, I would come to realize that the process through which one gets press and mainstream coverage is much more institutionalized than I would have ever believed.

I had studied the trajectory of other primary campaigns, and it was clear that Iowa and New Hampshire were the key. If you didn't perform in those states, you were done; most candidates would drop out even before the early states voted. But if you did well in those first states, it could catapult you forward into contention. Doing well in the early states struck me as fairly achievable. I had gone to high school in New Hampshire and felt confident that my message would hit home there; there's a healthy independent streak in the Granite State. And in Iowa only 171,517 Iowans participated in the 2016 Democratic caucuses. This was only 5.4 percent of the 3.1 million people in the state. You could assume that the number would grow somewhat in 2020, but the field would also be much more crowded. So my projection was that if I got approximately 40,000 Iowans on board I could win. (Indeed, Bernie Sanders wound up getting the most votes, with 45,652, so my working assumption was pretty close.)

Our system of electing a president operates such that each Iowan was worth his or her weight in gold. I started saying that every Iowan was worth a thousand New Yorkers or Californians, which was essentially true. Getting forty thousand Iowans on board to abolish poverty seemed very doable.

The first bridge to cross was trying to generate attention. And for that we needed the media. The initial *New York Times* piece had not generated as much follow-up as I'd hoped, but I figured other journalists would take an interest eventually.

That turned out to be much easier said than done.

IN THE SUMMER of 2018, I was invited to speak at a major Democratic grassroots fundraising event—the Wing Ding—in Clear Lake, Iowa. It was a huge coup for my fledgling campaign at that point. I later found out that I was invited because one of the organizers had heard me on the Sam Harris podcast—one of my first big breaks in terms of exposure earlier that year (more on this later)—and decided that I was worth hearing from.

For me, the Wing Ding was the first time I was getting the chance to address such a large group of people—a thousand—and in front of dozens of reporters. The venue, the Surf Ballroom, is most famous as the place where Buddy Holly, Ritchie Valens, and the Big Bopper played right before their plane crashed six miles away in 1959, which was later christened "the day the music died" by Don McLean in "American Pie." I tried not to dwell on that ominous history, though I absolutely love that song.

It was my first major political speech. It's not my custom to make emotional appeals, but I also knew, from the numbers, that a knockout performance would get me 2.5 percent of the way to forty thousand if I somehow converted everyone in the room. I approached it as a potentially make-or-break moment for the campaign—the speech of my life up to that point. My team approached it the same way; they had me practice until I could speak without notes, hit my major points, and not go beyond my allocated time.

The four major speakers were me, Tim Ryan, John Delaney, and the headliner—Michael Avenatti. John and I were the only declared candidates for president as of the summer of 2018. Most candidates were waiting until after the midterms to declare. It was clear that Michael Avenatti was the draw. The press was salivating over the pugnacious lawyer, who had rocketed to fame as the attorney representing the porn star Stormy Daniels in her lawsuit against Donald Trump, as a possible opponent for the Republican president. For his part, John Delaney had already spent several million dollars, including on Super Bowl ads in Iowa, and had opened ten offices in the state. I, of course, had zero staff and offices in Iowa at the time.

Approaching the ballroom, I saw it was surrounded by "John Delaney for President" signs that had been planted earlier that day. John's giant blue tour bus and sign spinners—two guys who were very talented at spinning giant "John Delaney" cardboard signs—were very conspicuous in the parking lot. The Wing Ding was my first brush with presidential campaign pageantry as a candidate. It immediately made me feel small and self-conscious showing up with my three young staffers and a meager table with our one brochure.

Still, I was careful not to project any vulnerability. You have to be rock solid because your team will take its cues from you.

I went into the darkened ballroom and began shaking hands with whoever was nearby. Most people didn't really know who I was, so it was a struggle to seem busy and not look awkward. One of my quick-thinking staffers started to bring people, including local officials, over to meet me.

The program was at least two hours long, with a procession of local candidates and luminaries who gave brief speeches in support of their races. I met local candidates like J. D. Scholten and Rob Sand. Eventually it got to Tim, John, me, and Michael Avenatti. Tim gave a rousing speech about America's never being knocked down. John spoke earnestly about consensus and bipartisanship.

It was my first time seeing their speeches, but not the last. Eventually, if you're a candidate, you see each other's stump speeches over and over again. Late in the cycle, I'd come to joke that Democratic fundraisers should have us draw names from a hat and deliver another candidate's speech. Donors would pay big money to see it. By the end, I thought I could do a decent rendition of Pete Buttigieg or Bernie Sanders giving their go-to stumps. I can imagine someone parodying my stump: "The robots are coming, we're doomed, give everyone money right now."

In the Surf Ballroom, I heard my name called and jogged up to the stage. I talked about how our economy was transforming before our eyes, and why Iowans needed to lead the country in a new and better direction. It felt great. I got a standing ovation from much of the crowd, though the level of applause was likely inflated by Iowa courtesy. (If you want to see the speech, you can judge for yourself by searching online for "Andrew Yang Wing Ding 2018.")

As I stepped off the stage, there was a small line of people who

Speaking at the Iowa Wing Ding on August 10, 2018

wanted to shake my hand. I wound up in conversation with John Delaney and his wife, April, who came over to compare notes. While we spoke, Michael Avenatti took to the stage to deliver the last speech of the night. Curious to see how it would go, I turned to pay attention.

Objectively, I thought Michael's speech was awful. He read from notes the whole time—word for word. He went on for *way* too long—a full five minutes over the allotted time. Though his speech was filled with cliché-ridden talking points, the Iowans in attendance politely applauded on cue.

Watching all this, I thought, "Okay, anyone seeing this will take from it that Michael Avenatti is not serious."

I could not have been more wrong.

As soon as Michael finished speaking, he was encircled by a dozen television cameras and journalists peppering him with questions about his presidential run. I didn't even know half of these journalists were in the room until they swarmed Michael. They followed him in a scrum as he slowly gravitated toward an exit.

The next couple days the headlines ran "Avenatti's 'Swagger'

Stirs Iowa Democrats" and "Avenatti at Iowa Wing Ding: Demo-crats Need to 'Fight Fire with Fire,'" with glowing quotes from Iowans in attendance about how Avenatti had fired up the crowd and was an appealing counterpoint to Trump.

These stories barely mentioned me or Tim or John. To the na-tional press it had solely been the Michael Avenatti show.

I realized that these journalists had come to Clear Lake, Iowa, for a story that had already been written in their minds. Avenatti, media darling, was exciting voters. His actual performance was in-cidental, and the speeches of any other candidates who happened to be there—including my big debut—might as well not have hap-pened.

THE MEDIA HAS ITS OWN STORIES IN MIND

There's a common assumption that people run for president be-cause they have big egos and it serves their sense of self. As can-didates, they are afforded numerous opportunities to get their messages across because people want to hear what they have to say. Later, they are rewarded with lucrative TV contracts, speaking gigs, and a larger following.

This is seriously off base. Generally the opposite is true. Run-ning for president is, by and large, an ego-destroying, humbling process. And the media is a very big part of that.

Imagine you are the author of thirteen books, including four *New York Times* number one bestsellers, and a spiritual leader with a following of millions. You count some of the most famous people in the world as your friends and confidants. You have founded a nonprofit that delivers food to people struggling with AIDS and co-founded a nonprofit for world peace. You have improved the well-being and spiritual life of droves of people and are adored and respected by them. You are wealthy, serious, and philosophical.

Then you decide to run for president.

Reporters respond with ridicule, scorn, and eye rolling. Journalists interview you with a patronizing air of skepticism when they decide to interact with you at all. Your past statements are taken out of context and used to ascribe to you beliefs that you do not hold. Eventually, you are denigrated as a wacko and a crystal lady. Everyday Americans contribute millions to your campaign, but that doesn't seem to matter. You move to Iowa in order to connect with people and campaign your heart out for months on end, and your efforts are essentially ignored.

As you probably guessed, I'm describing Marianne Williamson, whom I found to be warm, generous, thoughtful, and driven by a genuine desire to improve the world.

Or imagine yourself as a former three-star admiral in the U.S. Navy who served for more than three decades and commanded the USS *George Washington* aircraft carrier strike group in the Persian Gulf in 2002. You have led thousands of sailors who put their trust in you for their very lives. You have a PhD from Harvard and were second in your class at the U.S. Naval Academy. You were a two-term congressman from a swing state and led a nonprofit that promoted STEM education around the world. You see the direction that the country is going and its increased polarization, and you feel that a different type of leadership is needed.

So you decide to run for president.

You are ignored by most of the press. When they do talk to you, journalists regularly ask you, "Why are you running for president?" even though you spent decades in service and the answer ought to be pretty obvious. To the media, you are nearly a nonentity: major networks tell you they will not have you on air even to talk about foreign policy, which you are clearly better qualified to discuss than just about anyone, because they don't consider you a legitimate candidate. You walk across the state of New Hampshire as a way to generate attention and meet with people, and that is generally ignored too.

That's Joe Sestak, who struck me as a patriot and great man when I spent time with him on the trail. His daughter, Alex, suffered from cancer, which is one reason he got into the race late. She passed away in 2020.

I could go on and do the same exercise with perhaps a dozen other candidates. Running for president doesn't serve your ego generally—quite the opposite. It isn't much fun showing up to events that are poorly attended and stumping to disinterested audiences. I remember driving all day to New Hampshire to meet with a "crowd" of one person in a coffee shop or spending Labor Day in Iowa to address a tiny rally. The day-to-day positive reinforcement is spotty to say the least.

You believe in your message and hope that it will catch hold and that reporters will share your ideas with others who will then take an interest in you. And if you do start to grow a base of support, you hope that journalists will notice and cover you more.

Instead, many members of the national media feel they have a responsibility to reinforce particular candidates and their "narratives" and dismiss others. They don't just report on the news; they form it.

That was the case at the 2018 Wing Ding. My team was disappointed that my big debut speech in Clear Lake didn't get a mention in the press. I didn't let that discourage me. I traveled to both Iowa and New Hampshire every month from then on. I joked that the early states were like my children: if I visited one, I needed to visit the other one shortly afterward. My work in Iowa paid off in December 2018 when the Selzer Iowa poll included me in its list of candidates. It was the first nationally recognized poll to actually include me, which itself was a big deal after being ignored for months—thank you, Selzer and *The Des Moines Register*! The numbers were not great: I was dead last of the twenty-one candidates listed, including some people who weren't running, like Eric Holder. I had the lowest name recognition of any of the twenty-one candidates and was the only one with net unfavorables: of the 17 percent who had heard of me, 12 percent didn't like me. Zero percent said I was their first choice for president.

But buried in the poll were a couple signs that just about made me jump for joy. Seventy-six percent of those polled said they could consider supporting me or didn't know, which was comparable to other candidates. And 1 percent of polled caucus goers said I was their second choice. That was the same level of support drawn by established politicians like Kirsten Gillibrand, Jay Inslee, and Eric Swalwell. I figured polling would be the main criterion to eventually make the debates, and now there was a glimmer of hope.

To me, that was all I needed. If there were a few Iowans who were enthusiastic about me, I knew we could find more. But it was going to take a lot of work and ingenuity.

CHAPTER 4

ADVENTURES IN ADVERTISING
AND SOCIAL MEDIA

The early days of the campaign were rough. Days that felt like breakthroughs, or even break-evens, were in short supply. I had declared in February 2018, and it turns out no one wanted to talk about the presidential campaign of 2020 that far in advance.

I divided my priorities into three main buckets:

1. money and organizational growth
2. press and awareness
3. support in the early states

We needed money. I had raised a couple hundred thousand dollars from friends and family at the end of 2017 in order to launch, but that wasn't going to last forever. I knew if we didn't show growth over time, we would be stuck in the mud, become increasingly ridiculous, and disappear. I had hoped that more people would be excited about my run at first, but by late 2018 there were few signs of growing support. We got so few donations that I saw each one and sent an individual thank-you note. I did this for weeks. Most people thought I was a bot. You have to reward people who buy in early.

One of the things that my team asked me to do was "dial for dollars." The maximum any individual could legally give to a candidate was $2,800. Ordinarily people who give at that level play in

politics habitually. My team procured a list of traditional Democratic donors—these kinds of lists are publicly available—and said,
"Look, these are people who give, often to several candidates. If
you call them and work on them, you can get them to donate to
you. They know each other too, so it's how you start building a
network of donors." I tried making these calls a number of times
and was terrible at it. I also found it to be soul crushing and incredibly draining. It felt like a waste of time. Instinctively, I understood
that I was a poor fit for traditional donors. I also believed it was
never going to give us a chance at growing and winning. At best it
was a survival tactic.

But we needed money. I called friends and asked them to host
or co-host an event for me so I could make an appeal. I was not
cool enough for people to donate to up front. "Just tell your friends
to come meet me," I would say. Even this was very difficult; people
would ask their friends to come and get only a few to show up, and
then those people would hear me out but wouldn't necessarily donate. I would watch friends introduce me and say, "I don't really
think he has a chance, but he's a good guy. Let's support him because he could get some good ideas out there." And these were seriously the good ones, the friends who put themselves out on a limb
on my behalf.

AS I SAID before, when I started running for president, my email
list was simply my Gmail contact list. I probably had more email
addresses than the average person, but the total was still in the hundreds, not thousands.

At first, I knew everyone who donated and everyone on the list.
They were friends of mine, many of whom I had called personally.

The challenge was to grow the universe of people who were
interested in me and would donate to the campaign. The most efficient way to do that was online advertising. If the average online
donor was going to donate $37 over the life of the campaign and

you could attract their attention for, say, $15 in Facebook ads, then you would maximize your spend until it stopped working. We began using Facebook and YouTube targeting so that if someone watched a video of me or visited the campaign website, they would get served ads. The team had me constantly record different versions of Facebook and YouTube ads to test out different messages.

Part of the challenge was to identify what sorts of people would donate to the campaign. We had some guesses. Our early supporters skewed young, male, and tech savvy. After the success with Sam Harris, I would often go on podcasts and pursue interviews with tech figures and business journalists, the kinds of people who spoke to a similar demographic.

As time went on, we became increasingly hungry for data. Facebook offers an advertising tool—Custom Audience—where you can target ads across Facebook, Instagram, and a network of apps and sites that includes TikTok, Tinder, and Pandora. Ever notice how ads seem to follow you around the internet from site to site? This is why.

If we had enough data to identify our audience, we could scale more quickly. This is particularly true using an advertising feature on Facebook called Lookalike Audience. If you have identified between one thousand and fifty thousand fans on Facebook, you can create a Lookalike Audience—that is, other Facebook users who have the same characteristics as your current audience in terms of age, gender, education, location, media habits, likes, and other factors. This gave us access to a very large universe of people who should have been receptive to our message, based on what we knew about our current supporters.

My modest list of contacts pretty quickly mushroomed into a true mailing list.

As we grew, other organizations and candidates started offering to swap lists. Let's say I had 100,000 email addresses and you ran for Congress and had another 100,000 email addresses. We can give each other our lists, and then we both have 200,000 email addresses. This is one reason why you always seem to be getting on political lists you don't remember signing up for.

I vetoed these swaps for my campaign. I hated the idea of people who supported me getting emails from random other people. It felt like a breach of trust. And I figured that folks who didn't know much about me and my campaign were unlikely to donate anyway, so we weren't missing out on much.

Eventually, we would also be asked to buy lists of voters from the Democratic state parties. Each state's Democratic Party sells you its list of voters that includes mailing addresses, email addresses, demographics, and voting history. These lists were quite expensive, and in some cases you had no choice but to pay for them. For example, the New Hampshire Democratic Party would only let you speak at their big event the McIntyre-Shaheen 100 Club Dinner if you'd paid for their list, which cost $100,000.

When my list was small, I would write fundraising emails myself, often from a car or plane on the road. I enjoyed it, and it felt like a way to maintain a connection to the people who were early adopters to my idealistic little campaign. It felt personal. But as our operation grew, we brought on an email team that tested every message in multiple versions for subject line, timing, and appeal. They had hard data on which emails were most successful at generating donations. Asking for money with alarm or urgency boosted results; that's one reason why the emails you get always make it seem like the world is coming to an end. That wasn't my style, but I respect data and results. The first time I read an email that went out that I didn't write myself was a strange feeling. I didn't love the idea of my supporters getting bombarded by alarmist messages. But I understood that in order for our operation to grow, it needed to move beyond my homegrown communications. I was becoming too busy to write messages more than once a week anyway. Still, I insisted on writing an occasional message myself and asked that the message not include a fundraising appeal, just to feel human.

The email team and the digital team—focused on Facebook, Instagram, and YouTube—went to work testing and targeting ads and communications and growing the overall follower and supporter lists. After a year of grinding out small events and podcasts, we really took off. By mid-2019 we broke 100,000 individual donors to my campaign. By early 2020 we would have more than 425,000 donors who contributed about $40 million and a mailing list of one million voters.

By the end we had a full-fledged data team that was one of the biggest drivers of our campaign. It became a virtuous circle. More voter data meant better spend, a bigger list, and more donations. Data meant money, a dynamic we will explore in greater detail in part 2.

IN THE SPRING of 2018, in the midst of our flailing attempts at fundraising, my campaign manager, Zach Graumann, sat me down and said, "We've been inventorying different social media platforms. We think you need to become good at Twitter because it drives different forms of engagement, particularly the media. Every journalist uses it. Facebook, Instagram, and Snapchat we can manage through the team. But you need to get your Twitter game up." Plus, he added, social media was free.

I said, "Okay, I guess I will get good at Twitter." From my studying the rise of other politicians, it seemed like a great resource and powerful tool: Twitter had fueled the rise of Donald Trump and Alexandria Ocasio-Cortez on either end of the political spectrum. Still, adopting Twitter wasn't entirely natural for me. I had started a Twitter account a few years prior, but I wasn't especially active. I had around four thousand Twitter followers when this conversation took place. My handle was @andrewyangVFA, with VFA standing for the nonprofit I'd founded, Venture for America.

I'm forty-six years old, so I remember a time before social media. I had never been a heavy user; I had Facebook, LinkedIn, and Twitter accounts but wasn't particularly attentive to any of them. I did change my LinkedIn job description to "Presidential Candidate," which I thought was fun. The big principle I'd gathered was that you got what you put in; if you had an account that posted only occasionally and the content was corporate and dry, it would be a bit of a dud. I had never dedicated much time to my personal social media accounts. But I had never run for office before either, and I recognized the need to adapt.

I started tweeting several times a day and responding to people who were following me. People were very excited to get a reply from me, which was good positive reinforcement. Because our campaign was so small, there was virtually no one following me who wasn't positive. We were under the radar of the haters! I remember one person posting, "We should relish this time when Andrew is talking to us because pretty soon he will be too big for that." I thought, "Wow, that's awfully optimistic."

I resolved to enjoy Twitter; after all, if I had to do it, I might as well try to have a good time. My account became a stream-of-consciousness mini-journal when I was on the road or read an article that I felt was important. I tried to post a picture from any event I did so that people would feel like they were there. Virtually all of the other candidates had quite boring accounts that felt as though they were run by staff. So I tried to become more fun and human.

For most of 2018 and into early 2019 it was pretty modest. I would tweet and just get a handful of likes or retweets and responses. But it started to grow as I posted consistently.

I realized that journalists were looking for anything interesting to cover. The first time I tweeted and it made it to cable news, I was stunned. It was just a picture of a Waffle House sign with the caption "Back in the South" when I was in South Carolina. My staff told me that CNN randomly just ran the tweet on air.

Heartened by this, I started to tweet things from the road so that people felt as if they were getting a glimpse of the campaign trail at

every turn. I regularly went through my notifications and tried to reward anyone who was amplifying the campaign, particularly journalists. If a journalist wrote anything about us—even if it was mixed and had some negative commentary and even if it was the most minor outlet or website—I would retweet that journalist and thank them by name.

I also tried to make my Twitter voice more colloquial and casual, sometimes even a little sassy. "Before we buy Greenland we should take care of Puerto Rico" and "I'm literally trying to give everybody money" were examples of tweets that people seemed to like.

Unlike so many facets of running for president, there was no real rule book for how candidates should act on Twitter or other social media. I allowed myself to refer to nonpolitical things I like, such as sports and music: "Man I can't stand the Patriots" or "I'm sorry Ms. Jackson, I am for real." I thought that inserting my personality into it would both make the account more appealing and help me enjoy it more. I posted an image from a marijuana dispensary in Las Vegas in November 2019 that went viral.

I thought *Breaking Bad* was perhaps the greatest TV show ever made. Though I'm not a big user of marijuana, I think it's obvious that we should legalize it at this point given the way the laws are

> **Andrew Yang** 🧑‍💼 ✓
> @AndrewYang
>
> Say my name.
>
> 10:55 AM · Nov 18, 2019 · Twitter for iPhone
>
> ‖ View Tweet activity
>
> **20.3K** Retweets   **105.5K** Likes

administered and the fact that it's a lot less dangerous than many other drugs people are using to manage pain and other conditions. The dispensary said that they would name a strain of weed after me—"Yang Ganja."

I consciously kept my Twitter feed positive. I noticed that many people would react to Trump's outrage of the day, which I considered playing into his hands.

In August 2019, I tweeted,

Donald Trump: "Here's a dumb idea."

Press: "Can you believe his latest dumb idea? I can't stop talking about it!"

Trump: "I am rethinking my dumb idea."

Press: "Good! Give us another one to talk about please."

This is the reality TV show.

Twitter became a very effective way to meet with and engage supporters. I would often DM with someone whom I would see on the road, where I would then say, "You're Lacey Delayne!" or "You're @divinetogether!" It was fun "meeting" someone online and then seeing them in person.

I would notice that journalists would occasionally follow me on Twitter, and I would follow them back. Often, they would make requests to speak to me or interview me. When I was in press-seeking mode, this was very useful.

I would also occasionally notice someone follow me on Twitter whom I was a fan of. I'd look up and be like, "Huh, Rivers Cuomo just followed me on Twitter!" and it felt like magic. I would wind up occasionally making friends and acquaintances with people I'd admired from afar.

As my Twitter following grew, some folks responded to me negatively or angrily. In the early days, I'd try to engage with anyone who had a reasonable objection to something I stood for, particularly on the policy front. I would say something like "Thanks for digging in. Here is the point I was trying to make. I hope that seems reasonable." That worked on most people for a while, where they seemed pleased to have a conversation, even if they disagreed. And when I didn't have much of a following, most of the people who found me were genuinely curious and open-minded.

Over time, though, the number of people who seemed argumentative simply for the sake of it or genuinely uninterested in other points of view became hard to ignore. I experienced the occasional burst of negativity based on something I said. One of the earlier examples was a video surfacing of my saying to a group of Asian American supporters, "We are one generation away from people shooting up Asians because of racial hostility due to economic transformation, job loss, and a cold war with China." I had made the statement in part to try to motivate them to think bigger about the future of the country and to get involved. I also believed it.

For a couple of days after, I was attacked by various people on-line who saw my statement as inflammatory and alarmist. It's a lot to process when hundreds of people attack you online and call you nasty and disparaging things. Some were avid gun owners who saw my statement as anti–Second Amendment rights. Others were various online hangers-on, people you might politely refer to as "influencers," who used the perceived gaffe as an opportunity to attack in the hopes of drawing attention to themselves. I spent a little time responding to them but eventually gave up.

"I am running for president. This will come with the territory," I thought. I figured I should get used to it. But it's difficult to take a dip into a fountain of negativity and vitriol about yourself. Your natural impulses are to either ignore it and withdraw or get angry.

When I went on Joe Rogan's podcast in early 2019 (more on this in chapter 6), he casually commented to me afterward, "Yeah, you can't look at your notifications starting when you have about a million followers. It'll drive you nuts." I thought, "Well, no chance of that," because I had only about forty thousand followers at the time.

That number shot up to 1.2 million over the next twelve months as the campaign grew.

I continued to engage with people on Twitter. I amplified actions of supporters, particularly those who were volunteering or helping others. I would pass along articles that conveyed important statistics or ideas that related to the campaign. I would send messages of encouragement to uplift people and thrill to their excitement.

At the same time, I sometimes had to steel myself when I checked my notifications or replies, because there would often be someone who was attacking or ridiculing me or something I said. There is a great deal of negativity on social media; it seems that many people log on with the purpose of venting whatever hostility or skepticism they harbor. You tell yourself you'll ignore any negativity, even though sometimes that's not entirely possible.

Still, Twitter was a powerful tool and one of the only things I felt I could control and make optimal use of on the campaign trail at no cost. It made it possible for me to build a real connection with people organically and at scale and was one of the primary ways my campaign distinguished itself. Thousands of people would say to me in person or online, "I joined Twitter just to follow you." Thousands of them would add a blue hat emoji—to signify a MATH cap—to their Twitter profile and then advocate for the campaign online using the hashtag #YangGang.

My Twitter following became one of the major drivers of attention and coverage to the campaign. Journalists started to realize that if they wrote something positive about me, it would get a ton of likes and amplification on social media. It initiated a virtuous cycle that helped us compete with the top campaigns.

Other campaigns noticed and tried to emulate us. Senator Michael Bennet and Tim Ryan tweeted various GIFs at us. But it was very hard to create the same dynamic; it's not a tactic so much as a glimpse into a person's mind and day-to-day life and sense of humor. If you follow someone who's active on social media, you actually feel like you get to know them over time.

I was truly myself online. It's very difficult to simulate or replicate a human being's inner workings for public consumption. People can sense whether it's you or your team making a post or posting a picture. What started out as a way to compete with campaigns that were much better resourced became a key feature of our rise, largely because I was unafraid of trying to build a human connection with people, in public and for the world to see. It became a theme for the campaign: we were humans running against the machine and needed to embrace our humanity in order to get noticed.

CHAPTER 5

THE REALITY SHOW OF RUNNING FOR PRESIDENT

We kept on visiting Iowa and New Hampshire for several days each month throughout 2019, and our crowds started to grow. I joked that you could summarize running for president in two words: "camera angles." With every event my team would take a picture that would make the room or event look maximally crowded. Sometimes that was impossible because there were only five to ten people in attendance. On those days we would use a close-up photo of me talking to someone after the event. We would sometimes look at pictures from another candidate's events that were all close-ups and laugh and say, "That must have been a terrible event."

In Iowa, our state chair was Al Womble, a union representative, Democratic activist, and member of the Iowa Democratic Black Caucus. He and his wife, Sara, had met me at the Wing Ding; Sara got excited about me first. Al and Sara are amazing people with hearts of gold. Al is a power lifter who always has a camera dangling on his massive chest. One of their children had some developmental challenges, and we had bonded over that.

In New Hampshire, our state chair was Steve Marchand, a policy wonk and former mayor of Portsmouth who had run for governor in 2018. Steve and I drove around northern New Hampshire together for hours talking about the different towns and how to help them transition economically. Steve commented on how we were both forty-something sons of immigrants with two kids at home. I was incredibly grateful to Steve in part because he had met with just about all of the candidates and chosen me to support. "You're the only one who actually sees the future coming and can bring people together," he would say.

Khrystina Snell came aboard as our state director in New Hampshire at the same time. Khrystina had run Steve's gubernatorial campaign and was extraordinarily energetic and positive. No one knew the state better. Having Steve and Khrystina at events in New Hampshire elevated everything we did.

With additions like these to the team, we were forming more of an identity as a campaign. When I had launched, a friend in Brooklyn said to me, "The pendulum will swing your way because politics goes in opposites. We have to do the opposite of what we're doing right now. And the opposite of Donald Trump is an Asian guy who likes math." Shortly thereafter, I used that line at an event. It drew a ton of laughter and applause. Andrew Frawley, our marketing manager, started making "MATH" signs for our events and people snapped them up.

A supporter online posted, "You know, MATH is like an acronym. 'Make America Think Harder.'" I loved it. It seemed meant to be. Frawley said, "Let's make a MATH hat that's a blue ball cap." We sold more than $3 million worth of hats over the months that followed and gave rise to a whole vibrant set of merchandise, with the MATH cap serving as one of the campaign's most enduring symbols.

Merchandise was great because it accomplished multiple objectives at once: it raised money, it spread the word about the campaign, and it built a strong culture.

GIVING IT AWAY

At one point in 2018, a forward-thinking friend of mine said to me, "I wish you all could spend some of the money you are raising on something other than advertising."

The MATH cap—and our supporters—in action

I thought about it and realized she was right. I started to brainstorm. What could we spend money on that would speak to the substance of my campaign? We were all about giving people money, so it became obvious: we should start giving people money. I loved the idea of making our vision real to people.

As an entrepreneur, I know the difference between arguing about something in the abstract and demonstrating it in real life. The latter helps make everything much more concrete and appealing.

I asked my team to figure out the rules of how I could give away money, as a way to demonstrate the potential for universal basic income. They said, "Well, it's very possible. But the easiest thing would be to do it yourself. There are no rules against that." The campaign didn't have much money at this point anyway.

So in January 2019, I started giving Jodi Fassi and her family $1,000 a month for a year. Jodi was chosen out of hundreds of people who submitted an entry explaining their situation. Jodi cleaned houses in Goffstown, New Hampshire, and her husband, Chuck, had been dealing with job insecurity and health issues. Chuck was back working, but they had a daughter, Janelle, in college at nearby St. Anselm and were struggling to manage her tuition payments.

Jodi, Chuck, and Janelle came down to New York City for our small New Year's Eve party to celebrate their being chosen. CNBC covered it, and Jodi and Chuck became local celebrities doing interviews with NBC, NPR, and New Hampshire–based press. They were even on *The Daily Show.*

This initial experiment was so much fun that I wanted to do it again. I gave $1,000 a month for a year to Kyle Christensen in Iowa Falls, who had moved back home to take care of his mother, who was recovering from cancer. Kyle was a talented musician who had sold his guitar among other things to try to make it work for him and his mom. Giving Kyle and his mom the news while I was in Iowa was incredibly heartwarming. I also started giving $1,000 a month to Malorie Shannon in Florida, an older woman at home who was struggling with health problems and trying to go back to school. Over the next year I gave away $36,000 to Jodi, Kyle, and Malorie. Money to struggling American families was the entire point of my campaign.

Eventually, my team and I decided that we should formalize these efforts as one of the campaign's signature themes. At the September presidential debate in Houston, I announced onstage that my campaign was about helping solve our problems by getting bureaucracy out of the way and putting resources directly in our hands. And to demonstrate it, we would give $1,000 a month to ten different American families who went to our website.

This move was excoriated by the press as a gimmick. Some asked whether it was legal. I was named one of the big losers of the debate by commenters.

Meanwhile, more than five million Americans went to our

campaign website in the minutes after I made the announcement. We received 450,000 email addresses and raised more than $1 million. Our campaign grew substantially that night, positioning us to continue making the debate stage even as the polling thresholds kept going up.

When criticized about it by the press, I responded, "Campaigns can hire hundreds of people and have them staff events, knock on doors, canvass, and do everything in their power to help a candidate win. They can also hire marketing and media consultants for millions of dollars. In our case we are paying Americans $1,000 a month to talk about how receiving this money is positive in their lives to illustrate our campaign's policies. They certainly can vote for whomever they'd like. I know our donors vastly prefer their donations going to other people who can use the money rather than anything else. That's the point of this campaign."

Just as we had thrown out the typical campaign playbook with my Twitter efforts, it struck me that our UBI pilot program was another case of breaking the "rules" of what a campaign should look like, and finding that it was exactly what a wide swath of Americans wanted to see.

To me, that $120,000 we gave to people—and I would meet each of the recipients in the days ahead, each with their own phenomenal story that they were happy to share—was one of the best things we did on the campaign. Our supporters felt the same way.

THE REALITY SHOW

In April 2019, Zach said to me, "Hey, *New York* magazine is doing a profile on what all of the candidates were like in high school. They want a high school yearbook photo of you. Is that cool?"

I said, "Sure." I felt glad just to be included, because it wasn't a sure thing when national media did features on candidates. I told

Zach that my high school would have an archived copy of the yearbook.

They sure did, and pretty soon this photo materialized online.

My high school yearbook
photo from 1992

I was a little bit self-conscious seeing this image spread online. It didn't look like a standard yearbook photo of a presidential candidate. In high school, I was a little bit mopey and angry, like many young people figuring out the world, and I looked the part. It felt odd to have my teenage years splayed out for public consumption, and I was afraid people would take me less seriously.

Yet again, I would find myself confounded by the reaction of people on social media. People were excited that I seemed like a real person who had been a real teen. A lot of people liked the same bands I did. The reaction to my "goth" yearbook photo was so positive that Andrew Frawley, ever opportunistic, said, "We should make it a T-shirt." It turned into one of our top sellers.

We kept learning. In August 2019, I was invited to a gun violence forum in Des Moines, hosted by Everytown for Gun Safety,

Moms Demand Action, and Students Demand Action. Organizations hosted presidential forums in the early states timed for when candidates would be in town so as to make our attendance both convenient and somewhat obligatory. As soon as any of the major candidates said yes, everyone else would too. This forum had seventeen candidates scheduled to attend.

When so many candidates show up, each of us gets slotted for approximately half an hour. Even then, that's nine hours of programming, so it's a long day watching candidate after candidate show up and speak. I was one of the later candidates in the mid-afternoon.

My team and I rolled up to the back of the Iowa Events Center in a rented Navigator in the summer heat. As we crossed the parking lot, I saw a family on the storage dock coming out as we were going in. I made eye contact with the dad, a handsome middle-aged man in jeans with scruffy brown hair and a goatee. "Holy shit," I thought, "that's Eddie Vedder." I listened to Pearl Jam a ton in college, driving my secondhand Honda Accord, singing along to Eddie's vocals. I shook his hand and told him I was a fan.

Eddie thanked me and introduced me to his family. As we parted, he said to me, "Aw, man, we're missing the main event." It felt great hearing that from one of my personal rock gods.

We went backstage and waited to go on. Tulsi Gabbard was before me onstage answering questions. I watched and listened on a television monitor backstage. I snuck around the stage entrance and peered into the auditorium to get a sense of the layout. Tulsi wrapped up her remarks to moderate applause. As she came offstage, she saw me and we exchanged a quick greeting.

"Hey, Tulsi, great work out there."

"Thank you, Andrew. It's always great to see you." I had become friendly with Tulsi and her husband, Abraham, on the trail. Abraham doubled as her photographer. I envied their ability to travel together.

I went onstage and addressed the audience, consisting of hundreds of activists, about my views on gun violence. It was always better to stand: I felt I could project more energy and move around. I said that we needed to pass commonsense gun legislation, a point on which a clear majority of Americans agreed. But we needed to think much bigger, beyond the gun laws to the root causes of gun violence. We should acknowledge that more than 90 percent of school shooters were boys and that we have a disproportionate problem raising strong and healthy boys and men. That started with the family but continued into schools that were assembly lines and did not have the resources necessary to support boys who struggled behaviorally and academically. I talked about how one of my boys is neurologically atypical and that I knew that if you have the wrong boy in the wrong school, bad things could happen to that child and sometimes even to others. I talked about the links between the country's mental health crisis and gun violence, noting that a majority of victims of gun violence are suicides. I also talked about how we have an increasingly punishing and inhuman economy that makes many young men in particular feel like they don't have a stable path forward. Access to guns was the proximate cause in gun violence that we had to address, but there was often an entire chain of factors and events that we should try to interrupt and remediate at every level.

I felt my remarks were well received. Afterward, I took a seat and began answering questions from both the moderator and members of the audience.

One of the first questions was from Stephanie Pizzoferrato, a mother from Las Vegas. "My beautiful four-year-old daughter, Dayla, was struck by a stray bullet in 2011. My son—my daughter's twin brother—witnessed what happened that day. She died two days later." Stephanie went on to say that firearms were the second leading cause of death for children and teenagers and asked what we could do to prevent accidental shootings.

I heard this story and I had a vision of my older son getting shot and my younger son seeing it and surviving. I asked Stephanie if I could give her a hug and went to her to do so. As we hugged, I thought about how much I missed my children, and experienced a glimpse of the unimaginable sadness of losing one of them forever. My boys are eight and five, quite close in age to what Stephanie was describing. I imagined Evelyn telling the story in public years later, with a hole in her heart that nothing could ever fill. I heard the sadness in Stephanie's voice and her tearing up at the thought of her daughter even after years of mourning.

As I returned to the stage, the feeling stuck with me. I teared up, covering my face with my hand to compose myself. It felt like a long time, but in truth it was only a few seconds. I then answered Stephanie's question about how we can make households safer from unlocked guns by offering owners upgrades to personalized guns that can only be used by the owner. The answer was secondary to the emotion, though, of sharing grief with a mom who had lost a child. I concluded my response by saying, "I am so sorry."

After answering a couple more questions, I went backstage, where I would meet other survivors of gun violence. One had lost a classmate to gun violence in the streets. Another had lost a parent to suicide. I knew the numbers around gun violence, but seeing so many people whose lives and families had been torn apart by it was devastating.

Afterward, when we were back in the Navigator, Zach said to me, "Great work out there. Really proud of you. That was very difficult stuff."

"Thanks. Sharing in people's experiences was really tough. I feel for them."

"Yes. Hey, FYI the footage of you crying is now up online. It's already been seen by over a hundred thousand people. It will probably be over a million by the end of the day."

"Really?" I was dumbfounded. I felt very self-conscious about it; it's not as if I were used to having images of myself crying making the news.

Zach said, "Yes. I think it's going over well. It's probably a good thing because it's against type." CNN, *Rolling Stone,* the *HuffPost,* and others ran stories on it as the views multiplied.

A few hours later on the way back to the hotel I got a call from Evelyn. "Hey, I'm getting all of these text messages from friends who are saying they saw you cry and it made them cry too."

"Yeah. Have you seen it?"

"No. I know I'll cry when I see it."

"Yeah, if you'd heard this woman's story, it was heartbreaking. One of her children was shot in front of the other and died. Now the mom and the surviving sibling have that trauma they live with probably every single day."

"That's so sad."

My emotional reaction to Stephanie's story became a story in itself. In the next couple days I was asked to appear on CNN and MSNBC to talk about gun violence and my response to Stephanie. They even asked if Evelyn would come on TV to talk about my reaction. This human reaction I'd had to another parent's loss had struck a nerve; it had pierced through the ambient noise and become part of a public narrative. Very few journalists wanted to talk to the marginal candidate campaigning on automation and universal basic income, or even to hear my thoughts on curbing gun violence, but if I teared up over a story of a child being shot, it became newsworthy.

Something similar happened the following week in South Carolina, though in happier circumstances. My team and I went there to campaign for several days. We were led around by Jermaine Johnson, a Democratic activist and our state chair in South Carolina. Jermaine was a former professional basketball player overseas who had played locally at the College of Charleston. He's about six feet seven and 270 pounds with a big smile. I loved walking around with Jermaine, because people couldn't help but have their attention drawn to him and then eventually they would notice the

Walking with South Carolina campaign chair and current
South Carolina state representative Jermaine Johnson

normal-sized Asian man next to him. Jermaine joked that he looked like my security detail.

On our first day on the trail, we campaigned in Beaufort, South Carolina, a lovely coastal town of about thirteen thousand people. We visited the town's Black Chamber of Commerce to meet with voters. The building was mostly empty, and our stop there felt like a bit of a bust. But on the second floor behind a door we heard some line dancing music and a voice leading the group. "Step, and step!"

"Well, at least there are some people here. Let me go in and say hi," I thought as I opened the door. It was a nice well-lit studio with wooden floors. Jermaine did a great job trying to get people's attention, saying, "Hello, all. This here is Andrew Yang, and he's running for president." It didn't seem as though the people there recognized me, but they were very friendly. There were about fifteen middle-aged women doing a combination of dancing and Jazzercise.

The ladies said hello but were more intent on their workout

than meeting a presidential candidate. They had on sweats, T-shirts, and workout gear. I felt like I was interrupting. One of my staffers said half jokingly, "You should join in."

Their workout looked pretty simple and like a bit of fun. It also seemed pretty lame for me to just turn around and leave at this point. So I shrugged and took my place in an open spot in the line and started to imitate the steps of the ladies around me. The steps reminded me of the Electric Slide, which I had done at weddings. I got the hang of it pretty quickly. After I danced the Cupid Shuffle for a few minutes, the song ended and I jogged around the room high-fiving people and then left. I had the sense that some folks were recording it, but I didn't think much of it; on the campaign trail people are recording you all the time.

Minutes later we got into our rental vehicle—this time a big silver Chevy Suburban; we always rented American—to head to our next stop, which was about an hour away. At that point Erick Sanchez, my traveling press secretary, leaned over.

"Hey, Michael posted a video of you dancing to his Twitter account." Michael was a reporter who was writing a story about the trip.

"That's nice. I hope I looked all right."

Erick grinned. "Yeah, it was tight. I think it's up to 100,000 views already."

I shot up. "What?" It had been maybe fifteen minutes.

"Yeah, there are a couple different versions from different angles. Zach took one too. It's making its way through the internet."

I underestimated the interest people would have. The "Andrew Yang Cupid Shuffle" video circulated to millions in hours. Chance the Rapper retweeted it and said, "I can't be pandered to. But the confidence of that headbob: 11 seconds in mighta made me #YangGang." My doing the Cupid Shuffle became one of the defining images of the campaign.

Some of the cable networks played the video during roundups of the day's news. I did a network segment a few days later, and they ran the video of my dancing before the commercial break as a means of introducing me to voters.

By this point, maybe I shouldn't have been so surprised by this turn of events, but I was. I spent three days campaigning in South Carolina and went to town halls, Democratic clubs, a shelter for abused women, a Mexican restaurant, and a dozen other places. It turns out that the only three minutes anyone cared about was my dancing with the ladies of Beaufort. The machine craved content.

The next viral moment happened a couple weeks later. I was in Orange County, California, for an Asian American Pacific Islander presidential forum. The three candidates who were there were me, Tulsi Gabbard, and Tom Steyer. Not many candidates turned out for the Asians. The forum took place in the Segerstrom Center for the Arts, a very opulent concert hall that made me feel like an opera singer as I took to the stage. I spoke about my experience growing up in upstate New York and my pride in being the first Asian American man to run for president as a Democrat.

After my session I stood backstage with my arms outstretched while a technician took the microphone pack off me. Zach said to me, "Great job out there. We are supposed to be at the next event in ninety minutes, and it's more than an hour away given L.A. traffic. So we have ten minutes or so. But there are maybe a hundred supporters of ours gathered in the lobby." Zach knew I'd feel terrible if people came to support me and didn't have any chance to interact with me.

"Okay, let's go see them," I said.

"Great," Zach said. "But you cannot take selfies with everyone. We do not have the time, because we can't be late to the next event."

I rounded the corner and saw a large crowd of people holding campaign signs. They started cheering as soon as they saw me. I bounded toward them high-fiving people and thanking them. In moments I was surrounded by people chanting my name and clapping me on the shoulders. A number of people had their phones out to snap pictures, and I pivoted my head for a couple seconds in each direction so they each could get the right angle. Zach was right: there was no way I could take selfies with everyone in a reasonable time frame. I surveyed the crowd and tried to brainstorm a way I could mix with all of them. I laughed and said, "Maybe I should crowd-surf."

An excited man in his thirties heard me and said, "Yes! Let's do it! CROWD-SURF! CROWD-SURF!" Before long a dozen people were chanting the same. The first guy even cupped his hands together and crouched in order to give me a boost.

I saw there was a carpet on the ground, and the crowd was dense enough. People were chanting in my ears, and the people directly around me had their hands up. I started smiling and nodding and said, "All right, let's do it!"

Zach, nearby, was like, "Oh no."

I stepped forward and put my hand on the man's shoulders and my foot in his cupped hands. He boosted me up while several people then moved forward to support me from behind. I leaned back into about half a dozen hands. I put my arms out on either side so that it would be easier for people to support my weight as several other people caught me. They started to pass me forward feetfirst as people around them chanted my name. "AN-DREW YANG! AN-DREW YANG!" I pumped my fist in time with the chants.

The last time I had crowd-surfed was about twenty years earlier. I was at a Morrissey concert in New York City; I touched Morrissey's wrist when he reached down into the crowd. Back then I felt completely invincible.

The crowd passed me forward for about twenty seconds whooping and chanting the entire time. I remember looking up at the ceiling, thinking, "I'm glad Evelyn's not here to see this." Eventually, the crowd started to thin, and I could feel fewer hands on me and my altitude start to sink. There was a dip. I tried to shift my weight so that my feet touched the ground first. The main thing about crowd-surfing is to make sure you land feetfirst. I popped back up so that people could see that I was fine. People continued to cheer. Everyone was so happy that we started jumping up and down high-fiving and cheering.

I was quickly getting surrounded again. I tried to project, "Thank you! Thank you so much!" I felt as if I'd done everything I could to let people feel like we'd done something fun in a very brief period of time. People cheered and snapped selfies as my team took me by the elbows and ushered me toward the exit and out into the sun.

After we were settled in our rental car, Zach looked at me and said, "This campaign is absolutely nuts."

ONCE AGAIN, a video of mine went viral, with TV networks showing the footage and *The Washington Post, USA Today,* and CNN posting it online. Once again, I had become a meme, a piece of content, clickbait. It had become clear that we could pierce through the noise and get mainstream press if I did something that would make a casual viewer click a link and watch a quick video.

That was the nature of running for president. There were all of the things you were supposed to do that every other candidate was doing. Most of those things would not get noticed or covered if you were not a front-runner, and even a top candidate might not get attention for a forum or town hall. There was social media, a constant stream of images and videos. Then there was creating your own press by doing something fun, edgy, or interesting that arose naturally from the act of campaigning.

It was like a reality show that needed you to assume a role in order to survive. In my case, I became the MATH-hat-wearing, cash-giving, crying, dancing, crowd-surfing, basketball-shooting, skateboarding candidate in part as a means to compete.

I was running a substantive campaign based on big ideas like universal basic income. But the campaign required attention as its oxygen, and the mainstream media would not cover ideas so much as characters. People becoming familiar with me or even saying, "I kind of like that guy," was a necessary condition for anyone to actually engage with the campaign. Once again, I found that leaning into my relative humanity was one of the only ways to break through. In a campaign process that was largely formalistic and mechanical, it turns out everyone, including the press, craved a human being having fun on the trail.

CHAPTER 6

THE EYE OF SAURON

While we were campaigning around Iowa in the summer of 2019, my campaign manager, Zach, sat me down and said, "We need to improve your remote hits. You look uncomfortable, like you don't want to be there."

I responded, "That's because I don't. Those hits are awful."

Remote hits are when a news network like CNN or MSNBC beams someone in to do an interview from the road. Cable networks have a lot of programming time to fill, and a presidential candidate—even a second-tier one—would field periodic invitations to appear on camera and discuss the news of the day for five to six minutes. When you were a press-starved candidate like me, you took any opportunity to get on the airwaves, knowing that, even at weird times of the day, hundreds of thousands of people might be watching.

In order to participate in the interview, you would go to a remote studio, typically in a random office park thirty minutes away. The network would want you there at least thirty minutes early. Quite often I would show up for a segment at a particular time, and it would be moved back. MSNBC once bumped my segment entirely because Bernie decided to go for a walk and they cut to him.

You would arrive at the obscure studio for the remote hit, and there would usually be two people there: a makeup artist who would swab you down and a producer who would stick the earpiece in your ear and line up the shot. Makeup might take five minutes. They generally want you "in the chair" ten minutes before your segment.

When you sit in the chair, you can't see anything. You're facing a black screen with a camera inside. There's a voice in your ear from a person at the studio, which says things like "Could you move a tiny bit to your right, Mr. Yang?" or "You will be on after this segment and commercials, which will be about three minutes from now." You stare straight ahead and try to compose yourself for several minutes. Sometimes the makeup artist brushes you up at the last second or takes a lint roller to your shoulders. You stare at where you hope the eye of the camera is.

At some point you hear a whoosh of graphics, and the anchor's voice says something like "Over a dozen candidates are now on the trail making their case to primary voters in the early states. Joining us now from Iowa City, Iowa, is one of them, entrepreneur Andrew Yang. Mr. Yang, you have been on the trail now for about a year, but your name recognition is much lower than that of some of the other candidates in the field. What do you need to do in order to break through?" While the anchor fires off questions, you try to look attentive and form your response. You have typically been given a sense of the questions to be discussed: some news of the day with two or three questions about the campaign. You keep each response to about sixty seconds to maintain the cadence of the segment; if you go on too long, the anchor will cut in.

While you answer the questions, you still can't see anything but the black screen. By nodding your head to the sound of their voice and smiling, you act as though you were having a normal conversation with another person.

After four or five questions, the anchor says something like "Good luck on the trail. Coming up next, we will be talking to an expert on blah blah blah." Then the studio person's voice clicks back in, saying, "You are clear. Thank you." You sit there for an extra beat because you have been frozen like a statue in position for at least fifteen minutes. Then you take the earpiece out of your ear, and your heart rate begins to slow down to normal.

The entire process takes about an hour and forty-five minutes including drive time from the remote studio back to whatever you were doing. Almost two hours to sit down, stare at a screen, and answer questions for five minutes. (This was before we started Zooming into everything during the pandemic.)

Now Zach was telling me all the reasons why I was bad at remote hits. "Don't smile. Your smile looks weird and fake. Try a half smile. No teeth."

"Why do we have to do them in the first place?" I ask again. "Do we have any data that they are somehow moving the needle for us? It's not like we raise any money after I go on. I feel like people have cable news on for background noise, not actionable intelligence gathering."

"We need legitimacy. Being on the news gives that to us. And if cable news will have you on, then other reporters will talk to you," Zach says. "So you need to get better at them."

"Okay," I say. "But please see if there's something we can do to improve the settings. I feel like an idiot staring into the Eye of Sauron trying to seem compelling."

"The Eye of what?"

"Never mind. I'll work on it."

THE MEDIA GAUNTLET

I did slowly get better at cable news hits. And Zach started pushing for remote interviews to take place at campaign events. I still couldn't see the interviewer, but surrounded by supporters in the open air, I felt much more human. Plus my supporters were thrilled to pop up on national TV waving signs, even for a few seconds.

I'd run a strange gauntlet with the media. Upon declaring my (mostly anonymous) candidacy in February 2018, I had a hard time getting any attention at all. I would talk to just about anyone who would have me on—podcasters mainly. When a journalist would report on me, there would generally be some caveat saying, "This person is a long shot, but he has some very interesting ideas about automation and the future of work." One thing I noticed: a disproportionate number of the journalists who gave me the time of day early were Asian American. The major cable news networks generally acted like I didn't exist. This lasted for a year after I declared, until the beginning of 2019.

When I was being ignored by cable news, I went on any podcast I could. My first big break was when the neuroscientist Sam Harris interviewed me on his highly rated podcast in June 2018. Sam later introduced me to Joe Rogan, whose show launched our campaign into contention.

Everything changed after I appeared on Rogan's podcast in February 2019. Visiting his studio in Los Angeles felt like a turning point. Joe has a ton of energy. He was friendly and warm throughout and showed me around the building, which was like an airline hangar complete with a full gym and training mats. Our interview lasted nearly two hours, but it seemed to fly by in minutes. I left the building thinking, "That was more fun than I'd expected."

That interview made an immediate difference. Our fundraising surged from thousands a week to tens of thousands a day after my appearance on *The Joe Rogan Experience,* which has now been seen more than six million times on YouTube alone. I got recognized on the street much more often, and people felt comfortable approaching me, as if I were someone they knew personally. After that, more reporters noticed that I was running.

However, the national media initially presented me as the internet candidate and, bizarrely, the preferred candidate of alt-right white supremacists. One of the data points they cited was that I'd retweeted a *New York Times* article talking about the overdose rates in rural white communities, as if that were some kind of appeal to a racist element.

The white supremacist thing was completely confusing to me. I was literally the son of immigrants running on a platform (UBI) that had once been championed by Martin Luther King Jr. I had founded and run a nonprofit for the previous six years to help communities around the country, including cities like Detroit and New Orleans that are predominantly Black. None of that mattered. The media was looking for its own way to define me—to offer up a caricature that would serve to sensationalize or minimize me out of the gate.

When I launched the campaign, I assumed I would be regarded as the most "far left" figure in the field. After all, giving away $1,000 a month for everyone? Even Bernie wasn't going there. But it turned out that my approach—trying to solve problems, talking about real-life economic trends that people could see around them every day—wound up building a different type of following. My facts became their own kinds of symbols, forming a new political language that defied easy classification in the media.

Over the course of 2019, this initial post–Joe Rogan burst of curiosity faded, and I became the candidate that networks were hoping would go away, even though my campaign was becoming more popular than ever, in terms of donations and polling. MSNBC and CNN regularly omitted me from graphics that included polling or fundraising of major candidates. An MSNBC on-air graphic once called me "John Yang," which I found more amusing than my staff did. When I was mentioned in the media, I was often referred to as a technology executive or businessman, which served to diminish my nonprofit work in communities far from the "coastal elite" cities. Many people simply assumed I was from California.

To be honest, I didn't mind the "Asian tech guy" identity, because at least it was an angle. I wasn't that picky. One question I got over and over again was, "What makes you qualified to be president? You lack the proper experience." This is a question candidates loathe, because the truthful answer is usually a lot better than the sound bites disciplined candidates are made to serve up.

My usual response went something like this: "I have a sense of the real problems that got Donald Trump elected and are pushing Americans to the side. We are going through the most dramatic economic transformation in our country's history, the fourth Industrial Revolution. I have real solutions that will move our country forward. That's what workers and families are focused on, trying to improve their own way of life."

In other words, I would pivot the answer to address the substance of my campaign. But any number of alternative responses went through my head at different times, all of them at least equally truthful:

- "Well, I was editor of the *Columbia Law Review* and passed the bar on my first try, so I understand law and policy better than most."
- "I've run a private company that became number one in the country in its category and was acquired by a public company for millions of dollars, so I understand business."
- "I've worked in entrepreneurship and technology for more than a decade, so I understand technology."
- "I worked in health-care software for four years, including working on-site in hospitals in the Bronx, Newark, and suburban Florida, so I understand health care."
- "I was the CEO of an education company for five years and interviewed and hired hundreds of teachers and taught thousands of students, so I understand education."
- "I started a national nonprofit that impacts thousands of people to this day, so I understand philanthropy and social impact."

- "I'm a husband and the father of two young boys, one of whom is autistic, so I understand the realities of raising a family."
- "I grew up the son of immigrants, so I know what it's like to feel like the odd person out while trying to fit in."
- "Well, I have started a national movement that has raised tens of millions of dollars from hundreds of thousands of everyday Americans, so I understand fighting for people."
- "I'm under the age of seventy."
- "Well, I'm not a raging lunatic or an asshole, as much as this question suggests otherwise."

Often, what the questioner really seemed to be asking was, "You haven't spent years acclimating yourself to Washington, schmoozing donors, doing robotic press conferences, and generally insinuating yourself with the political leadership class, demonstrating that you will get very little done. How can we also trust you to get very little done and maintain the status quo?"

The primacy of the media's narrative control really hit home during the debates. During the first Democratic primary debate in June 2019, I got only two minutes and fifty seconds of speaking time over two hours, compared with twelve minutes for Joe Biden and Kamala Harris. Some of that was clearly on me; I should have muscled my way into more speaking time. But some of it stemmed from the fact that the moderators from MSNBC were far more interested in generating airtime for certain candidates and narratives they were pushing than they were for the new random interloper. The tens of thousands of Americans who had donated to my campaign to get me on the stage were irrelevant to them. At the next debate, I referred to the debate process as a "reality TV show."

I found out later that some campaigns were known to be in touch with debate moderators to suggest that certain questions get asked. If you don't have a direct line to the journalists, you can at least signal ahead of time to the press questions and topics that you would like to get, generally by attacking someone. When I realized this, in July 2019, I tweeted, "I would like to signal to the press that I will be attacking Michael Bennet at next week's debate. Sorry @MichaelBennet but you know what you did." Reporters contacted my team to see if I was serious.

I also found out later from the producer Ariana Pekary, who left MSNBC publicly in August 2020, that in April 2019 my name was on a list of candidates whom she was told not to seek an interview with without any explanation.

This persistent minimization occurred again when MSNBC moderated another debate in November. This time the moderators took thirty-two minutes to ask me a question—the statistical expectation would be about eleven minutes—and the handful of questions posed to me had nothing to do with any issue I'd campaigned on. "Mr. Yang, what would you say to Putin?" was the first. (I responded, "Sorry I beat your guy.") Once again, I received far less speaking time than any other candidate. When I walked offstage, I got the clear feeling that the moderators had wanted nothing to do with me.

The next day I was sitting in my hotel room when my team informed me that an MSNBC show had invited me for an interview. After reflecting on the previous night's debate experience and the dozen omissions from the network's graphics featuring candidates, I'd had enough. I said that I wouldn't accept MSNBC show invitations until they acknowledged that they had treated us unfairly and said that it would improve.

I expected this to be a quick affair. MSNBC would do what any normal high-functioning news organization would do. They would say, "We aspire to conduct excellent journalism here at MSNBC. We take seriously any complaints about the accuracy of our coverage, and any errors in our graphics were unintended. We apologize for any mistakes and omissions and look forward to working with Mr. Yang in the future." They could apologize for the graphics— one of which they had already apologized for—without copping to any systematic bias, and everyone would move on. I figured my boycott would last a few days or so while they issued a press release and sent a message.

Instead, they took my public complaints as an affront. At first, network sources told reporters that they had called and apologized to us when they had not. Then they refused to admit any fault and refused all comment. I disappeared from their coverage of the race. Weeks later, MSNBC would not even acknowledge that I'd qualified for the sixth debate when the field shrank to seven and I was the only nonwhite candidate left in the field, a major piece of political news reported by seemingly every other outlet under the sun.

The whole thing blew my mind. My supporters were furious and #boycottMSNBC trended on Twitter for days. A handful of Yang Gang even demonstrated outside MSNBC's headquarters in Rockefeller Center. But MSNBC had dug in its heels.

I eventually ended the boycott five weeks later and sat for an interview with Chris Hayes—who was always fair to me—because I figured I needed to reach Democratic voters any way I could. At this point we had 400,000 donors to the campaign, and I wasn't going to let my conflict with MSNBC keep us from talking to the public and maximizing our chances to win.

But the MSNBC flap offered another campaign trail lesson: don't expect TV news organizations to act accountable, fair, and objective. Many don't even see themselves that way. They're not there to report the news; they're there to make the news. They have set audiences to whom they are appealing and are comfortable making judgments as to what and how to present "the news" to that audience. They may not be eager to add new variables to the mix that may not line up with their audience's tested preferences.

This is not to say that there weren't TV journalists who were always very professional and conscientious. Ali Velshi, Erin Burnett, Van Jones, Dana Bash, Anderson Cooper, and others took an interest in the substance of my campaign early and gave us a real chance to take our message to the public.

For now, cable news—as the industry has for decades—continues to play a central role in shaping and sometimes distorting a presidential candidate's "narrative." The industry's dominance creates a wall; you're either on the inside, protected, or on the outside looking in. But there are signs that cracks are forming. It wasn't lost on me during the campaign that younger people are more likely to get their news from random articles in their social media feeds and podcasts than they are from cable news.

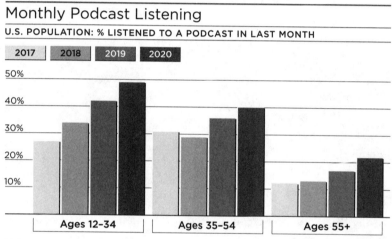

Monthly Podcast Listening

U.S. POPULATION: % LISTENED TO A PODCAST IN LAST MONTH

2017   2018   2019   2020

Ages 12–34   Ages 35–54   Ages 55+

Edison Research and Triton Digital

The audiences for the biggest podcasts now rival or surpass cable news with a much younger demographic. My interview on *The Joe Rogan Experience* has been watched more than six million times on YouTube and downloaded millions more as a podcast, and his audience has an average age of twenty-four. Around the same time, Tucker Carlson and Sean Hannity were setting records at around 4.3 million viewers, and the average age of prime-time Fox viewers is around sixty-five. The smart news organizations are investing in podcasts for this reason.

"Reading or watching the news is no longer immersive, as it was when you sat down with a bunch of papers or in front of a living room TV," wrote Bari Weiss in a *New York Times* op-ed column

Total TV Viewing by Age, Indexed to 2010

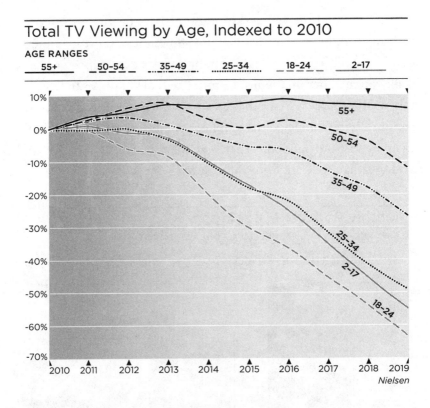

AGE RANGES
55+ | 50-54 | 35-49 | 25-34 | 18-24 | 2-17

Nielsen

in May 2020. Weiss's piece quoted Joe Rogan on how mobile devices had become central to news consumption: "Nobody ever thought: We need to gear our entertainment, our media, to people who cook, who jog, who hike, people who drive." A podcast is "really easy to listen to while you do other stuff."

As discussed earlier, I know full well the power of podcasts because that is how my campaign gained traction. In addition to Sam Harris's and Joe Rogan's podcasts, other enormous breaks included *Freakonomics, The Breakfast Club,* Ben Shapiro, Kara Swisher, Ezra Klein, David Axelrod, *Pod Save America,* and *The H3 Podcast.*

Podcasts were perfect for me. The conversations were typically long form—up to an hour or longer. Most of the ideas from my campaign took time to explain. Giving everyone money seemed radical unless I unpacked the transformation of the economy that had literally taken me hundreds of pages to fully describe in my book *The War on Normal People.* The content was a much better fit for an hour as opposed to a six-minute cable news segment.

Most of these podcast interviewers had a high degree of editorial independence. They didn't have any big company to answer to or set of relationships to safeguard. If a podcaster like Stephen Dubner or Kara Swisher wants to talk about automation or humanizing the economy, they can dedicate a show to it and dig in. And people trust them. When Sam Harris expressed support for my campaign on his podcast, we raised thousands of dollars a day for the entire week. With Joe Rogan it was tens of thousands of dollars per day. With the average blink-and-you'll-miss-it cable news hit, we raised next to nothing.

"Right or wrong, in podcasting you're getting that very pure, individual perspective" is how Joe Rogan put it. "On my show it's my opinion and the guest's opinion. That's it. On a network, it's a focus-group collective idea of what people are going to like. You don't get anything that will get you fired."

A friend who works in politics put it this way: "No one knows how we'll reach voters in twenty years when TV ads no longer work." They will be replaced by a patchwork of podcasts and tens of thousands of ads and influencer posts through YouTube, Facebook, Twitter, Instagram, Snapchat, TikTok, Clubhouse, and their successors. As people get their information and news in different ways, our politics are likely to evolve in new ways as well. When the gatekeepers go away, does that free up more oxygen in the media ecosystem for candidates like me, who don't fit so easily into the old guard's preconceived notions? Or do we risk extreme candidates like Donald Trump finding it even easier to gain traction, particularly as social media rewards more extreme viewpoints and conspiracy theories?

Some could take from the relative success of my campaign that the old barriers are crashing down. I believe they are getting weaker, but it is unclear what will replace them. The closest thing will likely be a collection of the top fifty to a hundred or so influential voices

online who have substantial followings and can steer public sentiment. Some of them are great and responsible—others less so. As
the cable news audience ages and people's news consumption frag-
ments, we are likely to see more outliers from outside conventional
politics making dramatic rises that would have been unthinkable
not that long ago. Institutional gatekeepers will be replaced by individual opinion makers, and politics will start to veer more toward
the extremes as candidates draw attention and resources directly
from people. If you are a fan of moderation, you will likely see less
of it as the media gatekeepers recede in prominence.

CHAPTER 7

POWER SCREWS WITH YOUR MIND

I t's your birthday. Imagine going into a room and finding dozens of people have gathered together to see you. They toast your arrival. There is much excitement. They ask you to give a speech. You are very flattered. You give a speech that speaks to how touched you are that they are there for you. You talk about the occasion that has brought you all together. You want it to be genuine. Not so short that it seems perfunctory, but not so long that it seems self-indulgent.

Your birthday speech goes great. People want to talk to you and congratulate you. You are happy to see them. You shake hands and greet the people you know. There are many people you don't know, perhaps because your friends brought their friends. It's that kind of party.

Now imagine if that happened to you every night. Not just every night but several times during the day as well. And in addition to it being your birthday every day, you periodically visit television sets to talk to a TV personality. The host greets you in the greenroom, and you find yourself studying a face that you have seen many times before. You are surrounded by people at all times. They theoretically work for you, but most of the time they are directing you, saying, "You have to be on the road in ten minutes" or "You have a call with this person in five." And you are on the road four days a week away from your family. You get back to the hotel room, and your face is tired from smiling or making expressions.

That's a bit of what it feels like, running for president.

. . .

AT SOME POINT in early 2019, Zach said to me, "We need to give you a different haircut. And update your wardrobe."

I said, "No one cares what I look like. Bernie looks like the scientist from *Back to the Future*. The point is just to stand for something. People know what I stand for and don't care about my hair."

Zach shook his head and said, "That's not true. Bernie's old. You're young. People care that you're wearing a weird button or a suit that doesn't look quite right. I'm going to set you up with a hairdresser and tailor."

I went along with it. I already had to get used to wearing makeup for television appearances that I often kept on for the rest of the day. The most irritating thing was using hair product again after taking a twenty-year break from it. Apparently, "hair gel" was upgraded to "hair wax" at some point, which seemed like an improvement from my old Studio Line gel from L'Oréal.

Before: It wasn't rare for my button to turn to the side and look like an *h*.

After: A tailor, a hairstylist, and a custom-made MATH pin later.

Imagine relearning how to groom yourself in your mid-forties. People talk about running for office or running for president as an act of leadership. I'm not so sure about that. I actually think that in many respects running for president requires qualities that would make you a terrible leader.

When I was the CEO of Manhattan Prep, I would often teach classes or conduct events without identifying myself as the CEO. In that case, it was better for the company if people didn't think of me as anything other than a random instructor. The more it was about me, the less it was about the company.

In my experience, if you see a CEO chasing press, that person's company is probably headed for trouble. The energy spent burnishing your image could almost always be better spent managing your people, ferreting out problems, clearing obstacles, honing processes, talking to customers, selecting vendors, recruiting team members, and working on new initiatives. With Manhattan Prep, the most important thing was to do a good job for each student. The most powerful growth driver would be a satisfied student telling his or her friend, "Hey, this company did a great job, you should give them a try." That is the way most businesses operate: if you do a good job and make people happy, then the business grows.

In the context of presidential politics it was the opposite. The job was simply the seeking of attention. You would seek press virtually all of the time. Interviews and press—or an in-person event that hopefully would attract press—were the job. When I wasn't on the road, I would wake up on a typical day and head to a television studio first thing in the morning, go to the office to film some digital ads, do several interviews, and then head to a grassroots fundraising event that night.

On a presidential campaign you make the big initial hires. But then as the campaign grows, it adds people quickly, often people who played a similar role for another campaign. It was jarring for me to show up to the office in New York or an event in New Hampshire and meet someone, only to be told, "This person is now working for you as a field organizer/digital outreach specialist/advance team/new role." I would thank the person and be genuinely grateful, but it felt strangely impersonal. When I ran my own company, I made sure to interview anyone we hired at any level, because hiring seemed like one of the most important aspects of leadership.

In national politics, it turns out, you're not as much the CEO as you are yourself the product.

The first time I was noticed in public I was taken aback. I was in a convenience store with one of my sons in March 2019. A hipster-looking guy in his twenties said to me, "Hey, are you Andrew Yang?"

"Yes, yes, I am."

"I'm a big supporter of yours. Keep it up."

"Thank you."

This was particularly surprising to me because I was wearing jeans and a hoodie. The fact that people recognized me out of my campaign uniform of a blazer and dress shirt was shocking to me. My favorite was when a young woman came up to me and said, "Are you Andrew Yang? No, no, you're not," and then walked away.

Things began to change over the course of 2019 as my public profile grew. After raising only $642,081 through all of 2018, our campaign raised $1.7 million in the first quarter, $2.8 million in the second quarter, $10 million in the third quarter, and a whopping $16.5 million in the fourth quarter. I remember in the fourth quarter we raised half of what Bernie raised, and I ran around yelling, "We're half a Bernie!" We had come a long way since the previous year. On New Year's Eve 2018 we had held a fundraiser party in New York that had actually lost money. Someone asked for their money back. That's not a good party.

Our media exposure had grown in tandem with our fundraising. We had graduated from podcasts to television. At first it was political comedy shows like *The Daily Show* or *Patriot Act with Hasan Minhaj* or *Real Time with Bill Maher*. Then it was *The Late Show with Stephen Colbert*, *The View*, and *Late Night with Seth Meyers*. Then eventually it was Ellen DeGeneres and Jimmy Kimmel. Jimmy and

I compared notes on playing Ted Cruz in basketball, because Ted had recently accepted a challenge from me before thinking better of it. Stephen Colbert joked that I went from "regular guy Andrew Yang" to "famous guy Andrew Yang." In many cases I went on a show more than once—like *The View*—and the first time I was on, the interviewers were a bit dubious. There was an undercurrent of "Who the heck are you?" But the second time around there was much more openness and even warmth.

We started spending money to increase my support in Iowa and New Hampshire, bombarding the airwaves in both states for weeks. We spent $6.6 million on television ads in Iowa and $3.9 million in New Hampshire alone. The TV ads were something else. The first ad had a lot of imagery of planet Earth. I joked with Evelyn that the voice-over for the ad should go something like this: "He arrived on this planet from a land far, far away. Andrew Yang—EARTH PRESIDENT 2040."

Recording political ads required hours. There's a lot of line reading and looking at a camera. The words have to be precisely measured to be exactly thirty seconds or sixty seconds. After you're done with a take, a producer will say something like "Hey, that was twenty-eight seconds; can you drag it out a little further?" or "Great, give it a more somber downbeat take." Recording those ads would typically take half a day because they would record multiple ads at a time with a full film crew. And it meant more time in makeup.

The fact that there were hundreds of campaign workers spending millions of dollars all in an effort to make you look good is a positively bizarre feeling. I joked with the digital team that they must have pictures of me emblazoned in their brain when they go to sleep at night.

The entire campaign was a massive adjustment to say the least. And it was more than just a head rush. There are psychological consequences to being treated this way for months on end.

POWER AND THE BRAIN

There is a great fear among many Americans that our leaders are out of touch. That they don't understand what is going on with the vast majority of people in the country.

These concerns are well-founded.

The historian Henry Adams described power as "a sort of tumor that ends by killing the victim's sympathies." This may sound like hyperbole, but it has been borne out by years of lab and field experiments. Dacher Keltner, a psychology professor at UC Berkeley, has been studying the influence of power on individuals. He puts people in positions of power relative to each other in different settings. He has consistently found that power, over time, makes one more impulsive, more reckless, and less able to see things from others' points of view. It also leads one to be rude, more likely to cheat on one's spouse, less attentive to other people, and less interested in the experiences of others.

Does that sound familiar? It turns out that power actually gives you brain damage.

This even shows up in brain scans. Sukhvinder Obhi, a neuroscientist at McMaster University in Ontario, recently examined the brain patterns of the powerful and the not so powerful in a transcranial-magnetic-stimulation machine. He found that those with power are impaired in a specific neural process—mirroring—that leads to empathy.

I'm a parent, and one thing you find very consistently with kids is that they reciprocate what you do. You smile, they smile. You laugh, they laugh. Among the powerful in various settings, their impulse to reflect what they are being shown emotionally has been numbed. They similarly lose the ability to put themselves in another person's shoes.

Lord David Owen and Jonathan Davidson called it the "hubris syndrome"—a disorder of the possession of power held over years and with minimal constraint on the leader. Its clinical features include contempt for others, loss of reality, recklessness, and displays of incompetence. Lack of empathy is part of the package.

Perhaps most distressing is that in lab settings the powerful can't address this shortcoming even if told to try. Subjects in one study were told that their mirroring impulse was the issue and to make a conscious effort to relate to the experiences of others. They still couldn't do it. Effort and awareness made no difference in their abilities.

Susan Fiske, a Princeton psychology professor, has argued that this change in attitude is adaptive and meant to aid efficiency. If you become powerful, you have less need to read other people because you have command of resources. The need to demonstrate empathy is behind you.

One behavior that did help some people relate to others was to recall a time when they felt powerless. Perhaps this is why so many of our leaders seem to recount their humble beginnings, because we sense that if those experiences are deeply ingrained enough, they can counteract their becoming progressively out of touch. It also may be why leaders—for example, women—who were perpetually marginalized in some way may be perceived to be more sensitive even after rising to positions of power.

On the campaign trail, I could clearly see how politicians become susceptible to growing so out of touch. You spend time with dozens of people whose schedules and actions revolve around you. Everyone asks you what you think. You function on appearance; appearance becomes your role. Empathy becomes optional or even unhelpful. Leadership becomes the appearance of leadership.

The process through which we choose leaders neutralizes and reduces the capacities we want most in them. It's cumulative as well; the longer you are in it, the more extreme the effects are likely to be over time.

CHAPTER 8

THE END OF THE BEGINNING

When I initially talked to Evelyn about running, she asked me, "Do you think we'll lose our privacy?"

I responded, "Well, you almost certainly won't. I mean, would you recognize Jeanette Rubio if she walked in right now? Or Amy O'Rourke?"

She said, "I guess not."

Over the course of the end of 2019, however, Evelyn did join me on the trail and became the campaign's most prominent surrogate. She began talking openly about what it was like being the mother of a special-needs child; she struck a powerful chord with many families. It was wonderful sharing the trail with Evelyn; it made me wonder how I had done it without her for the previous months.

Then, in January 2020, Evelyn was interviewed by Dana Bash on CNN. In the interview, Evelyn revealed that she had been sexually assaulted by her gynecologist, Dr. Robert Hadden, when she was pregnant with our son Christopher in 2012.

It was a devastatingly painful experience to recount for the world. After the abuse occurred, she didn't tell me for years afterward, and her parents still didn't know. When I found out, I felt sad and ashamed. She had changed doctors but never gave me a real explanation why. I had been traveling for Venture for America during her appointments. It felt as though I hadn't been there for her and had failed her when she was at her most vulnerable.

Evelyn had been grappling with coming forward for months. She values her privacy deeply, but she felt that telling her story could help bring a predator to justice and help other women. I always struggled when she was thinking about it. "Whatever you want to do, I'm 100 percent supportive." I wanted her to know that I was firmly behind her if she did decide to come forward, but equally behind her if she decided to keep it private. She said she was prompted to share her story by some of the messages I'd received from women on the campaign about how they felt empowered.

Evelyn sat with Dana and her team and told her story, speaking tentatively at first and then stronger and more forcefully as she went on. She described being in the exam room "dressed and ready to go" when, "at the last minute," the doctor "kind of made up an excuse . . . He proceeded to grab me over to him and undress me and examine me . . . I knew it was wrong. I knew I was being assaulted."

After the interview aired, we both got dozens of text messages and phone calls from friends and family. "I'm so sorry you had to go through that. I never knew." When I got these messages, an echo of the sadness I felt when I first found out several years before washed over me.

The outpouring of love and support that Evelyn received in the days immediately afterward was overwhelming. Everywhere we went, women would tearfully come to her and share their stories. I felt as if the woman I loved had become visible to the world, which in turn loved her too. I was so proud of her.

In the days that followed, more than forty women joined Evelyn in alleging that Dr. Hadden sexually assaulted them, generally when they were pregnant. Dr. Hadden was later indicted by a grand jury on six federal sex abuse charges. My wife had helped bring a criminal to justice and demonstrated that women could stand up and be heard. She changed so many lives for the better. Later, she would say to me, "This is another good thing that came out of this campaign."

. . .

IN JANUARY 2020, I headed to Iowa to fight it out. At this point many candidates I'd been running with for months had dropped out. Cory Booker, Kamala Harris, Julián Castro, Beto O'Rourke, Marianne Williamson, and others withdrew in the days before. John Delaney, who had declared before me, dropped out too. I felt for John because he had been at it longer than anyone.

While others were fading, we were growing. Our campaign raised $6.7 million in January alone as tens of thousands of Americans chipped in. Evelyn and the boys traveled with me to campaign in Iowa, which was a joy. Occasionally one of the boys would join me onstage and ham it up before running off.

Riding on the campaign bus was the first real time the boys enjoyed the campaign. When Evelyn had tried to get them to watch the debates, they would say, "Everyone but Dad is boring," and then wander off to do something else.

Evelyn and the boys outside the campaign bus in Iowa

Hundreds of volunteers came in from around the country to canvass and campaign for us for "Yang Month." A group of women who christened themselves "the Sorority of Yang," or SOY, rented a house in Davenport that hosted sixty volunteers from out of state. SOY started when Katy Kinsey from Washington, D.C., and Dani Hernandez from Chicago met online and realized that having a big house would facilitate volunteers. Cam Kasky from March for Our Lives arrived and held events on our behalf. Thomas Wu from Portland, Oregon, dislocated a kneecap slipping on the ice while canvassing in Oskaloosa and kept on working. I would see volunteers at every stop; it was invigorating and exciting. It filled me with gratitude every time, seeing someone who had come to Iowa to fight for the campaign.

Dave Chappelle came in and performed in Ames, Iowa, to benefit the campaign. Dave and I had met months earlier in Los Angeles after he had read my book. "A thousand dollars a month would be *the* difference maker to the people I live alongside in Ohio," he said to me during our meeting. When he decided to endorse me, it was an incredible moment for me. Dave was an idol of mine and someone I'd looked up to for years. Not only did he endorse me, but he scheduled a series of shows in Iowa and South Carolina just to help the campaign. That level of investment was above and beyond, but that speaks volumes about Dave. He wasn't a normal celebrity just giving a political endorsement; he was going to dig in and help. He and I did a *Rush Hour*–themed video ad before the Ames show. Sitting on the side of the stage in Stephens Auditorium at Iowa State while the greatest comedian of all time performs on your behalf was positively surreal. At the end, Dave brought me out along with Michelle Wolf and Donnell Rawlings and gave a rousing pep talk for everyone to go out and vote for their futures.

We ran polls in Iowa in January, days before the caucus. We had come a very long way, as evidenced by the latest polling. Instead of 17 percent of people having heard of me, 97 percent had heard of me. Sixty-one percent of respondents said that they were open to supporting me. A majority rated me warmly or favorably. My ratings were through the roof on "Will fight for the future we want for our kids," "Has good judgment," "Different kind of leader," and

"Parent, patriot, and job creator." My support skewed young, male, blue-collar, and, ominously, nonvoters. But despite all of the positive sentiments, my top-line support was stuck around 5 percent. The big barriers were "Has the right experience" and "Can beat Donald Trump."

On the bright side, support for my marquee issue, universal basic income, had grown tremendously; 61 percent said that they supported giving everyone $1,000 a month, which was up from 17 percent in the first poll we ran. That was an enormous forty-four-point increase. When we asked respondents why they approved of universal basic income, it was not that it would improve their standard of living or that they were concerned about the automation of jobs. Instead, it was that they heard from me and liked me or trusted me. People want a person to pin an idea to.

We crisscrossed Iowa that month, riding on a bus for seventeen straight days. We averaged about five events a day. On about day 8, I came down with a flu-ish bug. I felt feverish, weak, and nauseated. But we didn't want to cancel events; staff had been working frenetically to make them happen, and there would be a press cycle from the cancellations. We had embeds from all of the major networks assigned to our campaign. We needed to maintain a sense of growth and momentum. I told the team I could keep going. I started sleeping on the bus, drinking DayQuil, and taking ibuprofen. I was under a blanket as we traveled Iowa in our bus. My team would prod me awake when we arrived at an event. I would come out, do the town hall and take questions, thank everyone, come back on the bus, and then go back to sleep.

During this time, I had trouble putting contact lenses in because, in my weakened condition, they irritated my eyes. So I did the events nearsighted. I couldn't see terribly well. We dubbed it doing the events "Daredevil-style." The advance staff at events had to know that I wouldn't really be able to see people in the crowd who were asking questions so they should just call on people for me.

Perhaps in my delirium, I started talking to my team about an idea I had for a horror movie set in Iowa during campaign season: "Blood Caucus—Your First Choice Could Be Your Last." The plot involved all of the presidential candidates being killed one by one. Happily for the staff, after a few days of the illness I started to recover and stopped talking about the movie idea.

On January 28, the week before the big caucus, the Iowa Youth Straw Poll took place, and I won! I came out on top, ahead of Bernie and the other candidates. It felt like a great sign, because the Youth Straw Poll had often mirrored the finishing order in many prior caucuses.

The night of the caucus, there is a tradition of candidates speaking at different caucus sites. I was sent to speak at a high school in West Des Moines. Evelyn was sent to another site nearby; the thinking was that we could cover more ground.

When I walked into the gym, I knew it was not going to be my night. Out of a crowd of several hundred people in rows and rows of bleachers, there was a modest handful of supporters for my campaign and a small "Yang for President" banner. In the crowd drowning them out were throngs of blue-and-yellow "Pete Buttigieg" signs, teal "Warren for President" signs, and others. It looked as though my supporters were approximately 5 percent of the entire gym, which would wind up being a sign of things to come. I went up and down the bleachers high-fiving people, but most of the caucus goers were clearly there for other candidates.

The speakers were the precinct captains representing each campaign, so I went after various folks who were supporting other candidates. When it was my turn, I spoke to the crowd about the need to unite the country and solve the problems that people see around them every day. I told them that the future of the country rested in their hands. I received a nice ovation; Iowans were unfailingly polite. As I made my way out of the gym, a young man said to me that he had changed his vote to support me. An older woman in an Elizabeth Warren T-shirt grabbed my arm and said, "Please run again."

I left and walked into the cold February night thinking that I was going to fall below the 15 percent viability threshold in West Des Moines and wind up with no delegates from a significant district. I walked back to the bus to head to our celebratory event later that night.

On the bus to the convention center, we started to get a sense of the returns. I got 8,914 votes in Iowa, about 24 percent of what I said I needed for the previous twenty months and 5 percent of the popular vote. Because of the caucus rules, anytime you're below 15 percent, your delegates are reassigned, so my 5 percent got flattened to 1 percent of delegates for national reporting.

I knew hundreds of supporters would be arriving at our event that night, so I needed to deliver a positive message. I was granted a bit of a reprieve: Iowa had trouble actually reporting its results; the app they were using to compile votes malfunctioned, and it would be twenty-four days until the results were finalized. That allowed me—and every other candidate—to cast the results as inconclusive.

The fact that Iowa could not count the votes promptly and reliably was awful. Imagine being candidates who spent months and tens of millions of dollars trying to make your case in a state and then have that state be unable to determine a winner for weeks afterward. It sent a terrible message. Campaigns had every right to be angry, though in my case it didn't really make a difference. It later came to light that the problem was related to a DNC request to build a conversion tool for the raw data just weeks before the caucus.

The night of February 3 we flew straight to New Hampshire. We had eight days in the Granite State before the primary vote. Unlike in Iowa, the primary was going to draw 300,000 voters in a state of 1.36 million. We went back into sprint mode, doing five or six events a day with Steve Marchand opening up for me. There was also a CNN town hall and a presidential debate that week. Steve called it "the most exciting week in politics." New Hampshire roads aren't that friendly to campaign buses, so we were back to rental cars. Evelyn and I would either campaign together or meet up at the end of the night. Having her nearby made everything better.

One of my favorite places to campaign was Exeter, New Hampshire, where I went to high school. Students and faculty from Exeter would come out to hear me. I saw old teachers of mine and parents of high school friends. There were also some students from Exeter. I imagined high school me seeing candidate me out on the trail, and I wondered what he would think.

On my third day in the state, my team sat me down in a conference room in the hotel in Manchester. We were meant to do debate preparation. But instead, my team said, "Here's the deal. As always it is your call. But we think you should start taking steps preparing to drop out."

My heart sank. I had been going full bore for weeks. There were dozens of staff and volunteers in New Hampshire. Events were well attended. But on some level I knew this conversation had to happen. I breathed hard. "Why do you think so?"

"You didn't get any national delegates in Iowa. If you don't do well in New Hampshire, the press will treat you as if you don't exist unless it's to make snide comments about how you should drop out. What support you do have in Nevada and South Carolina will go down, not up. And then, when you do eventually drop out, it will be a tiny blurb or mention. Alternatively, if you drop out as soon as it's clear you won't win, you will get tons of positive press coverage and praise."

I responded, "I'm not running for the press. They can say what they want. I'm running to try to advance these solutions. Won't getting more votes and having events in other states give the cause more legs?"

They said, "Well, you're going to be on the ballot anyway, so people can vote for you no matter what. And you can do other things that will move your ideas forward. You can start an organization. You can influence the nominee. You can do lots of things."

I didn't like it. There were teams in Nevada, South Carolina, and around the country who were working hard on my behalf. I felt like I was letting everyone down. I said, "My entire thing is being the scrappy entrepreneur who works harder than everyone else. Doesn't quitting fly in the face of that? I don't mind grinding it out in the dark. That's the way we started; it almost seems fitting we end that way too."

They replied, "Your entire thing is being the MATH guy. The MATH says that you're not going to win. What does the MATH guy do?"

My team made a logical case. What was the better path—capitulate to the numbers or forge ahead? What was going to be better for the movement in the long term?

I talked to Evelyn and eventually concluded that if we didn't have a great result in New Hampshire—we needed 15 percent of the vote in order to get delegates and make the next debate—I would suspend my campaign. It was a very hard decision. I sat down to write my suspension speech, even as I was preparing for another debate in New Hampshire. I thought about everything I had been through the past two years. All of the nights away from my family. All of the people who had gotten behind me and believed in my campaign.

We campaigned hard throughout the state for the next five days. The night before election night my last event was around midnight. On Tuesday, when the results began trickling in, I was sitting in the conference center in Keene with CNN on in the background. I wasn't getting 10 or 15 percent. It was around the same level as Iowa. I certainly wasn't getting any national delegates. The message was clear.

I walked out to a group of enthusiastic supporters that night as election results came out. They seemed young. I told them that they had uplifted and inspired me and Evelyn at every turn and that I was incredibly proud of the campaign and all that we had accomplished. We had gone from my Gmail contact list to a mailing list a million strong, inspiring millions of people.

I shared some of what the people we had inspired had said to me just that week:

"Your campaign helped me out of a depression. Thank you."
"Working on this campaign has made me a better human being."
"I met my significant other because of you."
"Your campaign brought my family together."
"You got me excited about politics for the first time."

By raising the profile of universal basic income and focusing on issues like automation, we had accelerated the end of poverty in our society by years, perhaps even generations.

But the MATH was clear. We were not going to win this race. And I am not someone who would accept donations and support in a race I knew I was not going to win.

I told the crowd in New Hampshire that endings are hard and I've always intended to stay in this race until the very end. But I have been convinced that the message of this campaign will not be strengthened by my staying in this race any longer.

Endings are hard.

But as it turned out, that night wasn't really an ending at all. It was just the beginning.

PART II

THE ERA OF INSTITUTIONAL FAILURE

CHAPTER 9

SYSTEMS FAILURE

Coming off the campaign trail in February was a very strange feeling. It felt like I had been running a hundred miles an hour for months, only to find myself suddenly suspended in place. My goals of raising the alarm about job automation and the need to rewrite the social contract hadn't changed. But how could I best achieve them now? What would post-campaign life look like?

I talked on the phone with Pete Buttigieg after both our campaigns ended, and he said something to me that rang true: "You need a vacation. But it also feels like a vacation might not do the trick." The fatigue you feel after campaigning your heart out for months on end is something different. But it felt like there was no time to waste. I didn't want the energy around me to dissipate. I felt responsible to everyone who had supported my campaign to keep the movement growing. I had also learned things from the campaign trail about how the sausage gets made—about the relationship between public figures, their message, and the media—and I wanted to put my insights to use and to continue pushing for change.

A temporary answer arrived in the form of a phone call. The day after I suspended my campaign, an executive at CNN called and asked me to come on and do some political commentary for the next few months. I said sure, figuring it would keep me in the public eye. I also thought I could add value by giving a different perspective on what was going on through the rest of the primaries.

Soon after I got home from New Hampshire, a friend invited me to a Nets game one evening in February. Walking around Barclays Center was surreal. The crowd of New Yorkers seemed delighted to see me, and many requested selfies. I was happy to oblige. I was shown on the Jumbotron and got a nice round of applause. A number of people said to me, "Run for mayor, please!" It was a very dramatic change from past years, when I'd sat anonymously in the upper reaches of the stands.

I had achieved a level of celebrity, and the question was how best to use it. I knew that I wanted to start an organization that could further the goals of my campaign. That month I announced a new organization, Humanity Forward, that would continue to push for universal basic income and a human-centered economy.

I was also still involved in the race. Several of the remaining candidates called me to ask for my support, which was very flattering. Joe Biden called and asked me to endorse him in early March. A few days earlier, Joe had shocked all those who had written him off by winning a resounding victory in the South Carolina primary, after receiving a crucial endorsement from Jim Clyburn, the influential South Carolina congressman. I told Joe that I wanted to let the process play out. "Don't wait too long," he said to me as he said goodbye. Joe had called me the night I'd dropped out too.

Mike Bloomberg's team had also reached out about an endorsement after I'd dropped out. I had noticed that Mike's team was throwing around a lot of money getting support from mayors— probably a good idea when you're worth $60 billion. I joked to my team, "I'd very much consider backing Mike if they put up $1 billion for the biggest universal basic income trial in history." As soon as I said it, it didn't sound that crazy; Mike was already donating billions to charity, and this could come out of his philanthropic arm. When my team raised this as a possibility, Mike's team didn't shoot it down. After a few days, we got a response saying that they'd consider the commitment contingent on Mike's winning the whole race and becoming president. Talks died down at that point.

Joe's momentum continued. He did well on Super Tuesday and also in the following week's primaries. He won Washington, Missouri, Mississippi, and Idaho; most important, he won Michigan, a state that Bernie Sanders had won in 2016 and needed to win again. I was sitting at a CNN studio in Washington, D.C., that night offering commentary, and it was clear to me that Joe was going to be the nominee based upon the results of that night. It also hit me that we should unify behind him as quickly as possible; I love Bernie, but I didn't see a path to victory for him. I thought, "I have a TV camera on me," so I said to Anderson Cooper, who was seated several people to my left, "Hey, Anderson, can you send it to me after the break? I'm going to endorse Joe." I then gave my best pitch that Joe was going to be the nominee and we needed to come together to defeat Donald Trump in the fall. I felt a lot of responsibility in part because a survey back in January had indicated that 42 percent of my supporters weren't sure they were going to support the Democratic nominee. I always felt that defeating Donald Trump was the number one goal.

The Biden team reached out to me after the endorsement and said they were delighted and asked if I would be willing to be a campaign surrogate. I said emphatically "Yes!" and they began asking me to do events on Joe's behalf shortly thereafter.

THOSE LAST WEEKS before Joe Biden effectively clinched the nomination were the final weeks in which anything felt remotely normal. By mid-March, COVID-19 (we were still simply referring to it as "the coronavirus" back then) was shutting everything down. Back then New York City was the epicenter of the virus in the United States. CNN stopped having us in the studio for safety reasons around the same time, and the streets began to empty out.

It was hard to comprehend how quickly the coronavirus changed everything. It hit me what was happening when my son's school shut down. I had a call with Zach, who had transitioned from my campaign manager to the Humanity Forward team to try to figure out an appropriate response to what I believed was going to be a social and economic catastrophe as well as a public health crisis. With everyone staying home, it was clear that millions of jobs would vanish. We had a few million dollars to work with thanks to people who had donated to Humanity Forward upon our launch. We had planned on running a universal basic income pilot, but now the arrival of the pandemic had shifted us into a higher gear.

"We should give $1,000 away to a thousand struggling families in the Bronx," I decided. This would serve three purposes. One, it would get economic relief directly into people's hands in a time of grave need. Two, it would enable people to better abide by public health guidelines in a densely populated area; it's a lot easier to shelter in place if you're not as worried about next month's rent. Three, it would, we hoped, put pressure on legislators in Congress to follow suit and start giving cash to Americans quickly and broadly.

Now that we had a plan, the question was how best to execute. How do you identify a thousand struggling families in a particular area? In normal times, you might go knock on people's doors, but that was out given the pandemic, and we wanted to distribute the money as quickly as possible.

"At least some of these families must have bank accounts. Maybe we can have Citibank or JPMorgan Chase identify customers in the Bronx who are financially struggling based on their account activity." I called executives at both of these companies. After we were given the runaround at each of them for a couple days—even though I was in touch with senior people—each bank said they couldn't help us, citing privacy and regulatory concerns. Note that we were proposing giving a thousand of their customers $1,000 each. You'd think that would have been welcome news! But no. Even when I changed tacks, asking, "Well, can you give us $1 million in prepaid debit cards that we could potentially mail to people?" we were told that it would take weeks or months.

Fortunately, while we were talking to the banks, we were pursuing alternate routes. Always good to have a plan B. I reached out to Justine Zinkin, the head of a nonprofit called Neighborhood Trust that provides financial services to the working poor in the Bronx. It turns out that they had a technology partner, SaverLife, that was acting as the account intermediary for the families that Neighborhood Trust served. They could identify a thousand struggling families in the Bronx, transfer the money into their accounts, and even include a financial services counseling session for the recipients. We decided to transfer $1 million to be split among a thousand working families this way.

We announced the effort, hoping to drive energy and awareness. I said to reporters, "Many feel like they don't have money for groceries or rent, even as their child's school shuts down. Our goal is to get money into their hands as quickly as possible so they can focus on keeping themselves and their families healthy."

On our website, we designed a form for a separate relief effort that asked people for some basic info if they wanted a micro-grant of $250–$500. We got more than forty thousand requests very quickly. We asked for people's Venmo, PayPal, and Cash App IDs in order to expedite transfer. We then enlisted dozens of volunteers to call the recipients to confirm their info. We started with personal transfers from Venmo accounts; Venmo had a $3,000 per person weekly limit that we blew through very quickly. We set up a business account on PayPal, but our account kept getting flagged because it was unusual to be sending tens of thousands of dollars to hundreds of individuals. We spent hours on customer service calls with PayPal account managers. We were inputting the transactions manually and individually, which was a beast. Eventually, PayPal helped us figure out a way to send funds to up to five thousand people at once via a database. We were able to send money to thousands of people a day by mid-April. Between March and September 2020 we sent out about $5 million to struggling American families.

I had calls with some of these families. People were hurting. I talked to a single mom bartender who had never asked for assistance in her life but was now living out of her car. I talked to a driver who was so proud he'd bought his own limo, only to see his business disappear as people stopped traveling. There was the special education teacher who was told by her school that she no longer had a job because kids weren't coming to school. So many lives were disrupted. These people were thrilled to get $250 or $1,000, but I wished we could do more. I knew we were satisfying only a very small percentage of the need. At one point we were sending people we couldn't help otherwise just $20. Getting heartfelt thank-you messages for amounts that small was in its own way heartbreaking.

Occasionally journalists asked me about how we were measuring impact. I would answer, "I'm very confident that giving people $500 during a pandemic when millions are losing their jobs and are forced to stay home is having a positive impact for both the recipients and the country."

The idea did seem to catch on. When Congress started to discuss $1,200 stimulus payments to everyone, a dozen press outlets reached out to ask me some version of the question, "Do you feel like you have been proven right?" I would respond that I was grateful to everyone who helped advance a solution—putting money into people's hands—in light of the enormous need.

In April, the government began transferring $1,200 stimulus payments to people through the IRS; it was tied to whether you made less than $75,000 on your 2019 tax return. This had some problems. The IRS sometimes didn't have accurate bank accounts and mailing addresses on file. Adult dependents and non-taxpayers weren't included, so many people didn't get anything. It was hard to track your payment. When I talked to members of Congress, they bemoaned the fact that their offices were overwhelmed with people contacting them asking where to get their money.

This first relief bill also included enhanced unemployment benefits, which would be administered through the states. People who called state unemployment offices reported being placed on hold all day waiting for confirmation of their benefits. Days and weeks passed for many without getting help.

The federal government or individual state governments could easily have done the same things we did: set up a website, have a verification process, call people, transfer money to people's bank accounts or PayPal/Venmo/Cash App. Even the government of Togo, one of the poorest countries in the world, set up a digital cash relief effort that reached more than a million people in a matter of days. Ninety percent of Americans use the internet regularly, which is a significantly higher proportion than file taxes. How is it that our vast federal government with more than two million employees could not do something that the government of Togo and our brand-new nonprofit could both accomplish?

As I hunkered down with Evelyn and my two boys for quarantine, I asked the same question millions of Americans did: How did this happen to us?

If the system for administering a simple payment could go so wrong, what else was broken within the vast machinery of the federal government? What other systems within our society are operating on outdated or blown wiring?

We'll explore some of them in the rest of part 2. And in part 3, we'll talk about how to fix them.

CHAPTER 10

THE CENTERS FOR PASSING THE BUCK

When it became clear that COVID-19 was spreading from China to other countries in early January 2020, Dr. Robert Redfield, the head of the Centers for Disease Control and Prevention (CDC), gathered the leadership of the agency's nearly fifteen thousand employees in its Atlanta headquarters. He told them, "We are here in Atlanta because the CDC was originally the Communicable Disease Center, and we were formed to stop a malaria epidemic in the Southeast in the 1940s. Well, the mother of all pandemics is on its way. It is on the other side of the world right now, but it will soon be here. This will be the challenge of our lifetimes."

He turned to his deputy, Dr. Anne Schuchat, and said, "Anne, you and your team will be in charge of testing. Without a reliable test we will be fumbling in the dark, and it will be impossible to conduct contact tracing to identify people at risk of infection. It will be up to you to start ramping up our testing capacity to tens of thousands a day as quickly as possible and then get tests out."

He turned to his four other lieutenants. "Kate, you will be responsible for communicating the severity of the situation to key stakeholders in hospitals and public health officials around the country. We need to provide the right blend of guidance and urgency. Patrick, you need to monitor and coordinate incoming travelers and contact tracing. Everyone who comes in from an infected area needs to be monitored from the moment they touch down and instructed to self-quarantine. That's hundreds of airline passengers a day minimum. Mitch, you will be tasked with lining up information intake among hospitals. This is going to hit in different places at once, and we need to make sure that everyone is getting up-to-date information on infection rates and spread. Steve, you will be working with the NIH on vaccine development. Even if everything goes right, we are going to need a vaccine as soon as humanly possible."

He then concluded, "I served in the U.S. Army for nineteen years. I know that sometimes it's hard to get done what you need to with lots of different players. If you run into any red tape, let me know and I will clear through it for you. This will be the fight of our lives. But if we act quickly and judiciously, we will save hundreds of thousands of American lives. This is why we are here. Let's get to work."

Unfortunately, none of this actually happened. I made it up.

In reality, the response from the CDC, the agency responsible for pandemic control, was slow and cumbersome, a combination of inaction and errors clouded by bureaucratic mismanagement. Previously, the CDC enjoyed a world-renowned reputation as the authority other nations would turn to for guidance and expertise. That reputation would be shattered by real-life events and the disastrous response to COVID-19.

The CDC got off to the worst start possible. It set to work immediately on developing a test for distribution. But the coronavirus tests that it sent to twenty-six public health facilities in late January were contaminated and gave false-positive ratings in twenty-four out of the twenty-six labs; they even showed positive results for the virus when testing highly purified water or saline solution. The false positives pointed to contamination at the point of manufacture— at CDC headquarters in Atlanta.

The reports were so indicative of a screwup that Timothy Stenzel, a virologist from the Food and Drug Administration, was sent to the CDC to see why the tests were all giving false positives. He found that the CDC, in violation of its own protocols, had assembled the test kits in a room that also contained coronavirus material leading to contamination. Technicians were strolling in and out of the testing lab without even changing their lab coats. In other words, the CDC had assembled the testing kits in a lab that also housed the coronavirus.

Resolving the test-manufacturing defects took one month—a lost month during one of the most crucial periods in American history.

This was February 2020, when hundreds of Americans were starting to come down with COVID-19 in Washington and around the country. Without testing, there was no way to begin contact tracing. "It was just tragic," Scott Becker, executive director of the Association of Public Health Laboratories, told *The New York Times.* "Here we were at one of the most critical junctures in public health history, and the biggest tool in our toolbox was missing." The lack of testing kept public health officials from performing disease surveillance that could have tracked and minimized the spread of the virus. Travelers were returning to their homes after visiting infected areas, and there was no way to know if they'd brought the virus with them.

Those months in the winter of 2020 were the key window during which it might have been possible to keep COVID-19 from establishing itself in a critical mass of people and spreading through the general population, or at least delay the spread. If you had to measure the consequences of this failure, it would almost certainly be in tens of thousands of lives and hundreds of billions of dollars of economic value.

How could such a foundational error have occurred where we would botch the tests that were the vital first step in our defense against a pandemic? Stenzel, the FDA investigator, found that no one person out of the nearly fifteen thousand CDC employees in the Atlanta headquarters had personal responsibility for the test-manufacturing process. He couldn't identify who was supposed to ensure that the tests were properly put together. Literally no one was in charge. Weeks later, the director of the CDC still couldn't answer a congresswoman when asked who was responsible for testing.

Dr. George Schmid, who worked at the agency off and on for nearly four decades, described the CDC's culture in the *Times* as an "indescribable, burdensome hierarchy . . . It's not our culture to intervene." People at the CDC work "at the speed of science—you take time doing it," Dr. Georges C. Benjamin, executive director of the American Public Health Association, told the paper. The CDC was a sleepy bureaucracy with feet of clay in a race against time.

The breakdowns weren't limited to the inability to produce a functional test. When thousands of travelers who were possible carriers of the coronavirus landed in airports around the country, the CDC sent local health officials spreadsheets of passengers to be told to self-quarantine. But the data it sent was inaccurate, rife with bad phone numbers and incomplete addresses. Even this system went off-line in mid-February. "It was insane," said Dr. Sharon Balter, a director at the Los Angeles County Department of Public Health. When asked what health officials were supposed to do with potentially infected travelers, the CDC told the officials, "Just let them go."

Even when patients were identified, the CDC's response was behind the curve. When the agency was provided with the names of about 650 people who had contact with a confirmed patient or had been admitted to a hospital, the CDC agreed to test only 256. The agency typically declined to test asymptomatic patients, even though doctors were reporting that people could spread the virus without symptoms.

The same pattern played out when public health officials in New York and other cities asked whether there were plans to expand travel monitoring in February; their alarm was rising as passengers streamed into their communities. The CDC's response? "We're still actively considering that." It did not make a recommendation or act. It was later found that European travelers had brought the virus to New York that very month.

As the virus began to spread in the United States, officials around the country looked to the CDC to track the data of the spread so they could make decisions. It couldn't do that effectively either. There was no centralized system. The result was a confusing hodge-podge of faxes—yes, faxes—phone calls, and thousands of spread-sheets attached to emails each with different pieces of information being relayed back and forth. In California, state officials reported getting 146 emails a day, with one airline flight's info attached to each email. According to people in the field, the CDC could not accurately account for tests, patient demographics, and confirmed cases or even keep track of how many patients had died. "We got crappy data," Fran Phillips, Maryland's deputy health secretary, de-clared in *The New York Times.* Some CDC staff members were mortified when a seventeen-year-old in Seattle named Avi Schiff-mann managed to compile coronavirus data faster than the agency, creating a website that scraped data in real time from various sources, attracting millions of daily visitors. Other people desperate for data turned to Johns Hopkins University, *The Atlantic,* or other nongov-ernmental sources. "If a high schooler can do it, someone at CDC should be able to do it," said one longtime CDC employee. The CDC's official response was that more money should have been spent on its data infrastructure than the $50 million that was previ-ously allocated. Never mind that the high school student had a budget of approximately zero while the CDC's total budget runs into the billions.

As late as May, the CDC was publicly releasing testing data that blended together nasal swab tests that found active coronavirus in-fection with results from antibody tests that showed that a person had the virus in the past, even though these tests indicated different things and should have guided policy in different ways. "You've got to be kidding me," Ashish Jha, at the time a professor of global health at Harvard and the director of the Harvard Global Health

Institute, said of this practice, in an article in *The Atlantic*. (One reason to combine the tests in reporting is that the gross testing number appeared more robust.)

This was a total fiasco. After the disease got into the general population, we were all stuck with mitigation efforts—stay home, social distance, wear a mask, wash your hands, stay away from older relatives. We had a window during which we could have identified patients, traced contacts, and perhaps slowed the spread and given our health-care infrastructure time to build up. Other developed countries, such as South Korea and Australia, used this window of opportunity to contain the disease more effectively.

In response to this cascade of failures, the CDC sent out a series of soulless press releases.

Some commentators are quick to lay complete blame for these institutional failures on Donald Trump's shoddy leadership. While it's hard to imagine a president doing a worse job than Trump of leading the country through the crisis, if you examine closely the CDC's missteps, you'll find that they were serious, operational, and at multiple stages—the kinds of failures that happen in the lab or office. These weren't political failures so much as an organization being asked to do things that it theoretically existed to do but didn't have the actual experience or muscle memory to execute urgently in real time.

Others might argue, "Well, it needed a bigger budget. We've been starving government for years." While there are areas where dollars might have changed things, this doesn't seem to be one of them. The CDC had plenty of resources—$7 billion a year and some fifteen thousand employees and contractors—yet kept falling on its face. It's even possible that more money in the budget would have somehow made it even more cumbersome and bureaucratic by adding another layer of personnel and processes.

This wasn't a lack of resources. It was a lack of responsibility, decisiveness, and fast-twitch muscle fiber. No one knew who was responsible for the tests, even after the fact.

For thousands of Americans, it was literally death by bureaucracy.

This situation highlights one of the great sources of our collective frustration, anger, and despair in the twenty-first-century United States. Our bureaucracies are too often embarrassingly or tragically ineffective and inefficient, and generally no one is held accountable when they fail.

THESE BLUNDERS CROSS party lines. What was President Obama's signal achievement? Almost certainly the passage of the Affordable Care Act in 2010. In 2013, after years of buildup, HealthCare.gov was launched in order to implement the Affordable Care Act. You might remember the ad campaign in 2013 telling us about HealthCare.gov in the run-up to the website launch. An estimated $684 million was spent nationwide telling us to go to HealthCare.gov upon its launch on October 1, 2013.

Unfortunately, the website had massive problems on its first day, going down within two hours of launch. At the time, administration officials said that the problem was that more people went to the website than had been projected—250,000 in the first two hours—but there were design issues as well. The website log-in feature—the first step to using the website—could handle less traffic than the main website, which caused a massive bottleneck. Due to poor planning, this same log-in was used by website technicians, making it very hard for them to log in and troubleshoot problems in real time. Users also cited incomplete drop-down menus, and insurance companies said they were getting incomplete or incorrect data.

Out of the hundreds of thousands of visitors on October 1, 2013, a total of six users completed and submitted their applications and selected an insurance plan on the day of launch. The website became a national punch line. On *The Daily Show,* Jon Stewart joked to Kathleen Sebelius, the secretary of health and human services at the time, "I'm going to try and download every movie ever made, and you're going to try to sign up for Obamacare, and we'll see which happens first."

To fix HealthCare.gov and build up the website's capacity, private contractors, including Mikey Dickerson from Google, headed to Washington, D.C. By December 1, the website could handle 35,000 concurrent users, still far below demand but a big improvement. By the end of the year, which was the end of the open enrollment period, a total of 1.2 million Americans had signed up for a health-care plan using HealthCare.gov. This was a small fraction of the tens of millions of Americans who were expected to enroll.

Consider that millions of Americans were unable to sign up for health insurance as a result of these technical glitches. The result, undoubtedly, was illnesses and deaths that would have been prevented. Many Americans put off seeing health-care providers until they had their insurance squared away.

In part because of the resources being thrown at the website after its initial flop, the budget for the project ballooned from $93.7 million to a whopping $1.7 billion, almost twenty times higher.

This isn't that unusual. The Standish Group, an international IT research advisory firm, examined 3,555 technology rollouts in any context that had at least $10 million in labor costs from 2003 to 2012, which includes most significant government IT projects over the period. The firm found that 41.4 percent were total failures; these projects either were abandoned or had to be restarted from scratch. Fifty-two percent of the large projects were over budget, were behind schedule, or didn't meet user expectations. Only 6.4 percent were successful.

The federal government's success rate in large-scale technology rollouts thus seems very low. Meanwhile, our legislators haven't had any dedicated in-house technology policy advisers since 1995. That was the year Congress eliminated the Office of Technology Assessment, which had been founded in 1972 to give objective advice about technology and its impact. It was ostensibly abolished to save money, despite having a budget of only $22 million at the time.

Of course there were hearings on the failure of HealthCare.gov and numerous postmortems. Mikey Dickerson wound up a key figure. He was working for Google as a site reliability manager in October 2013. According to an account he gave in a speech at SXSW in 2015, after hearing the White House was looking for experts to help bail out the website, he dialed into a 5:30 a.m. conference call with Todd Park, the U.S. chief technology officer. "I had never met Todd; I looked him up on Wikipedia while on the phone. With a couple more phone calls, I was talked into flying to Washington, D.C., for a few days to evaluate the situation."

Upon arriving in D.C. to try to help fix HealthCare.gov, he found "some really surprising things" when he looked at the website's back office, as he told the SXSW audience:

> One was that there was no monitoring of the production system. For those of you that run large distributed systems, you will understand that this is as if you are driving a bus with the windshield covered. Second was that there were hundreds of people and dozens of companies involved, but nobody in charge. Third was that there was no particular urgency about the situation. As I would come to understand, nobody was acting like there was anything out of the ordinary because there was nothing out of the ordinary . . . The whole system had worked as normal and produced the expected result, which was a website that was overpriced by hundreds of millions of dollars and did not work at all.

Dickerson rolled up his sleeves and got to work trying to fix a site that was live and needed to be used by millions, with each day eroding public trust and enthusiasm. "I was hallucinating and having other problems from not having slept enough for three months. This was the hardest thing I have ever done and I hope nothing ever comes close to it again," he later recounted.

However, Dickerson said, the work he did wasn't really technically difficult. "There were simple problems with simple solutions. The solution to the lack of monitoring was to install monitoring. The solution to nobody being in charge was to make everybody come to the same room where we could coordinate. And so on. It was not a hard engineering problem, and any of you could have done it."

THE REGULATIONS FOR a company to get a government contract run for more than eighteen hundred pages, which serves to ensure that companies that win government contracts, like the ones who enjoyed the millions to build HealthCare.gov, are good at navigating the procurement maze but may not be the best at actually delivering product. And it's not as if the bureaucracy stops at procurement; it extends deep into every operational step.

Henry Chao, the former deputy CIO and deputy director of the Office of Information Services in the Centers for Medicare and Medicaid Services (CMS), writes in his book about his experience with HealthCare.gov that "it isn't possible for government to innovate at an accelerated pace" due to internal policies, the array of stakeholders and agencies involved with any major project, the need to integrate with existing systems, security requirements, political interference, and the long time horizons of career employees. Chao was among those asked to testify to Congress about the site's failed launch. He recalled in his book saying numerous times to his superiors that the launch was going to be very troubled without anyone listening or changing plans. Chao himself had been in government service for CMS for twenty-one years at the time. He describes a "public service environment that does not encourage taking calculated risks" and says that many government workers have adopted a world-weary "no good deed goes unpunished" outlook.

The CDC and HealthCare.gov stories are examples of bureau

cracy in action. In both, no one was sure who was in charge. No one acted with urgency, even as things went wrong. Large sums of money were spent to low or uncertain effect.

In his book *Try Common Sense,* Philip Howard, the lawyer and reformer, dates the country's prevailing governing philosophy to the 1960s, writing that "the decline of responsibility in Washington has been accompanied by a rise in apathy and selfishness in the broader culture." He went on to say that many Americans "are losing hope of a better future for their children. They don't matter to Washington, and they know it."

When I ran for president, I saw how these failures in Washington affect people's perceptions. Many of us on the trail made sweeping pronouncements about what we wanted government to do. But Americans mistrust our ability to make them happen because they understand our government's current limitations. One farmer in Iowa said to me, "I believe in getting health care to more people. But our government couldn't even get a website up. How can we have confidence that it can run something as complicated as health care?"

I told him that we need to demonstrate to him that we are capable of doing just that.

Bureaucratic failures will continue to recur because many of our governing institutions aren't built for efficiency, urgency, or accountability. They are built for continuity, stability, and the bureaucracy itself. They will fail us during the next crisis, and we will be left crying for answers time and again.

CHAPTER 11

THE INHUMAN ECONOMY

I ran for president based on a simple idea: the average American is being left behind by a rapidly transforming economy; automation is eliminating American jobs; and we need to take drastic actions to repair the economy. This was true even before the pandemic, though the coronavirus has now sent the inhuman economy into overdrive. The trends I feared and ran for president on have been greatly accelerated by the pandemic.

These forces have been building up for decades. While worker productivity has skyrocketed since the 1970s, worker pay has stayed more or less constant. As more and more value has been created, workers have not shared in the gains. On the other hand, the ratio of CEO-to-worker pay rose from 20 to 1 in 1965 to 271 to 1 in 2016.

The chances that an American born in 1990 will earn more than his or her parents are down to 50 percent and declining; in 1940 the same figure was 92 percent. People working multiple gigs to survive is increasingly the norm. Most Americans live paycheck to paycheck, with any unexpected setback enough to deplete their meager savings.

At the same time, vast fortunes—many built on software and other tech businesses that can be scaled in ways unimaginable in the brick-and-mortar economy of the past—have been generated over the past three decades. But the majority of the real income growth

Productivity Growth and Hourly Compensation Growth
CUMULATIVE PERCENT CHANGE SINCE 1948

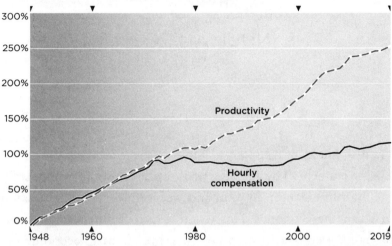

Bureau of Labor Statistics and Bureau of Economic Analysis

Cumulative Growth in Income, by Income Group
PERCENT GROWTH 1979—2015

Income Groups

— Top 1 percent   — Middle three quintiles

— — — 81st to 99th percentiles   ·········· Lowest quintile

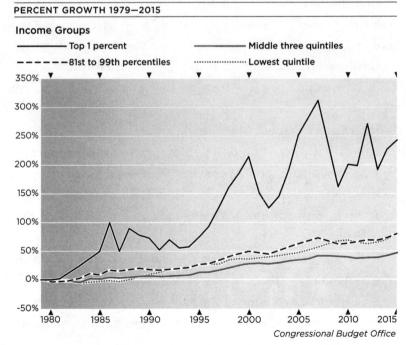

Congressional Budget Office

has been experienced by the top sliver of American society. Indeed, more than half of the real income growth in America accrued to just the top 1 percent of Americans since 2009. The bottom 80 percent of Americans own only 8 percent of stock market wealth, and the bottom 48 percent own zero.

We are in the midst of the most extreme winner-take-all economy in the history of the world. This disparity might be more tolerable for the average American if costs were stable even as their income and buying power stagnate. However, costs have ballooned for the foundations of American life—education, health-care, and housing costs have gone up and up, even as buying power hasn't kept pace. Wages have been stagnant even as the cost of a college education has gone up more than 200 percent. This is why the average American felt increasingly beleaguered, miserable, and left behind even before the pandemic.

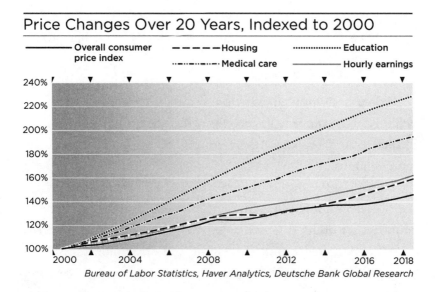

Price Changes Over 20 Years, Indexed to 2000

Bureau of Labor Statistics, Haver Analytics, Deutsche Bank Global Research

On the campaign trail I put it like this: "Yes, we are at record-high stock market prices and GDP. What else are at record highs?" People would think about it for a second and start listing things:

- "Financial insecurity." Forty percent of Americans couldn't afford an unexpected $400 bill. Seventy-eight percent of Americans report living paycheck to paycheck. Thirty-seven percent of Americans are living off credit cards, with an average credit card debt of $5,300.
- "Student loan debt." College has gone up 250 percent in price since the 1990s, resulting in more than $1.6 trillion of student loan debt, up from less than $100 billion in 1999.
- "Anxiety and depression." Prescription drug use and reported mental illnesses are both at unprecedented levels among young people in particular.
- "Suicides and drug overdoses." Deaths of despair have become so commonplace that America's life expectancy declined for three of the last four years pre-pandemic.
- "Health-care costs." Health-care costs have been overwhelming millions of families, playing a role in two-thirds of bankruptcies.
- "The temperature." Wildfires and floods contribute to the unease.

People have intuited that they and their families are being left behind despite the fantastic economy that they read and hear about in the news. They know their way of life has become more and more tenuous.

The Social Progress Index—devised by a global nonprofit called the Social Progress Imperative in 2014—measures how different countries are doing based on access to quality education, maternal mortality rate, freedom of expression, and other indexes. According to these composite measurements, the United States ranks twenty-eighth in the world and is dropping. We are behind countries such as Portugal and Slovenia overall. Here are some of the indicators and the U.S. ranking:

Access to quality education:	33
Access to basic drinking water:	31
Child mortality rate:	33
Life expectancy at 60:	27
Traffic deaths:	35
Homicide rate:	35
Discrimination or violence against minorities:	26
Equality of political power by socioeconomic group:	34
Freedom of expression:	23

Let these rankings sink in. There are thirty countries with better access to drinking water, thirty-two with better access to quality education and lower rates of children dying, and twenty-six countries where a sixty-year-old can be expected to live longer. This is pretty basic stuff that our society is getting worse at delivering, even while our economy has boomed as measured by worker productivity and stock market valuations.

These measures were declining even before the coronavirus came and eliminated millions of jobs. Economists estimate that 42 percent of those jobs aren't coming back.

If the U.S. economy were a patient, you would say we looked healthy on some levels—our stock market prices were a very nice tan—but we had a disease building up beneath the surface that had been weakening us for more than a generation. We were rife with preexisting conditions: rampant financial insecurity and income inequality; racial disparities; a cumbersome, expensive, and inaccessible health-care system; a depressed, anxious, and drug-ridden population; and a dysfunctional government bureaucracy, among others. Then we got a virus that ripped through our immune system as if it weren't there. We are in very bad shape.

One in six Americans struggled to get enough food to eat in 2020. Thirty percent of Americans missed their housing payments in June 2020. By the summer, the economy became a significant source of stress for 70 percent of Americans. Thirty-three percent of Americans experienced clinical signs of anxiety, depression, or both after the coronavirus pandemic began.

Meanwhile, companies have used the pandemic as a catalyst to invest in more automation. Half of companies indicated that they were going to increase their investments in labor-replacing technologies due to the pandemic. News reports have cited everything from Google's AI replacing call center workers to robot janitors in Sam's Club locations to robot butchers at Tyson Foods processing plants. By one measure, we experienced ten years' worth of job displacement in ten months.

The displaced were among the least equipped to manage a financial shock. Retail workers, bartenders, personal trainers, cruise ship workers, tour bus operators, hotel employees, nail stylists, hairdressers, servers, cooks, taxi drivers, security guards, food truck operators, musicians, stagehands, car rental agents, and many other workers were barely getting by before the pandemic. Then they had the rug pulled out from under them and watched their savings dwindle to zero, with little recourse in many cases but debt and desperation.

We talk about "the economy" as if it were one monolithic number that is going up or down. The truth is that the pandemic economy has been experienced in vastly different ways by people in different situations. For people who can work remotely on Zoom, things have been inconvenient and lonely yet, for most, economically sustainable or even prosperous. Some have moved to less expensive and more roomy locales. But most are not so fortunate. The most common jobs in the economy—retail, customer service, food service and preparation, truck driving and transportation, manufacturing—often require physical proximity and have fallen into lower demand when more people stay home. These effects will last for years. When will the bars, restaurants, concert halls, theaters, and bus tours be operating at full capacity? Will shuttered department stores ever reopen? Many of them won't.

Then there is the long-tail human toll. People who are unemployed for six months or more are likely to become unattached from the workforce entirely. This results in an increase in smoking, drinking, drug use, depression, domestic violence, child abuse, suicides, violent crimes, disability, and on and on. People who drop out tend to atrophy as communities disintegrate and opportunities disappear. You can see this clearly in postindustrial towns like Youngstown, Ohio, and Gary, Indiana, and Camden, New Jersey, all of which suffer from high crime rates. Social ills will surge everywhere.

Throughout the pandemic, I spoke to dozens of families who were struggling with economic insecurity. They tried to keep a brave face. But many were prone to despair and defeat. Often, if you pressed at all on their veneer, they would descend into tears. "I don't know what we're going to do." Some didn't pull through.

We have allowed our economy to become punitive and inhuman for millions of Americans. The pandemic and its aftermath have made it more inhuman still.

CHAPTER 12

HOW WE KNOW WHAT WE KNOW

I t was December 2019. I was sitting in the back of a black Suburban with Zach and a couple other campaign staffers. We were in Keene, New Hampshire, and I was outside the offices of the local paper, *The Keene Sentinel*.

I still had the same three metrics in mind to measure how the campaign was doing: our performance in the early states, Iowa, New Hampshire, Nevada, and South Carolina; how our fundraising was going; and national awareness. Each of these factors drove the others. If you had a strong national profile, then the people in New Hampshire took you more seriously. If you raised a lot of money, national publications paid attention to you. And if folks in the early states liked you, then it fueled fundraising because people thought you could win.

One way to get attention in early states was by making a good impression on local editorial boards of town papers. I loved these meetings. You were guaranteed an article. They were almost always small family-owned enterprises. And I enjoyed the conversation. I could talk to them about what was going on in their communities. Sometimes the conversation turned to how the local paper's advertisers and patrons were dwindling, or literally dying off, and how my policies would help.

The offices of local papers were always half-empty, with furniture from the 1980s that had never been replaced. The reporters and staffers were generally in their fifties or sixties and had been there for a long time.

The *Keene Sentinel* office building was no exception; it would make an ideal movie set for a New England newspaper. It has thick ivy draped across almost its entire facade. Around the side of the building as we approached, you could see the loading docks where the papers actually get thrown onto trucks. The newspaper was founded in 1799, making it the fifth-oldest daily in the country.

On the day of the meeting, I walked in the *Sentinel's* front door with my team, said hello to the receptionist, and went up the stairs to the editorial boardroom, where I was welcomed by the publisher and his team. The boardroom was decorated with a printing press plate of a map of Keene going back to the nineteenth century and a portrait of the paper's founder, John Prentiss. The editorial board consisted of Tom Ewing, the owner and publisher; Bill Bilodeau, the managing editor; Jake Lahut, a reporter; and Cecily Weisburgh, the digital editor. These meetings were recorded so the entire event would be available for the public to view them.

After some pleasantries and introductions, Bilodeau kicked things off. "Your best-known position would be the universal basic income. To what extent does the government have a duty to address income inequality?" I settled in for an hour-long conversation about technology, the economy, and my policy proposals; the exchange would eventually be seen by more people on YouTube than the population of Keene. I spoke about my years living in New Hampshire and what I saw coming down the pike, and how northern towns in the state had already been blasted by the closing of paper mills and other industries.

After the meeting ended, I thanked everyone and jumped back in the Suburban for my next campaign stop. I would run into Jake Lahut, the young reporter, again several times in New Hampshire. I found out later that reporter salaries were $12 an hour at the *Sentinel* and that they had canceled their Sunday edition earlier that year. After the campaign, Jake would relocate to Brooklyn to work for *Business Insider.* In a conversation we had later, he reflected on the fact that he might be "one of the last young reporters who got to experience a true on-the-ground New Hampshire primary," citing cost cutting at the bigger New Hampshire papers. He described to me how smaller papers like the *Sentinel* struggle to compete for entry-level journalists and said that they can't even afford to pay interns anymore, which is the typical pipeline of talent in journalism.

Jake's observations were depressing, but they weren't entirely new to me. I had some notion going into the campaign about the problems with the current media landscape, but the challenges crystallized for me over those months on the trail. As I experienced, there are several interrelated problems with our media ecosystem, all of them having to do with the changing business models in journalism, and they each have devastating effects: Local journalism lost its revenue drivers and is dying. National media rewards polarizing punditry over substantive news. And social media platforms are driven toward ever more extreme sentiments and perspectives. Taken individually, each of these developments would be a major problem. In tandem they have created a national crisis, an absence of an agreed-upon set of facts about reality that makes it more difficult for us to come together and agree on the nature of problems, much less implement meaningful solutions.

LOCAL JOURNALISM

Local newspapers took off back in 1833 when Benjamin Day of the New York *Sun* realized he could sell papers for only a penny each and make money off advertising. Based on this one idea, thousands of newspapers sprang up in communities around the country. That business model lasted for about 175 years and is now almost entirely gone thanks to the migration of ad dollars to the internet. Thirty years ago, if you were looking to hire someone or sell a car, you would likely call up your local newspaper and pay for a classified ad. Now you make a post on Craigslist or Facebook Marketplace, for free or a nominal fee. Those classified ads were the lifeblood of these newspapers, accounting for around 80 percent of their revenue; this ad revenue dropped 75 percent between 2000 and 2018. Meanwhile, local businesses that used to take out newspaper ads have also migrated online, using targeted ads on Google or Facebook. As newspapers' revenue dried up, quality went down, and circulation dropped as people went to the internet to get their news for free.

The consequences of these developments are disastrous for local journalism. In the last fifteen years, more than two thousand local newspapers have gone out of business. Thirteen hundred communities in the United States now have no local news source at all; they have become local news deserts. Thirty thousand reporters lost their jobs nationwide between 2008 and 2019, and that number goes up every day.

When I was a kid growing up in the suburbs of New York, we got a local paper, *The Reporter Dispatch*. I used to read the comics— *Calvin and Hobbes* was a favorite—as well as Ann Landers's advice column and the horoscopes. But I also glimpsed the headlines, which ran the gamut from local school board elections to a planned new roadway extension. *The Reporter Dispatch* is long gone; it was merged in 1998 with several other area papers.

I saw the aftermath of these closures and consolidations when I was campaigning. I visited New Hampshire and Iowa dozens of times each, with Nevada and South Carolina not that far behind. With every visit a goal was to generate local press. Any local paper, radio station, or TV station that wanted to talk to me was worth its weight in gold. I spent hours sitting for any interview that was requested. In the bigger markets there were still reporters who would show up. But when I went to the smaller towns, there was often no news media whatsoever.

Even in the bigger markets, journalism is withering. Every presidential candidate for generations has tried to court the journalists from *The Des Moines Register,* the biggest paper in Iowa. A beloved institution, the *Register* was owned by the Cowles family of Des Moines until 1985, under whom it won six Pulitzer Prizes for National Reporting. In 1985, it was sold to Gannett, which owns and publishes hundreds of newspapers, before Gannett itself was bought by GateHouse Media in 2019.

GateHouse is a holding company managed by the private equity firm Fortress Investment Group. Fortress, in turn, is owned by SoftBank, a Japanese conglomerate. The combined entity, which kept the name Gannett, owns and operates five hundred newspapers in addition to *The Des Moines Register,* including *USA Today,* the *Detroit Free Press,* and the *Milwaukee Journal Sentinel.*

When *The Des Moines Register* was changing owners in 2019, a reporter from the paper confided to me that "people at the paper are nervous. Any change in ownership will probably mean cost cutting and layoffs." Indeed, the combined company did wind up cutting reporters and staffers soon thereafter. And this was the flagship paper of Iowa.

The dismal truth is that the biggest operators of U.S. newspapers are private equity firms that are wringing them out for cash and cutting costs. No one is investing. The tide is going out. The demise of local media is, as Derek Thompson wrote in *The Atlantic,* "the opposite of a sudden and shocking calamity exhaustively covered by every media organization, it is, rather, a thousand local disappearances, with nobody left to report on what has gone away."

You might think, "So what, the local high school sports team won't get a write-up?" We have been conditioned to think that if the market doesn't place a positive value on something, then it ought not to exist. But there are a number of corrosive effects of not having a local paper. Local journalism is vital for a functioning democracy.

A decline in local journalism has been linked to fewer candidates running for mayor and lower turnout in state and local elections. Why vote if you don't know what's going on? The other effect is that more voters simply vote along partisan lines. Without local news—and reporting that would suggest reasons not to—you're likely just going to vote for the same people or side you always do, without thinking much about it.

The decline of local journalism has negative effects on governance too. The cost of municipal bonds went up without local news in one study. In one town in upstate New York, a former council person reminisced with me about the old relationship between the council and the local press. "I remember when we had city council meetings. A local reporter would come. People were very aware of the reporter's presence," the former council person said. "Then, because of budget cuts, the reporter stopped coming. You could sense a change immediately. People's professionalism slipped. The folks in charge started saying inappropriate things. We were more likely to cut corners. We got less done or more done with less care." It's not hard to imagine this same dynamic playing out in towns across America.

How can citizens begin to wrap their heads around their local government if literally no one is covering it? If the goal is to bring interested Americans together, reduce polarization, and sustain functioning, resilient local government, we need local journalism to survive. In part 3, we'll explore some ways I think we can help make that happen.

CABLE NEWS

In part 1, I wrote about the bizarre rituals of doing a live spot on cable news as a candidate. Now I want to dig into the business models that drive the culture and programming on the cable networks. If the problem for local journalism is that it doesn't make money anymore, the problem with cable news networks, which are plenty profitable, is *how* they make money.

On the campaign trail, most of the candidates' efforts to raise their profile on TV center on just three places: MSNBC, CNN, and Fox News. For all the talk of cord cutting in favor of streaming services, cable is still king—at least when it comes to politics. While there are other news programs out there (that is, the news divisions of the broadcast networks like NBC, ABC, and CBS and other outlets like PBS), they have relatively few hours of programming each week, and you were lucky to get covered once in a blue moon. By contrast, the cable news networks—with dozens and dozens of hours of live programming to fill each week, and audiences that still number in the hundreds of thousands or even millions—would have you on over and over again. Appearing on cable news outlets was one of the few ways we could successfully boost our chances of meeting polling requirements set by the Democratic National Committee to qualify for the debates.

Cable news networks have become massive profit drivers for their corporate parents. Their combined revenues were $5.25 billion in 2018, with $2.2 billion coming from advertising on top of about $3 billion in cable subscription fees. You'd probably think that most network revenues come from advertising, but the majority comes from cable subscription fees. These channel-specific fees are built into the cost subscribers pay for their cable package.

On average, cable providers have to fork over a reported $0.29 per cable subscriber per month to MSNBC. CNN gets about $0.96 per subscriber, which also includes its true-crime-oriented channel, HLN (formerly known as CNN Headline News). Fox (including Fox News and Fox Business), on the other hand, is getting $1.65 per subscriber per month.

Why such a massive divergence? Part of it is corporate bargaining power. Fox has traditionally had a lot of bargaining power, thanks to bundling its news with other appealing offerings like its FX network and sports. Part of it is ratings. Although there were some signs of slippage at the end of the Trump presidency, Fox News ratings skyrocketed over many years to a point where they dwarfed the other cable news networks' (although CNN and MSNBC made great strides toward catching up during the Trump years). The question is whether a carrier could get away with not offering viewers the particular channel, and in Fox's case the argument is that they could not.

Ratings matter for the network for two reasons: they increase bargaining power with carriers, and they command higher advertising rates. Fox, when it comes time to renew a carrier agreement, has taken their argument straight to viewers, saying, in effect, "Your cable company is trying to deprive you of your favorite news channel," as a negotiating tactic. Both subscriber fees and the cost of cable subscriptions have steadily risen over time.

Critics of its tone and coverage have made periodic attempts to influence Fox's programming by pressuring advertisers to pull ads from various shows. While Fox clearly wants to maximize advertising revenue, its true franchise is the cable fees. Between cable fees and advertising the network is wildly profitable, to the tune of hundreds of millions of dollars per year.

I went on Fox News multiple times during my campaign. Some anchors enjoyed having on Democratic candidates and were very evenhanded. Others were more contentious. I would often come in expecting to be treated negatively and walk out pleasantly surprised. I got the sense that some of the anchors enjoyed elevating a marginal Democratic candidate, and some were genuinely engaged with the arguments I was making around automation.

In general, however, catering to your audience and giving them content that reinforces their point of view are good for business. The ratings rankings pre-pandemic regularly went Fox, MSNBC, and CNN in that order, though CNN tends to do better when there are major breaking news stories like Trump supporters' January 2021 siege of the Capitol.

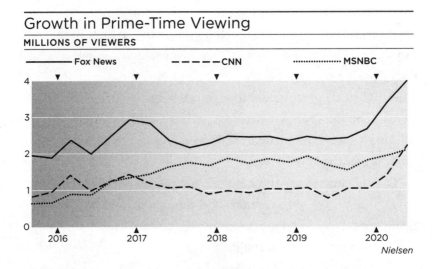

Growth in Prime-Time Viewing

MILLIONS OF VIEWERS

——— Fox News ————CNN ·············· MSNBC

4

3

2

1

0

2016 2017 2018 2019 2020

Nielsen

Gregory J. Martin and Ali Yurukoglu, two enterprising social scientists from Stanford, decided to analyze the transcripts of Fox, CNN, and MSNBC over a period of several years to try to measure partisan messaging. They identified certain phrases that were more likely to be used by one side or the other: For the Democrats/left-leaning, phrases included "civil rights," "social justice," "people of color," and "African American." For the Republicans/right-leaning, the phrases included "death tax," "illegal alien," and "Ronald Reagan."

The patterns played out exactly as you'd expect, with Fox skewing very conservative, MSNBC very liberal, and CNN in between with a slight liberal bent.

The business incentives of cable news channels drive polarization. If you invest in neutrality and evenhandedness and straight news, the audience does not reward you by tuning in every night. If you invest in personalities, strong points of view, criticism, and caricaturing of the other side, the occasional inflammatory or controversial statement, and a clear partisan or ideological bent, then your engagement numbers, ratings, advertising sales, and bargaining power all go up.

Curiously, even as their power over national political candidates

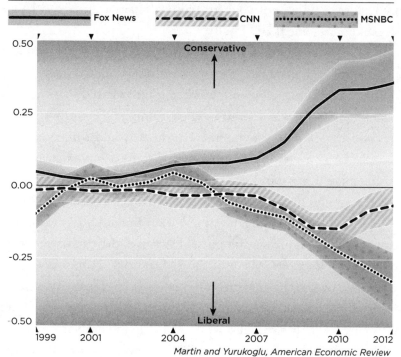

Predicted Ideology by Channel

IDEOLOGICAL RANGE: MORE CONSERVATIVE/MORE LIBERAL

Fox News   CNN   MSNBC

Martin and Yurukoglu, American Economic Review

and profits have grown, cable networks are actually losing a key demographic. The average cord-cutting young person is getting news from podcasts and their social media feed. The people sitting down and watching cable news every day are old. At Fox and MSNBC, the average prime-time viewer is sixty-six. CNN's is a relatively spry fifty-nine. While clips from cable news programs often make the rounds on the internet, particularly if someone says something offensive, adversarial, controversial, or problematic, the future of people regularly tuning in to cable channels looks uncertain, especially ones looking to produce middle-of-the-road, objective journalism.

Imagine if you were to start a new cable news channel today. If you were to say, "Hey, we're going to invest in quality investigative journalism and correspondents who really understand their issues or community," you would find a limited audience, high expenses, and an occupied space. If instead you were to say, "Hey, we're going to invest in representing an ideological point of view that a minority will love and others will hate," you would at least have a chance to build engagement and loyalty.

I have done hundreds of cable news "hits" as a CEO, then as a presidential candidate, and then as a commentator. In many cases, it was obvious to me when I was being interviewed that the host asking questions was trying to elicit something controversial or newsworthy from my response. The host would sometimes approach the conversation with a tone of conflict or indignation to try to spice things up. Even as a commentator, I would often be asked to weigh in on someone else's controversial statement.

Every major news organization makes hundreds of decisions a day around maximizing ratings, which drives their news coverage in specific directions. Many of those directions, in my view, have the effect of eroding information, details, and objectivity. I'm far from alone in this observation. Even people on the inside are throwing up their hands and acknowledging the problem.

In chapter 6, I mentioned an MSNBC producer, Ariana Pekary, who publicly quit MSNBC in August 2020. When I spoke to her about the network's decision making when it came to coverage, she told me that in her experience the network would gloss over more benign news events. "When there were peaceful protests for George Floyd, we would cut to something else," Pekary told me. "If there were some fire or conflict, we would cut to that and show the footage over and over again." In her impassioned farewell statement when leaving MSNBC, she wrote,

> The problem is the job itself. It forces skilled journalists to make bad decisions on a daily basis . . . The model blocks diversity of thought and content because the networks have incentive to amplify fringe voices and events, at the expense of others . . . all because it pumps up the ratings. Context and factual data are often considered too cumbersome for the audience . . . A very

capable senior producer once said: "Our viewers don't really consider us the news. They come to us for comfort."

Ariana received a lot of supportive messages from other journalists after she spoke out.

The public, too, has noticed that the media might not be airtight. Public trust in major media organizations has drifted down to 40 percent over the past number of years, where the media is now tied with banks (38 percent) and the presidency (39 president) and lower than the police (48 percent) in the public mind. Only 13 percent trust the media "a great deal," and 28 percent "a fair amount," significantly lower than in the past. The trust in media varies wildly depending on one's political leanings: 69 percent of Democrats say they trust the media, while only 36 percent of independents and 15 percent of Republicans say the same.

The bottom line is that the market is distorting our news in ways that are tearing us apart. The cable news networks are being rewarded via billions of dollars a year in revenue to separate us into ideological camps hungering for news and opinion designed to stimulate our sense of outrage and alarm. What is counterbalancing these mammoth financial incentives? A very thin layer of professionalism among producers who are subject to microanalysis of their decisions based on fifteen-minute ratings, which are then tied to advertising, continued employment, and their professional advancement. There is no reason to think that these trends will reverse themselves; media companies are businesses that benefit from heightening our polarization and giving us news that affirms what we want to hear.

SOCIAL MEDIA

If networks benefit from our polarization into camps, social media is often the engine of these divisions, making us unable to distinguish fact from fiction.

We each live in our own individual news silos today. We see different versions of reality in our news feeds on Facebook and Twitter and our YouTube video rabbit holes. The goal for each platform is to maximize our engagement and responsiveness to advertising, which results in more inflammatory content and controversy. Engineers at tech giants like Facebook and Twitter have designed their platforms to be addictive. "The brain fires off tiny bursts of dopamine as a user posts a message and it receives reactions from others, trapping the brain in a cycle of posts, 'likes,' retweets, and 'shares,'" P. W. Singer and Emerson Brooking wrote in their book *Like War: The Weaponization of Social Media.*

On social media, the stories with the greatest reach are not bound by fact; fiction actually travels further and faster than truth. In 2018, Massachusetts Institute of Technology researchers went through 126,000 contested stories that were distributed on Twitter, some true and some untrue. They found that a false story was much more likely to go viral; fake news was six times faster to reach fifteen hundred people than something accurate. This was the case in every subject area—business, foreign affairs, science, and technology. "It seems to be pretty clear that false information outperforms true information," Soroush Vosoughi, an MIT data scientist who led the study, told a reporter for *The Atlantic.*

The tendency seemed most acute in one subject category: political content. "The key takeaway," Rebekah Tromble, a professor of political science, told *The Atlantic,* "is really that content that arouses strong emotions spreads further, faster, more deeply, and more broadly."

Social media allows virulent and hateful ideas to fester and grow. On my social media platforms, the algorithms that determine which content I see are constantly suggesting social media posts to amplify; many of them express sentiments of outrage and hostility toward someone or something. I ignore most of them. Due to the insidious nature of these platforms' recommendation engines, however, that's hard to do.

You might be watching something relatively benign on YouTube—for example, a news documentary about the 9/11 attacks. In the list of suggested links next to the video you're watching, however, there is often something far more inflammatory, such as a video espousing conspiracy theories. Crackpot videos are featured right alongside videos by professional documentarians, and sometimes it's the deranged clips that receive millions of views. Conspiracy theories—like QAnon—can gain millions of followers who can even be driven toward violent action and protest.

Before the advent of nonstop social media use, if you had some awful ideas you wanted to share, you would have a hard time finding people to listen to you. What would you do? Write a letter to the editor of your local paper? Hand out leaflets? Stand in the town square? But today you can stake out your corner of the internet and find some people to listen to you: the more outrageous or toxic your ideas, the more likely they are to evoke a reaction.

In a TED talk, the technologist J. P. Rangaswami compared the information we consume to a diet. A work of great literature could be compared to an incredibly nourishing and fortifying meal. Social media snippets could be compared to snacking on junk food. Imagine if we surrounded children with an unlimited buffet of Cheetos and Twinkies. What would happen to their health over time?

Social media is affecting our mental health. In an interview about his book *Ten Arguments for Deleting Your Social Media Accounts Right Now,* Jaron Lanier, the technology futurist, said that "the behavior manipulation machine makes you cranky, makes you irritable, makes you paranoid, makes you sad."

The numbers bear this out. As you can see in the graph on page 132, teenage girls have seen an unprecedented surge in anxiety and depression coincident with their internet and social media use.

The dangers of social media are myriad, and yet it seems that we have little clue as to what to do about them. As Robinson Meyer put it in *The Atlantic* in 2018, "Social media seems to systematically

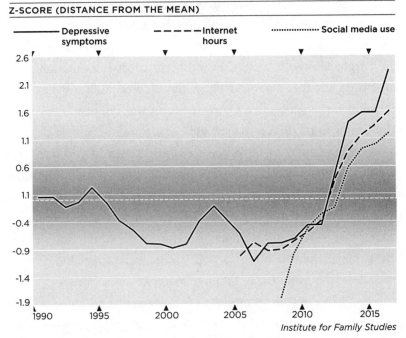

Teen Girls' Depressive Symptoms, Hours Using the Internet, and Social Media Use

Z-SCORE (DISTANCE FROM THE MEAN)

——— Depressive symptoms   — — — Internet hours   ·············· Social media use

Institute for Family Studies

amplify falsehood at the expense of the truth, and no one—neither experts nor politicians nor tech companies—knows how to reverse that trend. It is a dangerous moment for any system of government premised on a common public reality."

Social media will become all the more powerful in establishing alternate versions of reality as artificial-intelligence-enabled "deep-fake" videos become more ubiquitous. If you think there is a lot of disinformation now, what's coming will be even worse. Synthetic media—audio or video recordings that are altered or doctored by technology—is becoming more and more convincing as technology puts the editing capacities of a Hollywood studio into the hands of individual actors. In 2018, Jordan Peele and *BuzzFeed* released a video of Barack Obama uttering obscenities that has been viewed millions of times to illustrate deepfake technology in action. Victor Riparbelli, the CEO of a start-up that is generating synthetic media for commercial use, believes that synthetic video may account for up to 90 percent of all video content by 2025. But it's already happening. In 2020, Oxford University researchers found evidence that the governments of seventy different countries practiced online disinformation, often via social media.

Imagine a world where we are truly unable to differentiate fact from fiction, where you can show video recordings of anyone saying or doing something and they may simply deny that it happened. Nina Schick, the author of *Deepfakes: The Coming Infocalypse,* suggests that this could be the end of representative democracy.

You could think of the above as alarmist. But what I saw out on the campaign trail across the country between 2018 and 2021 reinforced my sense that we are living through a crisis in journalism and information born of both technology and market-based incentives. It's difficult to imagine building a consensus when so many Americans are seeing different versions of reality right now, much less five or ten years from now. But I want you to imagine America coming together to solve its problems with the current media landscape. We'll explore some ways to attempt this in the book's final chapters. We may yet have a window of opportunity to solve our problems, but that window will not be open forever.

CHAPTER 13

OUR DATA, WHOSE DATA?

Some of the broken machinery of American democracy doesn't, at least on the face of it, have much to do with government or bureaucracy at all. Take big data.

The experience of my campaign with data-directed online advertising is typical. Campaigns do it. Fortune 500 companies do it. Even local mom-and-pop shops do it with basic Google or Facebook ads. On my campaign we tried to be responsible, but all of the structural forces pushed us to gather as much consumer data as possible. Data has become big business.

How big? You might have heard the saying that "data is the new oil." That may be an understatement.

Consider that, as of the time of this writing in mid-2021, ExxonMobil is valued at $258 billion. What is Facebook valued at?

$1 trillion.

Google? $1.7 trillion.

Both Facebook and Google are built largely on the monetization of our data. Most of their revenue comes from advertising businesses that rely upon consumer targeting. If you're an advertiser on Facebook, you want to reach certain types of people in certain ways. Facebook can supply the audience. But it has gotten much more sophisticated than that.

It's not just that Facebook is saying to advertisers, "I can get your ad in front of a suburban housewife in Michigan who is looking for an organic laundry detergent." It's saying, "I can get your ad in front of a suburban housewife in Michigan who doesn't yet know she's looking for an organic laundry detergent but we're pretty sure she can be moved to buy based on her having joined certain affinity groups and liking similar things to a thousand other people who have bought your detergent based upon hundreds of thousands of interactions we have been tracking about her and the other people for years."

Facebook has become both a behavior modification machine and an artificial intelligence superpower. In his book *Zucked,* Roger McNamee, an early investor in Facebook who later became an outspoken critic of its business model, put it this way:

> The artificial intelligences of companies like Facebook (and Google) now include behavioral prediction engines that antici-pate our thoughts and emotions, based on patterns found in the reservoir of data they have accumulated about users. Years of Likes, posts, shares, comments, and Groups have taught Face-book's AI how to monopolize our attention. Thanks to all this data, Facebook can offer advertisers exceptionally high-quality targeting . . . Facebook has used surveillance to build giant pro-files on every user . . . It starts out giving users "what they want," but the algorithms are trained to nudge user attention in direc-tions that Facebook wants . . . [T]he goal is behavior modifica-tion that makes advertising more valuable.

How much is all of this data—our data—worth? Facebook's rev-enue in 2020 was $86 billion, about half of which came from the United States. Google, which has a similar portfolio of our interac-tions based on Gmail, Google Maps, YouTube, and its other prop-erties, generated some $182 billion in revenue, also about half from the United States. Our data is worth tens of billions a year just on the basis of these two companies.

But it's not just these two companies. Data tracking and selling have become an enormous business for a wide variety of firms, including automakers, retailers, restaurants, and software companies. It's one reason why everyone seems to want you to sign up for their club when you check out of a given store or restaurant. The average email address is worth as much as $89 over time according to one firm. Data brokerage—the buying and selling of our information—is estimated to be a $200 billion industry. It's a great high-margin way for a business to make some money on top of its traditional operation: just gather together customer data and sell it. You can sell it repeatedly because it's not as if by selling it to one party, you make the data less valuable to the next party. Some of the biggest players in this industry are the credit bureaus Experian, Equifax, and TransUnion, which you might have interacted with when you do a credit check.

How much your data is worth depends upon who you are. If you have a health condition, your value goes up; you might be in the market for some pharmaceuticals, which are quite expensive. And if you're a frequent traveler, your email address alone could be worth as much as $251 to the companies that want to reach you for airlines, hotels, and other services that cost a lot of money.

Your uniqueness can also add to your value. As James Zou, a Stanford researcher on data use, put it to a reporter for *Quartz,* "If I'm on Facebook and there are many other people who are very similar to me on Facebook, then my data is actually not that valuable, because there are many other people who could be substitutes." If you're unusual in some way, then your data can provide more utility to companies that are trying to predict behavior or more efficiently market to people like you.

There is also metadata—that is, information about the data itself. An example of metadata could be tags saying that these ten thousand retail customers have been sorted by certain characteristics— say, gender, location, and average purchase size. Many companies will say that there's no harm in harvesting metadata; it's often anonymous and doesn't include your specific name and address. But metadata is often layered on top of specific user data and then used to generate insights to target individuals more effectively, which has essentially the same impact on users.

Indeed, the more data sets a company has, the more valuable each of them is. In his book, Roger McNamee uses Google as an example of the rule that data sets become geometrically more valuable when you combine them. At first Google had searches on its search engine. The problem was that it didn't really know who you were; you just went to Google.com and typed in "air conditioner" and then disappeared. That made it tough to know how to advertise to you. Then they started offering Gmail, Google Docs, and other applications. If you used Gmail, it could then tie your Google search to your identity. Then with Google Maps it could tie in your location. Each data point made the earlier ones more valuable. The different data sets and metadata sets that companies sell have the same general effect: if you combine them, you can generate more value than if you have only one or two data points.

You may be thinking, "So what? I get a free social network, and advertisers know a lot about me. Seems like a pretty good deal. The last thing I want to do is pay for Facebook, Instagram, or other services I enjoy."

Unfortunately, the deal is not as good as we'd hoped.

When I say "deal," there was never any negotiation. Whenever we sign up for a new service, we typically see some long disclaimer language we scroll through, and then we click the "I agree to terms and conditions" button and move on. The very density and incomprehensibility of these disclaimers are intended to make us ignore them. No one actually reads that stuff. Not even lawyers unless they're getting paid to review it. We just click "I accept" and hope for the best. This is not a genuine choice.

Every once in a while you get a message from a company or site saying, "It would be a really good idea if you were to change your password," and you feel concerned. Also sometimes you might see a news story about a company that you use, like Yahoo, getting hacked. But the repercussions and impact of our data being harvested to this extreme are significantly worse than most people realize.

First, it has led to "surveillance capitalism"—a term coined by the Harvard professor Shoshana Zuboff—in which companies have an incentive to keep feeding us advertisements and keep track of us to the point where our attention is being bought and sold. Our email exchanges, direct messages, likes and clicks, and even phone conversations and voice commands are incorporated into building a profile that is used to target us no matter where we are. Facebook's ad network includes many other apps and websites; you don't even need to be on the Facebook app itself to be participating in Facebook's harvesting of your data. We are not the client or end user anymore; we are the product. Instead of having things sold to us, we are being sold to those with the means to buy access to every detail of our behavior and a financial interest to shape what we do next.

A second consequence of data harvesting is that democracy is being distorted, leaving us open to misinformation and manipulation by foreign actors and others who have the resources and smarts to activate a reaction from us. It has been well established that Russian agents and bots set up groups on Facebook to increase division in the run-up to the 2016 election. Those practices continue to this day. But you don't even need to look abroad. A contest of ideas has now become a contest of inflammatory content, data, resources, and targeting. As McNamee put it, "Microtargeting transforms the public square of politics into the psychological mugging of every voter."

To see how this played out in the 2020 presidential race, you need look no further than the vast misinformation campaigns that followed the election promoting false claims of voter fraud and other conspiracy theories. Trump raised more than $170 million in just the month of November after the election, much of it fueled by aggressive Facebook ads targeted at people who were sympathetic to his fabrications based on data that had been accrued for years. On the more benign side, earlier in the 2020 election cycle, Tom Steyer and Mike Bloomberg rode very robust spending online and on television to double digits in the polls.

A third ugly consequence of data harvesting is that it affects our mental health. All of the checking on old classmates, clicking, and posting makes us less happy. Social media use has been linked to a surge in anxiety, depression, and loneliness, fueled by the mechanics that maximize both engagement and data collection for the tech companies.

For a while, this correlation was noted, but causation was less clear. But starting in 2018, studies clearly indicated that social media use makes you less mentally healthy. In one study, 140 undergraduates reported better mental health when their use of social media was restricted. These effects were particularly strong among those who had started the study depressed. "Here's the bottom line," declared the psychology professor Melissa G. Hunt about the study's results: "Using less social media than you normally would leads to significant decreases in both depression and loneliness. These effects are particularly pronounced for folks who were more depressed when they came into the study." In other studies, overuse of social media has been shown to contribute to obesity, sleep deprivation, posture issues, stunted social skills, and blurred lines between real and virtual relationships. An unprecedented surge in depression, anxiety, and suicide and a marked decrease in sociability, particularly in teenage girls, have also been linked to social media use.

When I was a kid, I was very shy and awkward. When I came home from school after a tough day—and many of them were tough—I could at least close the door of my room and feel alone. Today, no one's alone. That kid goes back home, shuts the door, and pulls out her smartphone, and her classmates are all in the room with her, talking about things and looking happy. It's no wonder that anxiety and depression have skyrocketed.

Screen time is what's known in economic terms as an inferior good: the poorer you are, the more of it you consume.

As Jaron Lanier, the internet pioneer and futurist, put it in an interview, "A lot of the stuff that people experience when they're using social media is genuine and positive . . . [But] there's this other thing going on, this behind-the-scenes engine that's getting all your data, constantly surveilling you, and then tweaking what you experience."

Our data is being sold and resold for hundreds of billions of dollars a year—while we don't see a dime—in a manner that is reducing our autonomy, undermining our democracy, and diminishing our mental health.

GETTING OUR DATA BACK

In March 2020, I was approached by Enoch Liang, an old friend from law school. Enoch and I used to play basketball together, though he was more of a volleyball guy. Enoch had become a trial lawyer who litigated both on behalf of and against various technology companies. He represented Reggie Brown, the ousted "co-founder" of Snapchat who received a settlement of $157 million, among others.

Enoch had helped identify technology companies' legal obligations under the newly passed California Consumer Privacy Act (CCPA) of 2018. The law was championed by a California real estate developer, Alastair Mactaggart, who had become enraged and distressed by the systematic abuse of our data and resolved to do something about it. I was eventually connected with Alastair and found him to be an earnest activist trying to curb what he saw as modern capitalism run amok due to government negligence. One of the key provisions of the law was that tech companies owe consumers information about what they are doing with their data. It also said that consumers could authorize an "agent" to exercise their data rights on their behalf—a logical concession to the fact that the average consumer doesn't have the bandwidth or expertise to reach out to the dozens of technology companies and data brokers that access their data.

Enoch and his team had an idea—to act in the agent capacity, by banding together consumers to then negotiate with the tech companies for their data property rights. They believed that most technology companies didn't have the infrastructure in place to actually tell a consumer what they were doing with their data; sometimes they were getting data from different data brokers and then integrating it into their own and not really keeping track of which was which. One person likened it to going into a drawer and finding a ball of rubber bands that you had collected for years and then having someone ask you where each rubber band came from. Because they had never had the obligation to protect our data or report on it, most companies had just jammed it all together from different sources.

If a company was then forced to undertake an audit as to what they did with your data and create a report about it, they would have to create an internal process to sort through the different interactions. For some companies it would be pretty easy; say if you were a restaurant chain like Chipotle, you might have some user data, and you would be able to tell anyone what you did with it. But if you were a tech company that trafficked in data for advertising purposes and aggregated it from different sources—like Facebook—reporting on what you had done with an individual user's data could be a very difficult and expensive process.

If a big group of consumers were to show up at a technology company's door and ask for detailed records on what had happened to their data, what would the company do? Providing detailed audit logs would be both time-consuming and expensive. But if the consumers were willing to bargain, perhaps the technology company could simply pay the consumers a certain amount of money to waive their right under the CCPA for a certain period of time. If this money was multiplied by the myriad tech companies and data brokers, consumers could see a significant amount of money.

The California Consumer Privacy Act has already been emulated in Nevada, and other states like New York, Massachusetts, and Washington are considering adopting a similar law. This could apply to consumers around the country very quickly, even if Congress did not adopt it nationally.

When I heard about these efforts, I became very excited. We could potentially generate hundreds of dollars for millions of consumers for their data rights. Moreover, we might educate millions of Americans to understand what was happening to our data. We could encourage widespread adoption of laws similar to the CCPA around the country and federal legislation. I said to Enoch, "I love it—let's get people that data check!"

We decided to call it the Data Dividend Project.

In June 2020 we announced the Data Dividend Project to the world. The tagline was "If anyone is making money off your data, shouldn't it be you?" There was a lot of enthusiasm for it; we got twenty-five thousand people signed up in the first number of days. At the same time, we realized that Yahoo had settled a data breach lawsuit for $117 million and anyone with a Yahoo email address was entitled to up to $358 or two years of credit monitoring. The final settlement was only two weeks away, and only 1.2 percent of the people who were owed the money were collecting; most people are far too busy to fill out a form to participate in a class action. Facebook had just lost a civil case in Illinois for $650 million saying that they had incorrectly used people's biometric data; the Yahoo settlement was going to be the first of many over time. This could be another way we could help people get money for their data— helping them make sense of various civil suits and collecting whatever they were entitled to.

Some people took issue with our attempt to help people make money from their data, on the theory that people shouldn't be able to sign away their data rights. They thought that people who needed money would be more likely to take a few bucks and still be taken advantage of by the tech companies. I understood this perspective and agreed with aspects of it; it's true that if you drew regulations up from scratch, you might prefer hard-and-fast rules preventing abusive practices. But right now people are getting zero, and the laws let companies get away with abusing our data rights. I'd rather improve the status quo and get people some portion of the tens of billions a year being made off our data immediately and simultaneously lobby for better regulations than to just hope for the rules to change. The fact is both consumers and companies would be more excited for better regulations if we were able to start getting people some share of the value that their data was generating every day.

Right after we launched the Data Dividend Project, I connected with Alastair Mactaggart. Having helped pass the California Consumer Privacy Act, Alastair was now fighting for an updated law, the California Privacy Rights Act (CPRA), that would further bolster consumer protections. The new California Privacy Rights Act would expand company responsibilities to include sharing of data as well as sales, enable users to opt out of geotargeting, and create a new dedicated agency to enforce tech company compliance with the new regulations. The CPRA was set to go in front of California voters in November as a ballot initiative—Proposition 24.

Alastair asked me to help champion the CPRA, and I agreed to chair the effort's advisory board. I did regular interviews with California television and radio stations promoting Prop 24 as a big win for consumers. In November 2020, Proposition 24: Expand Consumer Privacy passed in California by twelve points. I was thrilled. Alastair and I had a congratulatory call; when he thanked me, I said, "You've been doing this for years. I just showed up at the end."

The CPRA gives consumers in California—almost one in eight

Americans—dramatic new rights to their data. They have to be informed as to what data will be collected and how it will be used. They can opt out of any data sales and sharing and any automated decision-making technology. They can have their data transferred to another entity and limit the sharing of personal information. Best of all, there's a new agency dedicated to enforcing these new rights.

One reason I am excited about the data and privacy protections of the CPRA is that I believe they will spread to other states quite quickly. Why do the people here in New York/Pennsylvania/ Massachusetts/[insert state here] have fewer data and privacy rights than the people in California? There's no satisfactory answer. When other consumers start seeing Californians begin to enforce and enjoy these rights, other state legislatures will catch on and follow California's lead.

The CPRA will also provide a spur to federal legislation. There have been bills introduced by Senators Kirsten Gillibrand, Josh Hawley, Mark Warner, and others trying to bolster consumer data rights. Senator Gillibrand's bill would create a new data protection agency, similar to what has happened in California. None of these bills has attracted enough support to pass. As consumer data rights grow in more states, Congress may eventually act to create a national framework that reflects a crucial truth: our data is ours, even if we decide to allow someone else to access it.

We should control our own data and destiny. It is not just about economics; it's about our dignity, human agency, mental health, and the future of our democracy.

CHAPTER 14

LOYALTY CUTS BOTH WAYS

Throughout the pandemic spring of 2020, I could sense the suffering. Every day on social media struggling families would reach out to me for help. The data shouted the same thing so many of us were feeling: a third of Americans experienced severe anxiety, and nearly a quarter showed signs of depression by July, according to CDC data. On top of everything, the public health crisis and the economic impact had become a mental health catastrophe.

Racism against Asian Americans surged, inflamed by Trump's terming COVID "the China Virus." Friends who were doctors described getting cursed out on the subway as they were going home from the hospital after caring for COVID patients all day. Others said they were afraid to leave the house or had been threatened while jogging. I felt it myself when I went to get groceries one night; two guys took a longer and more hostile look at me than was warranted. I started an online anti-hate campaign—All Americans—with Daniel Dae Kim, Lisa Ling, and a dozen other celebrities that received millions of views and raised thousands for COVID relief.

A staffer mentioned to me that just seeing a positive message from me on social media would uplift at least some people, so I tried to put good energy out there every day. As the weeks passed, my new organization, Humanity Forward, found other specific ways to help. We teamed up with a group of entrepreneurs in the

United States who had set up the $1k Project, a crowdfunded way to give $1,000 a month to families that had been identified by former employers as needing relief. Together we gave about $3 million to struggling families on top of the $5 million we had distributed directly. On another front, we followed through on our original plan to establish a small but long-term—five-year—basic income trial in the town of Hudson, New York, funded largely by the investors Albert Wenger and Susan Danziger and the NBA player J. J. Redick.

Joe Biden effectively became the Democratic nominee in April, though he didn't clinch the 1,991 delegates he needed until June 5. After my on-air endorsement on CNN, I attended dozens of Zoom events and Instagram live events for Joe and conducted numerous interviews with local press in places like Michigan, Wisconsin, and Pennsylvania. I took special pride in joining events that were aimed at the Asian American community, a group of voters I thought I could help activate. Asian Americans had historically voted at lower levels than other communities, and I wanted to change that.

I Zoomed for so many hours a day that I started to joke with Evelyn that Zoom was powered by human souls. It's free, but when you log off, you're like, "Why am I so tired?"

In mid-2020, Humanity Forward and I began endorsing political candidates. Most were congressional candidates, with some state and local candidates thrown in. I was determined to help candidates who were aligned with universal basic income, health care for all, and a human-centered economy win as many races as possible; I saw the election of 2020 as an enormous opportunity. I remembered how lonely it was for me as a candidate early, and the thought of helping people win local races was a thrill. Plus, I had a mailing list of hundreds of thousands of Americans whom I thought we could put to productive purpose pushing the movement forward.

When I was running for president, I received very few endorsements from elected officials. I found that the more politically plugged in someone was, the less likely they were to support me. I would have a long conversation with a state legislator or county chair, and at the end they would say something like "Well, I like what you're about, but my hands are tied. I've been working with this person who works for one of your opponents for ten years," or some message to that effect. Anyone who's been in the game for a while ends up developing relationships and obligations that make it very difficult for them to support someone new on the scene.

This dynamic extends to new candidates on every level; it turned out that very few people or organizations were endorsing local candidates or congressional candidates or putting resources behind them in many 2020 races, particularly in districts that weren't swing districts. We entered what was a pretty empty landscape hoping to move the needle.

Some of the candidates I endorsed were people who had worked on or volunteered for my campaign. The first candidate we endorsed was Dr. Jermaine Johnson, who had been my state chairman in South Carolina. It was a no-brainer. Jermaine is a former professional basketball player with a heart of gold who was running for state representative in South Carolina. He stumped for me in South Carolina hundreds of times, even back when hardly anyone had heard of me. He even turned down a huge pay raise from the Bloomberg campaign because he believed in me. "Y'all are the only person talking about the future," Jermaine would say.

There were a few factors I considered in making an endorsement. First, candidates had to apply; they had to actually seek and value the endorsement. Second, they had to complete a questionnaire as to where they stood on certain issues—specifically universal basic income—and sign a pledge to help advance our agenda. Third, they had to be someone we'd be proud to be associated with, win or lose.

I was unusual in a couple respects on the endorsement front. First, I didn't care what the Democratic establishment was going to think. I endorsed Jen Perelman, for example, an awesome public advocate in Florida who was running against Debbie Wasserman

Schultz, the former head of the DNC. I was an independent actor and figured I should act accordingly.

Second, I didn't mind endorsing people who were almost certain to lose. Heidi Briones was a volunteer on my campaign based in Oregon. She had me sign my book to her "I love lesbians." She had raised a not terribly significant amount of money for her race and was balancing it against a full-time job while running against a well-funded and well-liked incumbent. But she was a wonderful person and first-time candidate who was an exemplary representative of our values. I didn't want to lose every race, but I didn't mind a grim win-to-loss ratio.

I enjoyed talking to candidates a great deal. Most of them were phenomenal. Blair Walsingham was a military vet and mom running in rural Tennessee. Alex Morse was the mayor of Holyoke at twenty-two and was running for Congress in Massachusetts nearly a decade later. Jeremy Cooney was born in an orphanage in India and was running for state senator in Rochester, New York. Marilyn Strickland had been mayor of Tacoma, Washington, before running for the U.S. Congress.

It was very rare that two candidates in the same race would apply: What were the odds that there would be two candidates running on universal basic income in the same district? But it did happen in one very notable race—the Kentucky Senate primary.

The establishment favorite in the race was Amy McGrath, a military veteran and fighter pilot who had run for Congress in Kentucky two years earlier and had developed a national reputation. The Democratic Senatorial Campaign Committee had gotten behind Amy in a huge way; she had raised $40 million by June. On the face of it she seemed like a no-brainer to win the primary and challenge Mitch McConnell, the veteran Republican who was the Senate majority leader and had become a high-profile target for Democrats, thanks in part to his aggressive efforts to obstruct most significant Democratic legislation under both Obama and Trump.

He famously declared his mission was to make Obama a one-term president—not exactly compromise material.

Amy's opponents were Mike Broihier and Charles Booker. Mike Broihier had done it all. He served in the U.S. Marines for more than twenty years before retiring as a lieutenant colonel and moving to Kentucky with his wife. He became a farmer—raising livestock and growing asparagus—worked as a reporter and editor for the local paper, and served as a substitute teacher in the local schools. He was running on a progressive platform that included universal basic income. About half a dozen of my campaign staff had gone straight to Kentucky after my run ended and moved into housing on Mike's farm; his campaign manager was my former Iowa state director, Liam deClive-Lowe.

The third candidate, Charles Booker, was a state legislator who had grown up in Louisville, in the poorest zip code in the state. His parents had both dropped out of high school to take care of siblings. Despite this, Charles went on to get his college and law degrees from the University of Louisville. After working in government for a few years, he became the youngest Black state legislator in Kentucky in 2019. Just thirty-five, he was young and dynamic. Charles was unapologetically running on Medicare for All, universal basic income, and criminal justice reform.

I spoke to Mike first. He had a great story. He was smart and steady and had commanded large companies of soldiers but had a real humility to him. His years as a farmer made him highly relatable to rural Kentuckians. He expressed a ton of appreciation to the staff members who had taken up residence with him and believed in him. Mike was congenial, and I could imagine the people of Kentucky liking and trusting him.

Charles, on the other hand, was inspirational. He spoke passionately about his own upbringing and background in urban Louisville. He also talked about how he had supported universal basic income for years as part of a vision for a better way of life that would help others overcome some of the obstacles that he saw around him. It seemed like he actually embodied the message. He felt like a future national figure and a fixture in Kentucky.

I leaned toward Charles because it felt like he was going to be a force for good in Kentucky and beyond for a long time to come. But I literally had half a dozen former staffers who had campaigned with me in Iowa for months working their hearts out on Mike's campaign. Endorsing Charles would be devastating to them, and I felt I owed them better than that. Someone on my team who was advising me said, "Why not just stay neutral," but that felt like the ultimate cop-out given how much was invested in this race.

In the end, I called Charles and told him that I was going to be endorsing Mike, but that I believed in him and would support him in the future. Charles was disappointed but understood. Mike and his team—my former team—were thrilled. We announced the endorsement on May 22.

Three days later, on May 25, George Floyd was killed in Minneapolis.

When I saw the news, I didn't want to watch the video, but I knew I would have to. Watching a man's life get extinguished so casually was stunning and brutal. It was horrifying.

I spoke to Black friends both publicly and privately. Whatever I felt upon watching George Floyd die, it hit Black men and Black parents ten times harder. They were angry and saddened. They were heartbroken for their children. The experience truly was dehumanizing. It made them feel less than human, as if they didn't belong in their own country in their own skin.

One of Charles's primary campaign issues was police brutality and the killing of Breonna Taylor, which had taken place in his hometown of Louisville. Taylor had been shot in her home by police. Her story became part of a national movement. When the protests for police reform began, Charles was at the head of a wave that transfixed the nation.

Bernie Sanders and Alexandria Ocasio-Cortez both endorsed

Charles. Common and Jada Pinkett Smith came to rally for him. The national progressive organizations rallied behind him. He was facing off primarily against McGrath, who had out-fundraised him $40 million to $1 million prior to June and had been covering the state with television ads for months.

The voting on June 23 was neck and neck; the votes had to be counted a week after Election Day because most of them were mail in. Many of them had been mailed before Charles had his surge of enthusiasm. It went back and forth literally hour by hour. The final tally reported on June 30 was

Amy McGrath: 247,037
Charles Booker: 231,888
Mike Broihier: 27,175

Amy narrowly won, by fewer votes than Mike received.

It's unclear how many of Mike's voters would have gone for Charles; he got a lot of support in rural Kentucky, where Amy tended to dominate. It's possible he drew more support from Amy than from Charles in those areas. On the other hand, people who were looking for an alternative to Amy could well have chosen between Mike and Charles. My support had boosted Mike's fundraising and profile considerably. I couldn't help but wonder if my decision to endorse Mike over Charles had cost Charles the primary.

Amy would go on to lose to Mitch McConnell in the general election in November by 19 percent, despite outraising him roughly $95 million to $75 million. Would Charles have fared better?

In the days right after the primary, I reflected on whether I had made a mistake. The fact that my endorsement might actually have swung a race boggled my mind a bit. Literally no one had heard of me a year prior. I received approximately zero political endorsements from elected officials myself, after all.

If I had endorsed Charles, I would have been failing to honor and appreciate the work that my team had done on my behalf before going to work on Mike's campaign. And there was no way to know whether it would have changed the outcome. I consider myself both grateful and loyal to people who have meaningfully sacrificed for me.

But there was certainly a big part of me that wished I had supported Charles, particularly if it might have made the difference for him. He might or might not have defeated Mitch McConnell, but it would have been one hell of a race.

I had been in national politics only two years, and already I was facing choices based on loyalties and relationships and people who had fought for me and sacrificed for me. Imagine all of the relationships that accrue to people over ten, twenty, thirty years in politics. How many of their choices too would be shaded by trust and loyalty over the newcomer who might just be the right person at the right time? I consider myself a loyal person, but loyalty in politics has a way of keeping things from changing.

CHAPTER 15

WATCHING THE WATCHMEN

In August 2020, I got a call from Randy Jones, someone who had worked on my campaign. "Hey, boss. We are working with Jacob Blake's family. They would like to speak to you about their experience."

I felt a pang of pain. I, like so many others, had watched the video of Jacob Blake, a young Black father in Kenosha, Wisconsin, getting shot seven times by police in front of his children. I told Randy that I'd be glad to speak to his family; I was touched that they would think of me. Like many Americans, I had been profoundly affected by George Floyd's death and the protests that followed, and resolved to do anything I could to help change things for the better.

Hours later I was on the phone with Jacob Blake Sr., Jacob's father. He was with his brother when we spoke. I thought I should simply offer comfort and a helping hand.

"Thank you for speaking to us, Mr. Yang. Seeing my son in a hospital bed like this, I'm just glad to be able to touch him," Jacob senior told me.

"I'm so sorry for what you and your family are going through. No parent should have to see his child suffer like this," I said.

He paused. "You know the first thing he said to me when he woke up? He said, 'Daddy, why did they shoot me so many times?' How do you answer that?" His voice cracked with grief.

I struggled with what to say, choking up myself. As a father to two boys, the thought of one of them lying in a hospital bed paralyzed was overpowering. Eventually, I repeated myself. "I'm so sorry. No one should have to go through what your family is going through right now."

He continued, "Did you know my son is in chains? He's handcuffed to the bed. He can't walk. Where are we going to go?"

I shook my head. "That's not right. I'm sure that's a mistake. I'll do all I can to change that."

We spoke for several minutes. I asked him how I could be helpful. He said, "Please share my family's story with people. Tell them that my son is a human being." I told him that I would help in any way I could.

I spent the next couple days on CNN relating the Blake family's story to different anchors and connecting Jacob Blake Sr. to leaders in the Black community. Within the next days, Jacob's restraints were removed. Protests swelled in Wisconsin and beyond as Jacob remained bedridden and paralyzed and communities erupted.

One of the most basic interactions a citizen can have with government is encountering a police officer, and it's completely unacceptable that for millions of Americans even the most basic of these interactions, like a traffic stop, is grounds for fearing for their lives.

Police brutality has been a massive problem for decades, though the magnitude of the problem has been swept under the rug.

In 1994, Congress passed a law in response to the Rodney King riots requiring police departments to document how many people they kill or who die in custody every year. No police departments actually did so. Similarly, the Death in Custody Reporting Act of 2014 requires states that receive federal funding for law enforcement to report all killings by police officers on a quarterly basis. Many states have ignored this law without penalty.

The estimates we have of the number of police shootings per year come from compiling local news reports. The most commonly cited source is *The Guardian,* a British newspaper that has been cataloging shootings and deaths for years. The FBI even started to use *The Guardian's* reporting as a baseline that significantly increased their previously reported number. James Comey, the head of the FBI at the time, called it "unacceptable" and "embarrassing and ridiculous" that the FBI relied upon *The Guardian* and similar reporting in *The Washington Post* to determine how many police violence deaths there were each year.

Those reports say that more than 1,000 people are killed by police officers or while in custody each year. From 2015 to 2019 the numbers were 1,146, 1,092, 987, 992, and 1,004, respectively. That's about 3 Americans a day, comparable to the number of women who die from domestic violence or childbirth.

Another measure of the extent of the police brutality problem is lawsuits. Across the country cities are spending hundreds of millions of dollars a year paying victims of police misconduct. New York City spent a staggering sum—an average of $710 million a year—on payouts for police-related lawsuits in recent years (the entire NYPD's budget is about $6 billion, so the budget for payouts takes up a significant portion of it). Chicago spent $153 million per year on payouts. Police brutality is incredibly expensive, not just in human life and public trust, but in monetary costs that drain public money that could go to schools, health care, or infrastructure. Total payouts to plaintiffs cost communities more than a billion dollars a year, and that doesn't include litigation costs and insurance premiums, which cost hundreds of millions more.

In some cases, these costs have bankrupted communities. In 2018, a jury returned a $15 million verdict for the death of Leonard Thomas in Lakewood, Washington, who was unarmed when a police sniper shot him. The damages, after insurance, were the equivalent of 18 percent of the city's annual budget. In Sorrento, Louisiana, the police department was disbanded when a lawsuit against an overzealous officer resulted in the town's insurance company declining to cover the town further.

These costs are even more shocking given the legal barriers citizens have to overcome to successfully sue police departments and cities. A plaintiff has to sue officers in civil court for violating constitutional rights. The legal doctrine of qualified immunity shields government officials from liability for damages as long as they did not violate "clearly established" law. According to the Supreme Court, law is "clearly established" only when a prior court has held that an officer violated the Constitution under virtually identical circumstances. This turns out to be trickier than you might think. In one case, Nashville police officers released their dog on Alexander Baxter, a burglary suspect, who had surrendered and was sitting with his hands raised. A prior court had held that officers violated a suspect's rights when they released a police dog on him after he had surrendered by lying down. But the appeals court in the Baxter case ruled that there was a difference between a suspect who had surrendered lying prone versus one who was sitting with his hands raised. Another case distinguished between a woman walking away from an officer who had ordered her to come back—she was slammed to the ground, suffering a broken clavicle—and another who had walked away from an officer who did not give such an order.

In 2014, the U.S. Supreme Court in *Plumhoff v. Rickard* found that even egregious police conduct may not be enough to violate a citizen's constitutional rights. In that case, the police in Arkansas shot and killed the driver and passenger of a car speeding away from them with fifteen shots into the car. The Supreme Court said that the police were justified in shooting at the car to stop it because it posed a threat to public safety, even though law enforcement agencies discourage shooting at a moving vehicle. The standard the Supreme Court has offered is that "every reasonable official" would have to know that the conduct is unlawful. The Supreme Court has similarly held that a municipality cannot be held liable for the act of an official unless the city's policy violates the Constitution; the act of the official is by itself not enough.

Aside from the legal standard, the average plaintiff may not have much in the way of access to legal help or savings to be able to back a lawsuit for months; though plaintiff lawyers generally work on commission, lawsuits take time and energy. On the other side, the city will have a team of lawyers on staff who may be backed up by insurance lawyers looking to lower their potential liability; it's not a fair fight.

On the criminal action side, district attorneys work with law enforcement officers every day, and this creates a cozy dynamic between prosecutors and police. Said the attorney and activist Bakari Sellers, "The relationship between law enforcement and prosecutors is incestuous because every prosecutor relies on law enforcement to make their cases, and so it's kind of hard for you to then go in the family and ask that same prosecutor to prosecute somebody who's been helping them make cases." It's unrealistic to expect district attorneys to turn on their partners in law enforcement unless there are extraordinary circumstances and public pressure.

Against this backdrop and facing such a high set of standards, the fact that citizens have won more than $1 billion in civil judgments against police departments across the country per year in recent years is staggering, and evidence that the true scope of police damages against citizens is some multiple billions of dollars per year.

In 2018 there were 686,665 police officers in eighteen thousand local departments across the country, from the tiniest police department in rural America to the NYPD. How can one meaningfully reform behaviors nationwide?

Samuel Sinyangwe, co-founder of Campaign Zero, is a data scientist who has been researching police violence data and different policy responses for years. He has identified a number of changes that correspond to lower loss of life in encounters with police.

The first is direct and obvious: more restrictive rules and laws governing use of force. Police departments have rules and guidelines as to what techniques they can use in different situations. Banning choke holds, requiring a warning before shooting, requiring de-escalation and a continuum of force, requiring exhaustion of nonlethal alternatives, and banning firing at moving vehicles can all reduce deadly encounters. So can having a duty to intervene if another officer uses excessive force. Campaign Zero estimates that adopting these measures and reporting could reduce deaths by police violence by as much as 72 percent.

This would dramatically change the sort of training officers receive. One survey of 280 different law enforcement organizations reported that new recruits received an average of fifty-eight hours on shooting a gun and using deadly force and only eight hours on de-escalating violence. De-escalation is a set of actions to slow down an incident and allow officers more time and distance to peacefully resolve a conflict. Unfortunately, many officers right now are trained to speed up and escalate rather than slow down and de-escalate.

Tracking complaints about officers' excessive use of force would also reduce violent behaviors in other ways. Prior complaints indicate a higher chance for future complaints. So does being around other police officers who receive a high level of complaints for excessive force. Researchers studied more than eight thousand Chicago police officers named in multiple complaints between 2005 and 2017. Their analysis found that the more officers with histories of excessive force were in a group, the higher the risk that other officers in that group would have complaints lodged against them.

This makes perfect sense; if I'm a new cop and I'm around a bunch of guys who frequently use excessive force on suspects, I'm more likely to also use force in situations where it may not be warranted. One of the study's authors, Andrew Papachristos, described the dynamic in the *Chicago Tribune:* "How we pair and assign officers matters—a lot. Officers with a history of abuse have a pretty strong influence on subsequent behavior of other officers." Tracking behavior and separating officers can reduce the frequency of others' developing similar practices. So can tracking disciplined or fired officers so that they can't simply get a job in a new town.

The third method is eliminating language in police union contracts that restricts officer accountability. Police unions naturally seek to limit liability for the officers they represent. Common provisions in union contracts include restrictions on officers being interrogated after the fact, disqualification of certain complaints, officer access to privileged information while being investigated, erasing records of misconduct over time, and an appeal for reinstatement. One investigation found that 24 percent of officers—451 out of 1,881—who were fired for misconduct between 2006 and 2017 got their jobs back through appeal, in some cases over the objection of the police chief. For example, Sergeant Brian Miller in Florida was fired for hiding behind his car during the Parkland school shooting instead of intervening. He was given his job back on a technicality and reinstated with back pay due to union rules.

Another data-driven approach is to scale up other organizations to respond to emergency calls instead of the police. According to the Treatment Advocacy Center, one in every four people killed by police has a serious mental illness. One can easily imagine police officers giving orders that are ignored due to someone's mental incapacity. Many police calls involve domestic disturbances, substance abuse, or homelessness, which could be addressed by crisis workers or social workers.

In Eugene, Oregon, an organization called Cahoots—Crisis Assistance Helping Out on the Street—consisting of medics and mental health crisis managers, responds to nearly 20 percent of public safety call volume. "They don't need jail. What they need is to be de-escalated from their crisis, they need a ride to a mental-health facility or to a medical-care facility or wrapped around with services," Eugene's police chief, Chris Skinner, told a CBS News reporter. Cahoots is now expanding to Denver and other cities due to its success. The more non-police organizations respond to different types of calls, the lower the chances of an encounter that goes wrong. Ideally, more resources would go to these kinds of interventions within communities to diminish the need for police responses.

The fifth approach to alleviating police violence that has worked is federal oversight. Departments that went through federal investigations led by the Department of Justice and subsequently adopted new policies saw police shootings fall between 27 and 35 percent. Increased federal oversight and investigation is crucial given the incentives running against local district attorneys and officials confronting bad cops. If you're a local DA, you would love to have the Feds available to handle an investigation free from local pressure. The standards for federal investigation should change from systemic patterns and practices to triggers for elevated rates of police violence, and increased resources should be dedicated to the effort.

The sixth evidence-backed approach is demilitarization. Since 1997, eight thousand police departments have received more than $5.1 billion in surplus military equipment from the Department of Defense under Program 1033. This includes clothing and computers all the way up to armored vehicles and grenade launchers. One study showed that receiving more military equipment increased police-related deaths in a district. Officially, any received equipment must be used within a year or be returned. So if you have an armored vehicle and grenade launchers, you want to use them occasionally. The equipment is free of charge to the police department beyond shipping and upkeep.

President Obama reined in the program in 2015 and barred certain types of equipment, but this was reversed by Trump two years later. Restricting transfers of high-impact weapons would reduce civilian deaths and weaken the culture of militarization that has swept many police departments.

Far too many parents and families have gone through unspeakable pain and suffering with no recourse in sight. No family should fear for their child's safety from those who are sworn to serve and protect the public.

I appreciated what the legendary professor and civil rights activist Cornel West said in the hours following the eruption of protests for George Floyd: "I thank God that we have people in the streets.

Could you imagine this kind of lynching taking place and people were indifferent?"

As protests thronged the streets of Minneapolis, Manhattan, Brooklyn, and all around the country, West appeared on CNN and said,

> We are witnessing America as a failed social experiment. The history of Black people for over two hundred–some years has been looking at America's failure. Its capitalist economy could not deliver in such a way that people could live lives of decency The nation state, its criminal justice system, its legal system, could not generate protection of rights and liberties. And now our culture of course is so market-driven, everybody for sale, everything for sale, it can't deliver the kind of real nourishment for soul, for meaning, for purpose. And so when you get this perfect storm of all of these multiple failures at these different levels of the American empire . . . we can't take it any longer.

His words would prove prescient: despite the national spasm of grief, anguish, and anger that brought tens of thousands to the streets to protest, Congress proved unable to pass reform legislation. In late June, the House passed the George Floyd Justice in Policing Act of 2020 by a vote of 236–181, which would overhaul qualified immunity for law enforcement, prohibit racial profiling on the part of law enforcement, ban no-knock warrants in federal drug cases, ban choke holds at the federal level and classify them as a civil rights violation, and establish a national registry of police misconduct maintained by the Department of Justice. The Republican-led Senate proposed a much narrower bill and essentially refused to consider the House act. As of this writing, it is unclear what its prospects are in a fifty-fifty Senate.

All of that energy, passion, grief, anger, despair, violence, beauty, humanity on the streets and on our screens, and in our nation's capital nothing happened.

In the days that followed, I tried to collect my thoughts in a post I made on Medium, writing,

> These are heartbreaking times for the United States of America. The killing of George Floyd has given rise to a spasm of grief and anguish that has brought thousands to the streets to protest. George Floyd, Ahmaud Arbery, Breonna Taylor—they are just the latest names in a drumbeat of Black Americans whose lives were taken in brutal fashion.
>
> George Floyd's death is the catalyst but his dehumanizing death before our eyes was the latest bloody sign that we have been failing far too many people for too long. Police mistreatment of Black Americans is both a reality and a moral stain that threatens to tear our country apart.
>
> This must change. We all know that if there had not been a video shot of George Floyd's arrest his death would have gone unnoticed.
>
> Now is a time for mourning, for expressing our grief and humanity. People are hurting and have been hurting for far too long. Yet, no one's been listening. We have been pretending that we have been making progress in our country while people have been dying in the dark. We owe them, ourselves, and our families better.
>
> To those who have lost faith that we can do better, the weight of centuries of evidence and experience is on your side. It is difficult to argue with experience.
>
> Can we begin to right the inequities that have weighed down our country for generations? We have no choice but to try. We must try our hearts out, try until we burst, beyond the limits of our endurance. The wounds are too deep. It is our only chance. To cry for George Floyd and his family and to hope for an opportunity to do better.

CHAPTER 16

WHY NOT MUCH PASSES

et's say that you read this book and get really fired up. You say
to yourself, "Wow, things are not going well out there. I can do
something about it. I have a point of view. I would do the right
thing. I could do as good a job as the folks who are in charge. I'm
going to run for Congress!"

This isn't entirely hypothetical. (In fact, it's what public service
and representative democracy are all about.) Blair Walsingham, air
force veteran, mother, and small business owner, volunteered for
my campaign in rural Tennessee. Afterward, she decided she could
do more. She would run for Congress in Tennessee's First District.

As I discovered about running for president, just about anyone
can run for Congress if they feel like it. The Constitution says you
can run for Congress if you are at least twenty-five, have been a citizen for the past seven years, and live in the state—not the district—
you are running to represent. After that, the rules vary by state—
generally a certain number of signatures on a petition, a filing fee, or
both. These criteria are a very manageable threshold. Most people
could run for Congress if they get excited and completed the steps.

But then the problems begin to mount.

First, the odds are exceptionally high that you will be running
against an incumbent. Since 1976, an average of twenty-three
House members have retired each two-year election cycle. That's
only a 5 percent retirement rate; there is a 95 percent chance that
you will be running against an incumbent.

It turns out that defeating an incumbent is very, very difficult. Here are the reelection rates for incumbents since 1976:

REELECTION RATES FOR HOUSE MEMBERS	
Election Year	Percentage of Incumbents Reelected
2018	91%
2016	97%
2014	95%
2012	90%
2010	85%
2008	94%
2006	94%
2004	98%
2002	96%
2000	98%
1998	98%
1996	94%
1994	90%
1992	88%
1990	96%
1988	98%
1986	98%
1984	95%
1982	91%
1980	91%
1978	94%
1976	96%

See a trend? Over the last four decades, incumbents have a success rate of 94 percent in winning reelection. This is almost unthinkably high. The best NBA team of all time posted a win rate of 89 percent. Your opponent will have a better chance than the 1996 Bulls or the 2016 Warriors. The incumbent almost always wins.

Let's say that you are undaunted by this. "Where there's a will, there's a way." You start preparing for your run. It's the equivalent of taking on a full-time job for about a year. Do you have savings and the personal flexibility to drop everything and run around your district for months on end? That rules out most of us: Forty percent of Americans couldn't pay an unexpected $400 bill pre-pandemic, much less take on something as big as a congressional run that sucks up time and money.

You tell your friends and family that you're running. Because you're an upstanding person with a lot of relationships in your community, they are excited and supportive. They dig deep; two hundred people donate an average of $50 each to your effort. That would make you a very popular person; imagine people giving you $10,000 for your fledgling run!

Your $10,000 is about 1 percent of what you'll need. The average successful House campaign raised more than $1.6 million in recent cycles. In the Senate, it was more than $10.4 million. Amanda Litman of Run for Something writes, "Generally speaking, the 'experts' recommend that you shouldn't run for a seat in the House unless you can pretty quickly figure out how you'll raise at least $300,000 from your network." Her rule of thumb is that it costs $500,000 to $2 million to run a credible campaign for Congress. A lot of that money will go into advertising.

Think about this for a second. Who could raise $300,000 from their network? Someone older, established, probably rich themselves, and perhaps with ties to the business world, a group generally eager to make political donations, at least to candidates with a high chance of competing. The financial bar of running for Congress is one reason many candidates seem to have similar profiles. The contribution limit for any individual to a congressional campaign is $2,800, but this describes an infinitesimally small universe of donors. Only about 1 percent of American adults contribute more than $200 to a campaign, and about a tenth of 1 percent give the maximum. Getting someone to donate *anything* to a political campaign is a real feat.

Fundraising is crucial because many local races are largely built on a combination of party affiliation and name recognition. Studies have shown that name recognition and familiarity increase a candidate's likability. It's one reason why many ads and yard signs simply emphasize the candidate's name and likeness. "If voters haven't done all the research that we hope they will do before they go in, they'll often default and go with the person whose name they recognize," said Professor Andrew Downs at Purdue's Center for Indiana Politics. It's another advantage of incumbency: more voters will find the name of their current representative familiar.

You press on, undeterred. "I'll use social media and get tons of people behind me," you think. "The money will come. Besides, this race isn't about the money; it's about the message and the people."

Along with a volunteer or two, you start showing up at grocery stores and transit stops handing out pamphlets that cost you $2.50 apiece. A contact who worked in local politics agrees to become your campaign manager. You buy some new clothes and develop a website, a logo, and a set of positions. You are indefatigable, showing up to any block party, garage sale, piano recital, anyplace you think there will be a gathering. When you're not going to an event, you are on your phone calling someone or on a Zoom call. The hours add up—hundreds and then even thousands. You emphasize a couple of big ideas that you think your community will love and hope that the local media will pick up on your inspirational campaign.

Unfortunately, as we learned in part 2, since 2004 more than two thousand newspapers have closed in the United States. It turns out that in many communities there isn't much local media anymore to cover congressional races; maybe the local PBS station or radio station will have you on. Incumbents routinely decline to debate their challengers, figuring it's only a losing proposition to give the upstart any visibility and voters won't really care or notice. Many conventional journalists will avoid covering politics. Brynne Kennedy, a former tech CEO who ran for Congress near Sacramento, described it like this: "When you're a tech founder or CEO everyone wants to talk to you and says, 'Come to my dinner party.' The minute you run for office everyone's like, 'Why would you want to do that? Are you an alien?'"

Not much attention is paid to congressional politics in part because most races are not competitive across party lines. Thanks partially to gerrymandering, the common practice in which states draw congressional district boundaries that favor candidates from one party over another, more than 80 percent of congressional districts are considered safely Republican or Democrat; there is almost no chance of the other party winning. Think rural Alabama or midtown Detroit. People aren't terribly keen on hearing about their local congressional race, because they know which party— and typically candidate—is going to win.

Because the vast majority of seats are safely red or blue, the biggest threat to the incumbent is not someone from the other side; it's that they will be challenged in the primary within their own party. This is one reason why members of Congress are pushed away from compromise; reaching across the aisle to work with the other party will increase the prospect of a viable challenger from the extreme flank of your own party. Less than 20 percent of eligible voters participate in most congressional primaries, and this group is disproportionately ideologically extreme. Any form of compromise will be more likely to be punished than rewarded.

This is the landscape you are entering. You're running against an incumbent with a million-dollar advantage in a media-unfriendly environment where most everyone thinks the outcome is irrelevant or predetermined.

This is the experience that Blair Walsingham had in Tennessee.

She is awesome and compelling; when people hear from her, they come away convinced. Blair ran on improving rural broadband access and improving education. She won the Democratic nomination against two other first-time candidates. I endorsed her through my organization Humanity Forward, and No Dem Left Behind, which supports candidates in rural Republican-leaning districts, endorsed her as well. She raised more than $125,000 from people who were excited about her both in Tennessee and around the country. But she had trouble getting any attention in eastern Tennessee and lost to the incumbent by a very wide margin.

Blair's experience is all too common. But let's say, for the sake of your hypothetical run, that you catch a break. Your local congressperson has retired or gets mired in scandal. People get enthused about you. You dedicate thousands of hours to stumping and showing up and handing out leaflets making your case. You defy the odds and win your primary and then the general election. It has happened, though so seldom that you can almost rattle off the most prominent examples in recent cycles. Cori Bush in Missouri, Jamaal Bowman in New York, and Alexandria Ocasio-Cortez in New York all defeated incumbents in primaries in safe Democratic seats. On the other side Steve King in Iowa lost his primary in 2020 when Republican leaders in Congress turned on him for being overtly racist.

You do the nearly impossible and win.

You are now a newly minted member of Congress.

You've got some big ideas and you're ready to roll. The hard part is over, right? Think again.

YOU'VE JUST JOINED a body of 435 representatives as the new kid on the block.

"Freshman members of Congress are a bit like freshmen in high school: low on the totem pole and, for the most part, expected to be seen and not heard," wrote John Delaney, who served three terms from Maryland, in his book, *The Right Answer.*

Ro Khanna, current member of Congress from California's Seventeenth District, which covers Silicon Valley, described the dynamic this way in an Instagram Live with me in 2020:

> Your power in Congress is very much based on relationships . . . Who is going to have the best chance of convincing people to vote for them? The people who have been in Congress the longest time . . . If you've been in Congress, twenty, thirty years, you probably know 150, 160 of these members of Congress. So what you have is actually institutional static, basically a governing institution that is governed by people who won twenty, thirty years ago catering to people who won ten to fifteen years ago, and they actually hold the power in the institutions . . . Congress is being governed by people who won elections in the '80s and '90s. The antidemocratic character of these institutions probably isn't understood enough, that it's so seniority based.

The average age of a member of the 116th Congress is 57.6. For senators it is 62.9. The average member of the House has been there nine years, with twenty-seven members having been there for more than thirty years. Nancy Pelosi, the Speaker of the House, is eighty-one years old and has been in Congress for thirty-four years. Steny Hoyer, the House majority leader, is also eighty-one and has been in the House for forty years. Mitch McConnell is seventy-nine years old and joined the Senate thirty-six years ago. Chuck Schumer is seventy years old and has been in the Senate since 1999.

It is a seniority system. There are a lot of egos to navigate; more than half of the members of Congress are millionaires. No one wants to hear your ideas. You are told to settle in and fundraise in the hopes of working your way up toward an important committee seat . . . in about eight years.

You take office in January. From day one, you get reminded daily that you are up for reclection the following year. It's time to get yourself a million-dollar moat to make sure that you are able to defend your seat. You are told by party leadership that this is the path to advancement; since 1975 committee assignments are controlled by the Speaker and party leadership, and they favor members who raise money for the party. Members of Congress spend between 30 and 70 percent of their time fundraising; there are cubicles in party headquarters set aside for you to "dial for dollars." You thought that you might be able to put that behind you after your campaign, but it continues to be a big part of your waking life. The Democratic Congressional Campaign Committee and the National Republican Congressional Committee, which help fund races, raised $296 million and $205 million, respectively, in the 2018 cycle, and you're expected to raise your share.

Okay, you think, I can do this too. You start to settle in and make friends. You start thinking longer term. You resolve to become better at fundraising. Occasionally you have an opportunity to get on your local TV station or even cable news. Your staff has ideas on how you can build your social media following. You try to stake out one or two ideas for legislative accomplishments, even symbolic, you can talk about when someone asks you what you've accomplished in Congress.

Your salary is $174,000—a great deal by national standards. But you are now commuting from your home district to Washington, D.C., several times a year and need a place to stay in town. Washington, D.C., is one of the wealthiest metro areas in the country, ranking number three after Silicon Valley and San Francisco. You are around businesspeople and highly paid lobbyists much of the time.

Indeed, you are now at the center of a staggering vortex of money and influence. Approximately $6.4 billion was spent on lobbying Congress and government agencies by companies, trade associations, unions, and other special interest groups during the

2016 election cycle alone. Your office is constantly swamped by lobbyists and your schedule is filled with events organized by various firms that put money into your coffers in return for you politely listening to industry representatives with a policy recommendation. I attended a lobbying breakfast as a guest a number of years ago; the congressman was bored out of his mind listening to people talk about import policies while he ate pancakes.

The army of lobbyists surrounding you has two agendas: enabling changes that further advantage their clients and keeping things from changing in a way that would hinder them. Any legislation that will cost an industry or firm money will hit fierce resistance from members who will jump to preserve jobs and activity in their district. Francis Fukuyama calls the current system a "vetocracy": *I may not be able to get something done, but I can keep you from doing anything.*

You pay strict attention to the companies based in your district. If employers in your community or state don't like something, you're almost certainly going to have to do all you can to kill it. You can't have lost jobs in your district on your record.

Each party has a fairly strict hierarchy. You are actively discouraged from working with the other side. Your incentives are to avoid compromise in part because your party elders frown on it, and also to avoid giving the primary voters in your district any reason to back a viable challenger. Laws are drafted increasingly by one party—the party with a majority—without meaningful consultation with the other side. You are commonly asked to vote on legislation that runs hundreds of pages long that you and your team are given mere minutes or hours to read. Between 2006 and 2008, there were sixty-seven conference committee reports on legislation that reflected input from both sides for reconciliation. By 2016–2018, that number was down to eight.

Since the 1990s there has been an informal rule in the House enforced by several Speakers—the Hastert Rule—that a bill can only be voted on if it has the majority support of the majority party.

This means that even if a bill could pass because some members of the majority support a bill proposed by the minority party, it will never be brought to the floor. If you are in the minority party, you know you will likely never get a vote on anything you put forward.

You put that aside and decide to be a team player. You like the people in your party after all. And some of them have been at it for decades. You have been there for only a year or two. It's time to make friends. You can't get anything done in this town without friends.

Let's say that you win a couple races. You start to climb within the party hierarchy. Your team settles down in Washington, D.C. Your staffers get married and have kids. You are beginning to get noticed within your party. You get named to a committee that will have real impact for your district. You have relationships with a few national reporters. Your name recognition is rising.

You talk yourself into the fact that change doesn't happen overnight. You have to be patient and play the long game. When there's a big problem, you learn to defer to your party's leaders. They are the key to it all. You think you're friends with the party's future leaders, and there will be a place for you when they take the reins . . . about fourteen years from now.

In a jointly written foreword to the book *The Politics Industry*, the Republican congressman Mike Gallagher from Wisconsin and the Democratic congresswoman Chrissy Houlahan from Pennsylvania, both military veterans, ask, "Why is our status as members of different political parties seemingly more potent than our shared love for America, our many areas of agreement, and our shared responsibility to solve problems and get results? Why are we more often opponents than colleagues? . . . Because the system is built to tear us apart. In American politics, winning isn't winning unless the other side is losing, and losing badly."

The best members of Congress are frustrated. One congressman said to me privately, "You get to the Capitol and you see all the marble, as if it's there to remind you that nothing will change."

Jared Polis, who served five terms as a member of Congress from Colorado, said to me in his office a few years ago, "The goal is to get something significant done so you can go home." Jared is now governor of Colorado.

The partisanship was hard to miss in Congress's response to economic relief during the coronavirus. At first, there was a whiff of bipartisanship: Congress nearly unanimously passed the CARES Act in March 2020 that put $2.2 trillion back into the economy in the form of cash benefits, unemployment benefits, the Paycheck Protection Program, and aid to large corporations and to state and local governments. It was a rare display of bipartisanship in a time of crisis.

But when the enhanced unemployment benefits and other provisions, which lasted until July 31, were running out and another stimulus measure was proposed, sharp sides were drawn. The House passed the Heroes Act on May 15, 2020, by a vote of 208–199, along strict party lines. The headline cost of the bill was $3 trillion; it included $1 trillion for state and local governments, hundreds of billions of dollars for medical equipment and costs, and continued unemployment benefits. Only one Republican, Peter King of Long Island, New York, voted for the bill. Fourteen Democrats declined to support it, with many describing it as excessively partisan. Of the Democrats who didn't support the Heroes Act, most were new members of Congress from swing states or right-leaning states. Sharice Davids of Kansas said, "The partisan nature and wide scope of this bill makes it doomed upon arrival in the Senate—only further delaying the aid that Kansans desperately need." Abby Finkenauer, a freshman from Iowa, similarly said, "This legislation only serves to push real relief down the road."

Unfortunately, these statements proved prescient, because the Heroes Act stalled immediately upon arriving in the Senate. Mitch McConnell signaled that Republicans would consider a bill at around $1 trillion, but negotiations ground to a halt. June, July, August, September, October, and November passed with no bill, even as benefits expired for millions. In September, the Senate Republicans passed a scaled-down version of around $500 billion, which Democrats vetoed, and the stalemate continued.

Americans around the country sensed that our government was failing us. "The United States distinguished itself with its remarkable mishandling of the medical side of Covid-19. It has independently distinguished itself with its equally extraordinary mishandling of the economic consequences of the pandemic. This is incompetence/indifference squared," wrote the columnist Nicholas Kristof of *The New York Times,* capturing the frustration many felt around the country.

How could Congress fail in such a basic way, when more than four out of five Americans—including a majority of both Democrats and Republicans—wanted an extension of coronavirus relief and other stimulus measures? First, any individual member of Congress has only a marginal role in negotiations; the real conversations take place among leadership hammering out the bill and trying to reconcile it with the other side. Rank-and-file members of Congress rarely get to touch the decision-making process, beyond a yes or no vote, as demonstrated by the fourteen Democrats who declined to support the bill.

Imagine yourself as an individual member of Congress trying to answer for the inaction. What are your choices? You can either try to initiate a revolt within your own party or blame the other party.

The choice becomes easier to understand when you consider that, in the vast majority of cases, each member of Congress is not actually going to pay a price if a bill isn't passed. Their incentives are not tied to congressional performance or popular opinion.

Americans' approval of Congress has steadily been declining over time, from highs in the 50s and 60s a couple decades ago to 18–30 percent today. Think about that: three-quarters of Americans disapprove of Congress as a whole, while individual members sport reelection rates of 94 percent.

If you are a member of Congress, your clear incentives are to go

Congressional Job Approval

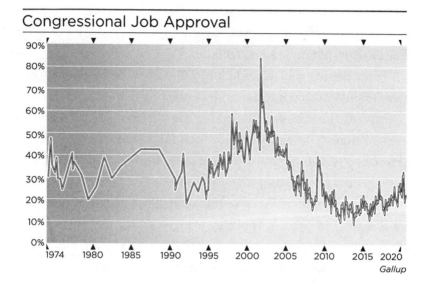

Gallup

along with party leadership, raise money, elevate your own profile, avoid a primary challenge, and bide your time. The nature or quality of legislation—or the way of life of your constituents—is increasingly irrelevant. If you blame the other party, you'll win reelection. If you break ranks, you'll likely be cast out or challenged in the primary.

I was staggered by the near-total lack of criticism for Nancy Pelosi over Congress's inability to pass a coronavirus relief bill for most of 2020. Hundreds of Democrats in Congress didn't breathe a word. I vastly preferred her approach to Mitch McConnell's and think the House bill had it mostly right, but at some point you have to try to get a bill passed. On December 27, President Trump finally signed a watered-down relief bill, giving some Americans a meager $600 check.

It wouldn't be until March 10, 2021, that another relief bill would pass. It relied on a process known as budget reconciliation, a tie-breaking vote from Vice President Harris, and a revote in the House to accept a Senate amendment, but the American Rescue Plan Act of 2021 was finally signed into law. The $1.9 trillion relief bill included $1,400 stimulus checks for many individuals and the expansion of the child tax credit, as well as an additional $300 boost to weekly unemployment benefits. Still, it would pass almost a year after millions of families had fallen into distress.

We are getting angrier and more despondent or frustrated as our government continues to be unresponsive to the needs of the vast majority of the country. Expecting the dynamics to change is a waste of time. The machine is broken. The incentives are wrong. This is why well-intentioned people grow frustrated and jaded after being elected to Congress.

What is required is first recognizing that this system is not actually designed to produce policies that maximize the public well-being or resemble the will of the people. It is designed for stasis and inaction, for cable news television appearances blaming the other side and fundraising dinners that make sure nothing changes. It is only by meaningfully changing the system of incentives that we could start to expect a different result.

CHAPTER 17

THE WAVE THAT WASN'T

As the summer of 2020 wore on, my team at Humanity Forward and I decided to endorse more state and congressional candidates who were aligned with cash relief. I became fixated on the hope that Congress could pass a new relief bill. I interviewed each candidate and was blown away by the folks who were running for Congress. Kara Eastman, an award-winning nonprofit leader, was running for the second time in Omaha, Nebraska, and Moe Davis, a retired air force colonel and judge who had resigned as chief prosecutor at Guantánamo over the use of torture, was running in western North Carolina. Truly remarkable people were running for Congress in many districts that the national party wasn't paying much attention to. I made a personal donation to each candidate I endorsed; it was the kind of gesture I would have appreciated when I was running.

In August, the Democratic National Convention went virtual. When the initial speaker list came out, I wasn't included. I was surprised. My team had been told that I was speaking and was upset at the omission. I tweeted, "I've got to be honest I kind of expected to speak." My tweet—and seeming snub—created an online furor led by the #YangGang. Later that day, my team got a call saying that the announced list hadn't been finalized and that I'd be speaking on the last night.

I thought, "Wow, now I'd better say something good." I built my remarks around the fact that 72 percent of Americans thought we were going through the worst time in living memory and we needed new leadership to turn the page.

I was the opening speaker of the final night of the convention. They had me come in and do a dress rehearsal earlier in the day in a New York studio. It was odd pretending to speak to millions. When the real thing happened, it felt great. It was a high-water mark—getting to address the American people. We had come a long way from the beginning of my campaign. I got a flurry of texts congratulating me. I walked a number of blocks to CNN to watch the rest of the night's speeches and then comment on them. I considered joking, "Sure, Joe was great, but what about the opening remarks? They really set the tone."

The following week I watched the Republican National Convention. It was like a parallel universe. The messages were well presented and often started from something compelling and then took a different direction. The entertainment and production values were high. It reminded me of the movie *Starship Troopers*. An unfailingly keen observer, Evelyn watched it with me and said, "I think people will respond to this law-and-order message more than Democrats might think."

In October there was hope that there would be a second relief bill. The last bill passed in March, and unemployment benefits and other benefits had elapsed in July. There were millions of families in distress, and I knew many of their situations would get much worse through the winter. Steve Mnuchin, the Treasury secretary, publicly made a $1.8 trillion offer, almost twice what the Senate was prepared to accept. I began to comment on CNN that I thought Nancy Pelosi should take a deal before the election, because I thought her leverage would be at its highest and I feared that a relief bill wouldn't pass in a lame-duck session and people would need to wait for months. I was struck by how few Democrats were making the same case; Ro Khanna was the only other one I saw.

Much to my surprise, Nancy Pelosi went on Wolf Blitzer's show, seemingly to respond to my comments. Her appearance was not reassuring; there was a sense that Democrats didn't really want a bill to pass before the election. My fears that Americans would enter the winter without relief grew stronger.

I'm friendly with Nancy Pelosi; she and I have met several times and she was very kind. But you are allowed to disagree with people you are friendly with if it's sincere.

During this time, Joe's team asked me if I'd campaign in person as a surrogate in Pennsylvania down the stretch. I visited Philadelphia's Chinatown one weekend and western Pennsylvania the next. Campaigning with a mask on during COVID felt strange, as if you were operating with a giant mute button suppressing crowds and excitement.

Election week I was on CNN almost every day. There was live coverage twenty-four hours a day in the studio; we were warned that we would have some crazy hours and not to expect much sleep. I drew the early morning shifts, so I worked from 3:00 a.m. to 8:00 a.m. or 4:00 a.m. to 9:00 a.m. for most of that week. It helped that the anchors were Don Lemon and Chris Cuomo, who were always energized and engaging.

On election night I watched the early returns with Evelyn and other family. The early results filled me with dread. I knew there was a wave of early reporting states—Florida, Ohio, North Carolina—that could result in a quick knockout win for Joe. The next set of swing states—Michigan, Wisconsin, and Pennsylvania— had rules on mail-in vote counting that suggested we would have to wait a few days for full results. So my hope going in was that Joe could win one of the first set of states.

As it became clear that Trump was going to win Florida and likely Ohio and North Carolina, it felt like déjà vu to 2016. I had been quite optimistic going in, and even though I knew the mail-in votes favored Joe, it was concerning.

The following morning, as votes continued to be counted, we had a longtime Michigan congresswoman, Debbie Dingell, beam into the CNN studio to comment on what was going on in her district. Debbie said that a plant in her district had closed and laid off fifteen hundred workers. She was concerned about how working-class voters were voting in the election.

After Debbie's comments, Don Lemon turned to me and asked if Democrats were having a hard time connecting with working-class voters. I responded,

> I had that experience countless times on the trail, Don. I would say, "Hey, I'm running for president!" to a truck driver, a retail worker, a waitress at a diner, and they would say, "What party?" and I would say, "Democrat," and they would flinch, like I'd said something really negative or I'd turned another color . . . There is something deeply wrong when working-class Americans have that response to a major party that theoretically is supposed to be fighting for them. So you have to ask yourself, "What has the Democratic Party been standing for in their minds?" And in their minds, the Democratic Party unfortunately has taken on this role of the urban, coastal elites who are more concerned about policing various cultural issues than improving their way of life that has been declining for years . . . This to me is a fundamental problem for the Democratic Party because if they don't figure this out, then polarization and division will get worse, not better.

Don asked me, "Is that real or messaging? Or both?"

I responded, "It's real! Debbie just said they lost a plant that had fifteen hundred workers and if you're a laid-off worker from that plant and you look up and say, 'What is the Democratic Party doing for me?' it's unclear. And we can talk about a unifying message . . . but then there's the reality on the ground where their way of life has been disintegrating for years, and if we don't address that, you're going to see a continued acceleration toward the institutional mistrust that animated the Trump vote and will continue to do so."

This was around five in the morning, so I wasn't sure many people would notice. But later that day, a blogger, Matt Skidmore, posted a video clip of the exchange on Twitter. It quickly went viral, racking up five million views over the next two days just on Twitter; it was viewed millions more times on other platforms. Other news outlets picked it up and rebroadcast it. The critique struck a chord. I wasn't the only one who felt like our political conversation was highlighting certain types of issues that pit us against each other while ignoring a lot of the underlying economic conditions that could actually bring people together.

THAT SATURDAY, after a labored four days of vote counting, Joe Biden was declared the president-elect by CNN and the other networks. People celebrated in the streets of New York City, whooping and hollering. It was as if a cloud had started to lift for millions. I felt both exhilaration and relief. That night, Evelyn and I went to see Dave Chappelle host *Saturday Night Live;* he had invited us the previous week to be his guests.

In the car, I said to Evelyn, "I'm sure glad that Joe won. But if Mitch McConnell is the Senate majority leader, it's going to be a rerun of the Obama years when Joe can't do anything because it's being blocked."

"That would be terrible," Evelyn said. "Is there anything that we can do?"

"Well," I said, "if the Democrats win both seats in the special Senate races in Georgia, then the Senate is tied and Kamala is the tiebreaker."

Evelyn said, "We have to do everything we can to help them win!"

I nodded. I confided to Evelyn that I was considering heading down to Georgia to campaign and that I wanted to talk to her about it. "It seems like the most important thing we can do," I told her. Having spent months campaigning for Joe, I thought it would be odd to walk away and not follow through.

Evelyn touched my hand and said, "We should totally do that.

It feels like Joe's presidency could depend on it." We decided then and there to head to Georgia to campaign for the Democratic candidates.

I tweeted out, "Great news #yanggang—Evelyn and I are moving to Georgia to help @ossoff and @ReverendWarnock win!" I did so in part to focus people on the Georgia races even as they were celebrating Joe's win.

We parked near Rockefeller Center. Fifth Avenue was boarded up; the fronts of about half of the stores were featureless planes of wood. The level of foot traffic in midtown on a Saturday night was negligible. It was eerie. It reminded me more of Detroit, a city I've spent a fair amount of time in, than Manhattan.

There were a couple of police officers on Fifth Avenue keeping watch. We asked them to direct us to the correct entrance. One of them recognized me and said, "Are you Andrew Yang? Man, I'm a big fan. Ever since I saw you on Rogan." We took pictures with them and thanked them.

SNL was a lot of fun. We convened beforehand with Dave's family and friends. I also got to meet Bowen Yang, who had played me on *SNL,* which was a treat. The cast members were very friendly backstage. It was tremendous to give Evelyn such a quality date night given the past couple of years of endless campaigning.

EVEN THOUGH THE networks had all called the race for Joe, election returns continued to pour in. In the following days, it sank in more and more that Trump's support had grown by more than ten million voters. It was likely that he might even have won if not for the coronavirus, which had killed 230,000 Americans by the time of the election. Democratic hopes for states like Texas, Iowa, and Ohio were misplaced. House Democrats, who had expected to win five to fifteen seats, instead lost thirteen seats and had thirteen incumbents lose. The vast majority of the candidates Humanity Forward and I had endorsed in places like Florida, Ohio, Iowa,

California, Texas, and western New York lost. Kara and Colonel Moe lost. It was a very tough election for folks who had hoped for a repudiation of Trump.

Seeing these candidates lose had a huge impact on me. Julie Oliver, a very impressive mom and lawyer, got 136,385 votes in 2018 in the Twenty-Fifth District in Texas, which is near Austin, about 27,000 fewer than her incumbent Republican opponent Roger Williams's 163,023. When I interviewed Julie for an endorsement, I admired her grit, character, and intellect a great deal. Many people were impressed with her campaign in 2018, and she decided to put the work in and do it again. She got 165,697 votes in 2020, which was about 29,000 more than in 2018 and more than her opponent had in the last race. The problem was that her opponent got 220,088, over 57,000 more than he had gotten the last time. The same thing happened to Kara Eastman in Omaha, who got 155,706 votes in 2020, up from 121,770 in 2018. But her opponent, Don Bacon, similarly went to 171,071 from 126,715. Imagine losing by fewer than 6,000 votes, coming back to run again, working your heart out, getting 34,000 more voters, and then losing by more than last time. People on both sides were getting more energized, despite what one would imagine would be a desire to turn the page.

When I was campaigning, I spent a significant amount of time in Ohio and Iowa, both of which were quintessential swing states until quite recently. They both went to Obama in 2012. In 2020, they both went to Trump by 8 points, despite Joe making appearances in each one. To me, these two states mark the plight faced by both the industrial and the agricultural Midwest. Ohio in particular has demographics that are strikingly similar to Michigan's—13.1 percent Black in Ohio versus 14.1 percent in Michigan. In Iowa, suicide among farmers has become a growing concern.

The temptation for Democrats is to say, "Who cares about Ohio and Iowa? We won Arizona and Georgia, both states that are diversifying to become more Democrat-friendly. Let's just go where the demographics take us." Many people online made this point to me when I mentioned these states. There are several problems with this line of thinking.

First, in theory, your goal as a party is to improve people's lives as well as win elections. Even if you can eke out a national election by trading Iowa and Ohio for Arizona and Georgia, you should try to figure out why you are losing battleground states that you were recently contesting by perhaps addressing why people feel like their quality of life is declining rather than improving.

Second, it sends a terrible message. I met literally thousands of Democrats in Iowa and Ohio while I was campaigning, including county chairs and activists as well as elected officials. In both states, there are people who have done enormous service for the party for years. Iowa, for example, launched Barack Obama's campaign in 2008. Saying to the folks who have fought for you tooth and nail for years, "We give up on your state; it's no longer winning territory for us, because of your demographics," is not exactly an inspiring party line.

Third, acceding to these pressures exacerbates and accelerates the political polarization that is tearing the country apart. Iowa is a predominantly white agricultural state. Ohio is more diverse but is 81.7 percent white, significantly above the national average of 60.1 percent. Saying that Democrats can't compete in white-majority states and/or rural states accelerates the definition of each party, where Democrats lay claim to urban and racially diverse areas, primarily on the coasts, and Republicans dominate in shrinking rural economies that are majority white. Not competing in battlegrounds will heighten division and harden the lines.

You could of course reverse this line of argument and say that Republicans should be adopting policies and messaging that allow them to compete in diversifying places they used to win, like Virginia and Nevada. I'd agree: if each party was actually fighting for the other party's territory, you'd see more moderates elected to office and lower racialized rhetoric.

Fourth, winning over at least some proportion of these voters is necessary in order to not just win an election but pass legislation. The current congressional rules require a real majority that will be very difficult for Democrats to muster without some new voters. David Shor, a Democratic polling and data expert who worked on the Obama campaign, told *Politico,* "We have an election system that makes it basically impossible for Democrats' current coalition to ever wield legislative power . . . We are legitimately in a position from here on out where [Democrats] would need to get 54 percent of the popular vote—which we did not even accomplish this time—for multiple cycles in a row, for us to be in a position to really pass laws."

If Democrats are going to get a majority big enough to pass laws, there's a need to grow their coalition. And to grow their coalition, they might as well start with places that they were recently competitive in, like Ohio and Iowa. Figuring out how to compete there would almost certainly benefit the party in neighboring Michigan, Pennsylvania, and Wisconsin.

The party dynamic unfortunately cuts away from this kind of introspection. Party leaders represent safe seats on the coasts and often are only superficially responsive to Democrats in swing districts. One midwestern congresswoman said to me, "The fact is that, in a seniority system, folks like me who are from genuine swing districts won't last long enough to ever make it to House or party leadership."

This is not just to blame Democrats; at least the Democratic Party still has a platform. A series of structural reasons makes it difficult for either side to achieve a governing majority, namely:

- A geographic imbalance is baked into national elections now, where states that account for only 42 percent of population account for more than 50 percent of electoral votes. Wyoming has the same number of senators as California, despite having one sixty-eighth the population. Democratic voters are clustered into the same states, while Republicans are spread out. This has the effective impact of making the average state six points more Republican than the average voter. This also means that if the popular vote were close, the Republican candidate would be expected to win the presidential election 65 percent of the time. Simply put, Republican voters have slightly more weight because they are allocated to lower-population states where their votes count more.

- Conservative self-identification remains high. Self-described conservatives consistently outnumber liberals—35 percent to 26 percent as of January 2019. Three-quarters of Republicans identify as conservatives, while only half of Democrats call themselves liberals. If that isn't enough, in December 2018, 57 percent of Republicans wanted the party to become more conservative. Perhaps of equal importance, 54 percent of Democrats wanted their party to become more moderate. This is not a nation prone to dramatic shifts by the numbers.

- Partisanship has risen to a point where most people will simply vote for one party or another regardless of the individual candidates. One study showed that the number of people who were actually independent and who could be persuaded to vote for one party or the other is now only 7 percent of voters, down from 22 percent in the 1980s and 1990s. Instead of trying to attract a shrinking middle, both parties now focus on getting out their bases as a better return on investment. One Republican candidate for the state legislature in South Carolina did nothing but put her name on the ballot and won easily. These sorts of things happen every election because so many people now will just show up to vote for the R or the D.

The parties have now "sharply split across racial, religious, geographic, cultural, and psychological lines," as Ezra Klein puts it in *Why We're Polarized.* "There are many, many powerful identities lurking in that list, and they are fusing together, stacking atop one another, so a conflict or threat that activates one activates all." Klein stipulates that demographic and social changes are activating increased conservatism among many white voters. In 2008, 54 percent of the country was white and Christian. By 2016, that had fallen to 43 percent. About 70 percent of all senior citizens are white and Christian, compared with less than 30 percent of young adults. These changes both reflect an evolving electorate and drive reactions in the opposite direction.

When I was in Georgia for the Senate runoff races, the airwaves were dominated by political advertisements. The Republican ads would intone solemnly, "Radical leftist Jon Ossoff wants to team up with radical leftist AOC and radical leftist Nancy Pelosi to destroy America. You have one chance to save America. Vote for David Perdue to Save America. David Perdue to Save America. I approve this message." The ads were rife with images of Jon Ossoff walking with Black voters and then David Perdue walking with white voters. The "America" that David Perdue was "saving" seemed to be white America. I thought, "Wow, these ads are pretty much straight-up fearmongering." The fact that these appeals failed in Georgia—barely—does not mean they have lost their strength or power.

Democrats could barely eke out a governing majority against Donald Trump, a historically unpopular figure who mismanaged a pandemic that killed hundreds of thousands of Americans. There are reasons to expect that not to change. Polarization is getting worse, not better—unless we somehow change the terms of engagement.

CHAPTER 18

CONSTRUCTIVE INSTITUTIONALISM; OR, THE PRIESTS OF THE DECLINE

During the six years I spent running Venture for America, part of the job involved speaking regularly about the mission of the organization—in our case training entrepreneurs and creating jobs in communities around the country. Over time, I became aware that the economy was transforming in fundamental ways that would displace millions of workers, requiring larger changes to society than my nonprofit could address. Our nation's $22 trillion economy was turning against people, and there's no nonprofit on earth that operates at that level; the largest nonprofit in the United States has a budget of less than one-hundredth of $1 trillion.

Despite my epiphany, it was very difficult to acknowledge this thinking in my role. My job was to motivate people and to be grateful. People were volunteering, working hard, and donating money every day to keep the organization going. And we were doing phenomenal work that was changing lives. I had to be a can-do guy. The last thing I, as the CEO of a nonprofit, could do would be to stand up and say, "The problems are getting worse, not better."

There are many people stuck in versions of this same situation. You do good work. You're proud of it. But part of you knows, "There are deeper problems here than I can solve."

One example of this is schoolteachers. We expect schoolteachers to do amazing work. Millions of teachers do just that every day.

But the data shows that two-thirds of our kids' educational outcomes are determined by many factors outside the school: number of words read to the child when they're young, parental income, parental time spent with the child, stress levels in the house, quality of neighborhood, and so on. Teachers know this. Imagine being asked to do a very important job when you know that you can control only about one-third of the result.

The economist Eric Weinstein has posited that our failing economic system is making liars out of many people. Two examples he cites are academia and law firms. In academia, it used to be the case that someone could go to graduate school, get a PhD, get an academic post, and aspire to a full-time professorship. But today, tenure-track positions have dramatically shrunk in number relative to the supply of graduates. Since 1980, the number of teaching positions has increased by more than 100 percent, but the number of tenure-track positions has increased by only 22 percent. Most academics will never get tenure or even be considered. PhDs keep getting produced every year, though, so the vast majority leave the field or become underemployed as permanent underpaid adjuncts in a sort of nebulous purgatory.

The same dynamic is playing out in the legal industry. Graduating law students incur well over $100,000 in school loans. I owed about $120,000 myself when I graduated from law school in 1999. It made sense when you could be confident you'd have a high-paying job waiting for you when you got out of law school. Today's graduates have far less certainty about their financial rewards, yet their tuition is significantly higher than mine was. Similarly, young attorneys agree to work themselves to the bone for eight to ten years in the hopes of being named a partner, getting a corner office, and making even bigger money. But law firms aren't growing as they used to. If profits don't grow, partners will not want to anoint new partners, because they will just be cutting the same pie of profits into smaller slices. They can't come out and admit that to the associates who are joining the firm. So they wind up telling them eight years later that it turns out there's no room for them at the top.

No one wants to admit the above realities in academia and law. As a result, institutions and the people who make them up keep proceeding as if opportunities will exist that won't be there.

I call this dynamic constructive institutionalism—a tendency among leaders to state publicly and even hold the belief that everything will work out, despite quantitative evidence to the contrary, coupled with an inability to actually address a given institution's real problems. Maybe you even acknowledge the failings and struggles, but you do so in a way that ends up increasing both your credibility and trustworthiness. Imagine a gathering of twenty university presidents to talk about why colleges are so expensive and why the underprivileged don't have a higher level of access. They would say very smart and compassionate things about the perverse incentives put forward by the *U.S. News & World Report* rankings and the financial pressures of maintaining competitive appeal. You would think, "Wow, these people really get it." But not one of them would actually go back and change anything important.

"How will we train Americans for the jobs of the future?" or "How will we overcome polarization and bring Americans together?" I've been asked these questions innumerable times over the past several years. The honest answers are "We probably won't. It will almost certainly get worse." I then talk bravely about the caring economy, vocational programs, changing the language of politics, or circumscribing social media. But none of those things will actually happen. By talking about them as if they were possible, I'm giving people a mistaken sense of reassurance. We have become a whole network of people bullshitting each other into believing that *smart people are thinking about it* and *good things are happening that will address the problems.* And then we all just go back to whatever we were doing.

Government is largely about this kind of theater. When I talk to government officials, oftentimes they lack the power to do anything about a problem, particularly in a time of legislative gridlock and dysfunction. You know what many of them say? "We do have the power to convene." They will send fancy invitations to a bunch of powerful or well-known people who are involved with or knowledgeable about the issue at hand, and everyone will come together to discuss "the future of work" or "elevating entrepreneurship" or whatever the issue is. Their big delivery will be to get a mayor or senator or member of Congress to show up to said event as an enticement.

I was named a Champion of Change by the Obama administration in 2012 and a Presidential Ambassador for Global Entrepreneurship in 2015. Both of these honors involved meeting President Obama. When I was running for president, I sometimes made use of the photos I had from these gatherings to great effect. I still use them today.

Meeting with President Obama to discuss job creation and entrepreneurship

But it turns out the photos were the main deliverable. Champion of Change was a designation given to people doing work that the White House Office of Public Engagement was looking to spotlight. When I went to the Champions of Change event, it was as one of a group of nonprofit leaders to meet the president. We did an interview with the Office of Public Engagement afterward where we were asked for feedback. The first speakers expressed their gratitude for being there. By the third or fourth leader, though, people started saying things like "I wish that we were given a contact who could help our organization" or "I wish that I was getting resources so that we could grow our work." Many of these nonprofit leaders were running small grassroots organizations and were constantly scrapping for money. The power of the keepsake photo was already wearing off.

The Presidential Ambassador for Global Entrepreneurship program, on the other hand, was for business titans, including several billionaires and household names. If I was one of the coolest Champions of Change, I was certainly one of the least cool Ambassadors for Global Entrepreneurship. I joked that they must have needed an Asian American for the photo. I met Daymond John, Mark Cuban, Barbara Corcoran, Hamdi Ulukaya, and Nina Vaca at the White House. (Also there—Elizabeth Holmes, the since-disgraced Theranos founder. She struck me as odd, but I was like, "Who am I to say?" Meanwhile, Daniel Lubetzky, the founder of KIND Snacks, at one point asked us if we were hungry. A bunch of us said yes, and he opened his jacket pockets and produced all of these experimental KIND Bars that none of us had seen before; he was the Batman of snacks.)

Even for people at this level, our function was mostly ceremonial. We convened at the Global Entrepreneurship Summit in Palo Alto in 2016. The highlight of the event was Mark Zuckerberg sitting on a stage and advising young entrepreneurs from around the world. Some of these entrepreneurs were from Africa and clearly of modest means. I felt like screaming out, "Mark, cut these folks a check!" from my seat in the tenth row. But no. It seemed that the entrepreneurs walked away with a photo of being onstage with Mark and some advice.

If running for president consisted of camera angles, our current approach to governance rests significantly on photo opportunities and performances that demonstrate our understanding. I found out later that at least one major entrepreneur who was a public company CEO turned the honor down because he was more about action than ceremony.

As someone who's been a part of this theatrical tradition, my incentives are to continue the fiction. If I was on a panel or attended a conference, it's much better to suggest that the panel really did make a difference. If I have a photo with Obama, I must have his cell-phone number or at least be able to get in touch with him.

Indeed, two groups that are especially prone to constructive institutionalism are those that we rely upon both to give us a sense of the problems and to solve them—journalists and politicians.

Journalists are typically trained to be impartial observers, which inhibits them from expressing emotion or opinion. They are supposed to calmly document and present the news. For many, there is an implicit perch of authority and stability. Unfortunately, this has also turned many into market-friendly automatons and cultural guardians who make pro forma gestures about decorum, virtue, and propriety while ignoring the disintegration of trust, the dissipating integrity of their own organizations, or the decline of the American way of life.

I've been blown away by how so many journalists seem to keep a stiff upper lip even as their industry has been decimated. Talk about bravery—or bizarre institutional acceptance—in the face of real-life distress. More than sixty thousand journalists have lost their jobs over the past ten years, with over half of that in 2020 alone. Digital media companies that were supposed to be the future have hemorrhaged employees along with the old-line businesses. On their way out, many tweet out chin-up messages about it: "It's been an honor reporting alongside the most talented colleagues in the world for these past 10 years. I learned so much. Thank you."

The most visible figures command enough of an audience to make the industry seem healthy, even while the rank and file disappear. Top journalists continue to make good money; there will just be a lot fewer of them, with others looking up at them. The winner-take-all economy is subsuming the field as it is so many others.

If you ask a journalist about the secular disruption, you're likely to get a response like "Don't worry, journalism will continue to reinvent itself via a combination of Substack and podcasting"—the kind of response that is the epitome of constructive institutionalism. There's nothing wrong with the institution after all; it's just that the journalists are not adaptable enough. Perhaps if they pivot quickly, you will subscribe to their new newsletter on coronavirus vaccine news.

That's a much more common response than the correct one: "Help! I'm sad! Our sector is being blown up, and we need either massive philanthropy or public funding if it is to survive in a way that approaches the needs of a modern functioning democracy!"

If journalists are conditioned to calmly document dispassionately, politicians are conditioned to invoke profundity, resilience, and the greater good at every turn. As a politician you're like a totem or shaman. You show up to a gathering or charity event to speechify and elevate the proceeding: "Thank you for the incredible work that you're doing. It's so important." Which it is, of course. Though it would be if you didn't show up too.

You are meant to embody the concerns of the community. You listen patiently to all. You are present. If someone asks you a question, you answer it reassuringly. You express values and aspirations. You are a human security blanket, and your job is to make people feel better.

You make false promises regularly or lay claim to powers you do not have. "Together we can ensure that every child has the kind of opportunity that they deserve in our community." "If we come together, there's no limit to what we can accomplish." "If we listen to each other, we can create a bright future for all." You are all about the singing of brighter horizons.

Perhaps the biggest example of this magical thinking is the political conversation around retraining workers, often expressed, absurdly, as "teaching people to code." The actual success of government-funded retraining programs has been found to be near zero in a majority of cases, with many workers simply holding valueless certificates afterward. Has the politician ever tried coding before? Have they tried to retrain a thousand former manufacturing and retail workers? Would they hire those thousand people if they needed a thousand coders? How about a hundred thousand?

We accept ridiculous statements on their face because we have grown to regard them less as real actions or policy statements and more as simply value statements and political representations of the world as you wish it to be. The country has lost more than four million manufacturing jobs since 2000, devastating hundreds of once-thriving communities in the Midwest and the South. That's fine; if ten politicians stand in a circle holding hands and chant in unison, "You'll like to code, heed this refrain, despair not, you shall retrain," those millions of workers shall all move to Seattle and become Amazon Web Services technicians.

You can't solve the problem, so talking assumes the role of solution. Right before he left office, Justin Amash, a Michigan congressman, said, "I'm seeing all of these campaign ads right now, and everyone's saying, 'I'm going to do this, I'm going to do that' . . . No you're not. You're not going to do that, because you have no power to do it. The system is not designed to allow you to do that." It's much easier and more compelling for a politician to say "I'm going to fight for each and every one of you!" than "There's not much I can do about that one."

Of course, politicians and journalists reinforce each other's fictions. I'm reporting on you because you represent the people. I'll catch you if you misspeak, because your speaking right is the most important thing; if you spoke right, all would be solved. This is important.

Politicians are increasingly reduced to well-liked or poll-tested stewards who tend to our emotions rather than figures who can actually improve the situation. There's a negation of the self: you are not a human being; you are our weathervane and expresser of grief, outrage, celebration, sorrow, sports allegiance, or whatever the occasion warrants. You can't actually amend the institution that you represent, but you can make us feel better about it temporarily as we go home.

If there is a big hairy problem—climate change, automation of jobs and a dehumanizing economy, dysfunctional government—you can attend a conference about it. In a world where preserving your role means playing along, who is left to tell us the truth about either the organizations they represent or what is happening to us?

The mistrust that is building up in American life is born in large part of the pervasiveness of constructive institutionalism. We have conversations about what we can do better while the reality degrades around us, increasing the divergence between the world we're talking about and the world as it is. We're paid to be positive and market-friendly and can-do. We say something like "We must solve these problems" while counting our book royalties. The people who are on the outside of these institutions lose trust in us. Their instincts aren't entirely wrong.

Can this dynamic be changed? It's an open question whether we can reinforce more disciplined communications that call out the reality of our situations without descending into happy talk. We must start distinguishing between compassionate and conformist statements, on the one hand, and actually improving the facts on the ground in a world where action and statement have become the same, in part because very few are capable of actually taking steps that would improve the reality on the ground.

The previous sentence was constructively institutionalist. You see how it works. Or doesn't.

IN PART 3 we will survey a number of improvements that I believe would genuinely help change things for the better.

PART III

FORWARD

CHAPTER 19

THE HUMAN ECONOMY: MAKING WHAT WE MEASURE

I was campaigning in Iowa in January 2020. We were crossing the state in a tour bus, conducting town halls in every other town. Some of the events were quite modestly attended, but my team assured me that getting a dozen people in Panora in Guthrie County was quite an accomplishment.

I felt good about the conversations I was having with people. Some were showing up out of curiosity or obligation, but others seemed very engaged. Many said they would caucus for me. After one event, a fit, middle-aged man with a beard came up to me and said something that has stuck with me ever since.

"Thank you for your talk," he said. "Things aren't working for a lot of people here. I should know. I'm the town doctor."

I perked up. "Wow, thank you for being here! What do you mean?"

He said, "Well, a lot of people here work on farms. They used to work for themselves, but now they work for a big holding company. When they get sick, they generally can't work anymore. They lose their health insurance because they lose their job. They typically then file for Medicaid or another program, but they don't have health care in the meantime. A lot of them die while they're waiting, because they're sick. The health-care system around here means a lot of people get no care at all, just when they need it the most. It's like it's designed for people to die. If you can do something about that, you'd be helping a lot of people."

"Thank you," I responded. "I'll do my best."

Think about this story. Here we are celebrating being the richest society in the history of the world. Meanwhile, people are routinely dying because of a system that doesn't prioritize their health or well-being so much as whether there is money to be made from their care.

In the United States, GDP has exceeded $22 trillion even as income inequality has reached unprecedented levels. Meanwhile, life expectancy and mental health are declining, and stress levels are through the roof.

NEW MEASURES FOR A NEW ECONOMY

We rely upon the market to tell us how much things are worth. But the market misses the mark all of the time. For the past several years, my wife, Evelyn, has been at home with our two boys, one of whom is autistic. We say that she is the CEO of his care. The market values her work, and that of millions of stay-at-home parents, at zero. I would say it is obvious that her work, as well as that of parents and caregivers around the country, is among the most important, difficult, and valuable work that anyone will ever do.

In our extreme economy, even the handful of winners feel more anxious and depressed. Jamie Dimon, the CEO of the banking giant JPMorgan Chase, and Ray Dalio, the influential founder of the hedge fund Bridgewater, have both argued that we should declare our economy a national emergency because it is not working for most Americans anymore. And that was before the pandemic.

So what are we missing?

It's pretty simple. The purpose of an economy should be to improve the way of life of its people—that is, to improve the measurable quality of life of each and every person in a society.

I've run several organizations, and one of the lessons I learned is "you make what you measure." If you don't measure the right things, you won't solve the right problems.

Right now, we're measuring the wrong things. We trumpet gross domestic product as the barometer of economic progress. Even the inventor of GDP, Simon Kuznets, said at its invention in 1934 that it was a terrible measure of national well-being and cautioned against using it as such, and here we are riding it into the ground eighty-seven years later. Bobby Kennedy famously echoed this idea, saying that GDP "does not allow for the health of our children, the quality of their education, or the joy of their play . . . [I]t measures everything, in short, except that which makes life worthwhile." We're like a car spinning our wheels in mud while the driver argues everything is okay because the eighty-seven-year-old speedometer is showing progress.

So what measures should we use? Let's pose this question another way: What do you care about in your own life? Positive mental health and freedom from substance abuse? Health and life expectancy? How your kids are doing in school and whether they are addicted to screens? Average income and affordability of basic needs like health care and housing and education? Clean air and clean water and a stable future for our children? These are the measures of progress in a modern society and should be our new economic measurements. We are the purpose of the economy, not its fuel.

If we used these measures, instead of focusing all our energy on GDP and the stock market, we would see that we have been facing a crisis on many fronts since before the pandemic. Our physical health, mental health, financial security, and expectations for the future have all been declining or at multi-decade lows for years. Suicides, drug overdoses, and deaths of despair have become the new normal in towns across America.

Some might argue these are social problems and not economic ones. That line of thinking ignores that each of these issues has a crushing impact on our economy in addition to its human toll.

Our revenue-maximizing cost-driven health-care system has led to the United States spending double that of comparable nations while facing lower life expectancy and higher infant mortality rates.

The cost of the opioid epidemic has been estimated at more than $78 billion every year, not to mention the hundreds of thousands of lives lost and families ruined, some of whom I met on the trail every day. Mental health issues at work alone put a $550 billion drag on the economy. Not having a middle class will be devastating for our economy over time, as businesses catering to these consumers shut their doors as their customer base erodes. And climate change, by the year 2100, will be costing us nearly $2 trillion per year. It's already costing us hundreds of billions of dollars just in disaster mitigation and cleanup, much less the lives and livelihoods lost.

These are the numbers that matter, and yet we have leaders who tout a record-breaking stock market as if it were indicative of a successful economy.

I propose an evolution of our current system of corporate capitalism to one that I call human-centered capitalism, or human capitalism for short. Human capitalism has three core tenets:

1. Humanity is more important than money.
2. The unit of an economy is each person, not each dollar.
3. Markets exist to serve our common goals and interests.

We don't exist to serve the economy. The economy exists to improve our way of life.

Such systemic rethinking may seem as if it would take a lot to implement. But it's not that difficult to advance our measurements. It would simply take the Bureau of Economic Analysis of the Department of Commerce to start reporting economic data that included measurements of well-being and human progress. I spoke to an economist at the bureau, and he said that he and his colleagues have actually been asking to update these measurements for years.

We've been using GDP as our North Star since 1934. Isn't it time for an upgrade? I am going to suggest some measures that would at least help us get a read on the depth of our problems and start moving our communities forward.

UNIVERSAL BASIC INCOME

Okay, this one may seem a little familiar to those who read my last book or supported my presidential campaign. Making the economy work for us starts with implementing a universal basic income. Universal basic income is a policy where everyone in a society gets a certain amount of money to meet their basic needs. During my campaign, I championed UBI as the freedom dividend, which would have meant $1,000 a month for every American adult.

When I was running for president, this proposal struck many as futuristic or extreme. But since I first started talking about UBI on the campaign trail in 2018, more than 160 million Americans have received checks for $1,200, $600, and $1,400 from our government as a result of the pandemic. This has put to bed the two main objections I heard on the trail:

- Where will we get the money? It turns out we had it all along if we decided to treat ourselves as owners and stakeholders of our own society.
- How will it affect people? Now more than 160 million Americans know what they would do with the money—pay for groceries, fuel, rent, day care, car repairs, local businesses, and maybe sock a little bit away.

So, we've effectively been experimenting with UBI during the pandemic, and by all accounts these small sums have made a big impact. But onetime payments are not enough.

A basic income would make us stronger, healthier, mentally healthier, more optimistic, more trusting, and less stressed out and make it easier for our children to learn. UBI would also be a boost to creativity and entrepreneurship, supporting the creation of millions of new jobs. We should free people from the constant fear of losing their home, of deciding between paying for heat or paying for food. We need to get the economic boot off our throats so that we can get our heads up and start planning for the future. In a time of unprecedented wealth and technological progress, we must recognize the inherent value of each and every person.

I'm thrilled to share that dozens of mayors have now committed to universal basic income trials throughout the country. From Los Angeles to Newark to Atlanta to St. Paul, people are standing up and saying that we will need new ways to provide for ourselves and our communities.

This would be the largest, most fundamental shift in modern history, and one that would finally unlock the potential of the American people. Let's stop valuing people based on the market alone and instead recognize our intrinsic value as humans.

People can tell immediately when you are actually investing in them. Think about every company you have ever worked for: you knew if they cared about you after the first day. It is only by investing directly in our people that we will begin to dispel the confusion between human value and economic value, and restore the trust that Americans have in our institutions that is quickly disintegrating.

HEALTH CARE FOR ALL

As the Iowa doctor's depressing description of the health predicament facing many of his rural patients highlights, our health-care system in this country is broken. We spend twice as much as similar advanced countries to worse results. Studies have found nearly fifty thousand Americans die each year directly because of a lack of health insurance. Our mental health system may be in even worse shape; 70 percent of children live in mental health care deserts, and teen suicide rates are up 56 percent over the past decade.

Tying health care to employment makes zero sense in an environment where millions are not working due to a pandemic. And as literally every other advanced nation shows, it doesn't have to be this way. Our employer-based system is derived from a World War II–era decision to implement pay caps that led employers to start offering health insurance as a way to attract workers. Connecting health care to employment never made sense, but we keep doubling down on it, creating a bizarre patchwork system that freezes workers in place or fails to cover them during a transition.

Consider that 66.5 percent of all personal bankruptcies are related to medical costs. People can't leave bad or abusive jobs because they need to keep their health care, and it prevents taking a risk on a move, launching a new career, or starting a small business. It incentivizes businesses calling everyone a contractor or part-timer to avoid having to pay for health insurance that gets more expensive every year. We have parents sitting with feverish kids in emergency room parking lots, wondering how their child's illness will be "coded" by a hospital bureaucrat because they can't afford non-emergency care.

In short, America's health-care system is a massive anchor on our people, our businesses, and the economy. Without a fundamental restructuring of this 18 percent of our economy, we're going to see costs continue upward, outcomes stagnate, and more Americans out of work, bankrupt, or uncovered.

If we get it right, however, we can save trillions of dollars and thousands of lives. We should have universal health care in the United States where insurance coverage is not contingent on your employment status.

TAXING THE ROBOTS

How do we pay for these measures? The biggest winners in our modern-day economy are enjoying unprecedented returns while paying very little back into the system. There are at least three big reasons why our labor/income-based taxation system should evolve.

- The first reason is structural. A society should seek to tax things that it wants less of, like cigarette consumption or giant executive bonuses. We don't want less labor from regular workers—quite the opposite. In taxing people's labor incomes, we're putting a tax on the thing we should be trying to encourage most.

- The second reason is political. Because many people experience their income tax as the largest tax they face, people focus on what *they* are paying instead of what other people are getting away with in other parts of the system that are more abstract, such as corporate tax rates and loopholes and capital gains rates for wealthy investors.

- The third reason is the current automation of labor. As more and more work is done by robots and AI, more and more of our economy's value is generated by things other than people. We are facing a situation in which there will be fewer and fewer human workers capable of paying income taxes over time.

Take the example of Google's AI doing the work of call center workers, which was announced in mid-2020. How much will Google pay in taxes? Certainly much less than the more than two million Americans working in call centers right now making between $10 and $15 an hour. The same will be true of self-driving trucks and the more than three million Americans who currently drive a truck for a living. If we truly want to use our economic prosperity to build a stronger country, we need to harvest these kinds of productivity gains in order to fund real changes. That doesn't happen with an income tax, particularly because the biggest companies currently pay minimal or even no income taxes. Amazon famously paid zero in federal taxes in 2018, which was not unusual. Amazon is joined by Netflix, Starbucks, and other household names in not paying federal taxes in recent years.

So what can we do? One mechanism that could capture those

gains is a value-added tax (VAT), a policy that's currently in place in 160 of the world's 195 countries. As the name suggests, these taxes tax the value that any company adds at every step of the production process. If you buy a blender from Amazon, every company that touched the blender from manufacturing to distribution would pay a portion of the tax based on how much value they added to the blender before it got to you. Because it's baked into the supply chain, it's impossible to wriggle out of. A value-added tax is easy, effective, and proven, and it works.

Why are VATs so popular throughout the world? They're easy to implement and difficult to dodge. Because each company is responsible for paying taxes on the value it adds to a product, each company has an incentive to prevent other companies from cheating the system. You could dial down the VAT on consumer staples, like food and diapers, to avoid hurting middle-class consumers, and dial it up on luxury goods, like yachts and artificial intelligence.

I said this to people on the trail: "Jeff Bezos is worth more than $150 billion. Let's say I raised the income tax to something very high, like 75 percent. How much of his money do we see?" They think about it for a second. "Next to nothing. Because he's not dumb enough to pay himself $10 billion in salary. Instead, most of his wealth is in Amazon stock, and Amazon currently pays zero in federal taxes."

The legendary bank robber Willie Sutton was supposedly once asked, "Why did you rob the bank?"

His simple answer? "Because that's where the money is."

Where is the money now? We need to focus less on the town dentist and more on the Amazons of the world.

Right now, our largest and most successful companies are paying next to nothing in taxes. They're sucking value out of our economy, using our infrastructure and data, and giving little back. It's time that we shift to a tax system that makes them pay their fair share. If we install a value-added tax, we will close all of the tank-sized loopholes that our biggest companies run through and generate trillions in new revenue from the organizations that are benefiting most from new technologies.

WE'RE SHORT MILLIONS OF JOBS, BUT NOT SHORT OF WORK

During the pandemic, unemployment spiked, but our labor force participation rate remained at historically low levels. We simply have too many people out of work, which is ridiculous considering all of the important work we have to do.

Our infrastructure is crumbling. We received a D-plus from the American Society of Civil Engineers, with $4.6 trillion of work needed to be done by 2025 in order to get it up to an acceptable B. Our roads, bridges, schools, and water treatment facilities are all criminally underfunded, leading to preventable deaths and the poisoning of our children.

And all of this is costing us more over time. Outside the economic costs of having such outdated infrastructure, everyone knows that fixing something once it breaks is significantly more expensive than maintaining it. We're well past the point where we can actually save money by investing and building.

Infrastructure projects have the opportunity to solve so many of our problems at once. A massive jobs program to rebuild our country would increase labor force participation and get people back to work. We can use this opportunity to improve our environmental sustainability, which would set us up for the future while also alleviating the health impact of pollution. We can expand broadband access and affordability to more Americans, a necessity for functioning in modern life that is currently inaccessible to eighteen million Americans and unaffordable for another twenty-four million. I saw this when I traveled rural America: almost one-quarter of rural Americans don't have access to high-speed internet.

We also have almost eight million openings for in-home health aides. As our population ages, the need for workers is only going to increase, but the private sector simply isn't providing the necessary workers. People are working for $10 an hour, at a physically demanding and emotionally taxing job. There's a lot to be proud of in working such jobs, but it's hard to make a career out of it when you're making little more than minimum wage, developing back problems, and not even receiving benefits. As a society, we need to recognize that the value provided by these workers simply isn't realized by the free market and support them.

The pandemic has also shown that in a country this large there's always new work that can get done. We needed an army of contact tracers to get this pandemic under control, with estimates of required workers being between 98,000 and 180,000. We didn't get them. While the pandemic is an outlier event, it highlights that there are outlier events that could use an easily mobilized workforce. Whether it's working through our national lands to prevent forest fires, helping with cleanup after a natural disaster, contact tracing during a pandemic, or helping develop the next generation, we will always have more work to be done.

New measures for a new economy. Universal basic income. Health care for all. Taxing AI and the robots. Rebuilding our infrastructure. Many of these measures are quite popular but would obviously require a functional Congress willing to enact bold solutions to the problems that we see around us. As we've noted, that's going to be a challenge in our current system. The question is, what would it take to help make our government more responsive to both the needs of our time and popular will?

CHAPTER 20

REWIRING GOVERNMENT

O ur government isn't working. How do we get it working bet- ter?

In chapter 16 we looked at some of the obstacles that keep well-intentioned people from running for office successfully and, even when they win, being able to accomplish the things they promised on the campaign trail. We need to realign incentives and change the software of government so that our elected representatives can actually get something positive done.

This is of course much easier said than done.

I ran for president on universal basic income and other things. Now a majority of Americans agree with universal basic income, but we are nowhere near passing it, in part because the will of the people and our government's legislative process are no longer bound together. A number of big changes are necessary to reconstitute the connection between people and our representatives.

What do these changes look like? Let's take each one in the order that you would encounter them as our hypothetical congressional candidate from chapter 16 and then focus on the ones that are most achievable in the short term. This reform agenda could be put under the rubric "Democracy Reform." Some items you've likely heard of; others will be a little bit new. They're each important, and when you see them together, you realize how big the task is.

Here's the takeaway: the most impactful change that is easiest to make is the adoption of ranked-choice voting and open primaries. This can be done at the state level in many states with ballot initiatives that require as few as fourteen thousand signatures depending on the population and rules of the state. This is the opening in the system—like the thermal exhaust port in the Death Star.

MONEY FOR CAMPAIGNS

The biggest reason why legislation and policy do not reflect the will of the people is that they reflect moneyed interests. This is because candidates and parties need money to compete, which allows wealthy donors, corporate lobbyists, and interest groups who donate to have massive influence.

Less than 10 percent of Americans contribute to federal candidates, and most of them are very small donors. The percentage who give more than $200 is about 1 percent, and those who give $2,700 are about 0.1 percent. The rich thus have outsized influence, and they have very different priorities from the rest of us. "If there is one thing that political scientists have learned about the small slice of Americans who give money to candidates, it is that they are nothing like their peers who do *not* give money," the Harvard Law professor Nicholas Stephanopoulos has written. Generally the wealthy are more conservative, respect current authority, and encourage a less radical or rapid approach to change. Candidates and politicians quickly become subject to the donor class.

This doesn't even account for the flood of money from corporations, the parties, PACs, and special interests. In 2016, election-related spending for all federal races from these entities and the campaigns themselves totaled around $6 billion.

"The currency of votes has consistently less relative value than the currency of money," explain Katherine Gehl and Michael Porter in their book, *The Politics Industry.* "The utility of votes has a limited upside (i.e., all you need to win an election is one more vote than your competitor) whereas the utility of money has no limit (i.e., more is always better)." This is particularly true because you can roll over money into future campaigns while you can't bank votes for a rainy day. Thus, "money in politics gets a great return on investment (ROI)—votes, not so much."

Here is the basic problem: in America today, the money speaks more loudly than the people. All of our politicians and institutions respond accordingly.

The solution is to put the money into people's hands to reflect popular preferences.

Many politicians will express sentiments like "We have to get the corporate money out of politics. We have to repeal *Citizens United,* the terrible Supreme Court ruling that said that corporate donations are speech, enabling companies to contribute millions to these races."

I agree with this: I think we should repeal *Citizens United.* But there are at least three major limitations with this approach:

- The first is practical: repealing *Citizens United* requires a constitutional amendment, which requires a supermajority.
- The second is the fact that companies have plenty of ways to exert influence even if their contributions to super PACs have a limit. They can donate to issue areas or special interests or encourage employees to give to a particular candidate. It's not like companies were devoid of influence prior to the *Citizens United* ruling in 2010.
- The third is that money would still dominate politics, just to a less egregious degree. As noted above, political donors would yet reflect a tiny band of the population that tends to have distinct preferences and characteristics.

What is required is tying the money to the will of the people.

The best plan—the plan that I believe would work—would be to issue a hundred "democracy dollars" to every registered voter that they could give to any candidate they can vote for in a given year. They are "use it or lose it": if you don't use them, they simply expire.

There are presently 250 million voting-age adults in the United States. If only 20 percent of eligible voters allocated their $100 to given candidates in an election cycle, that would be $5 billion, enough to counterbalance all the money that is currently being sourced by companies and special interests. If a congressional candidate got ten thousand people excited, he or she would get $1 million, enough to be competitive.

One exciting thing about this idea is that it can be adopted by a city or state instead of just the federal government. A number of communities have adopted measures that either match small-dollar donations or simply grant voters money. For example, New York City matches small donations eight to one for those candidates who agree to contribution and spending limits. Maine has a robust system of publicly funding state candidates who gather $5 donations and then eschew further private funding. And Seattle in 2016 approved four $25 democracy vouchers that voters could use on local candidates who abide by spending limits. An analysis the following year showed that the vouchers enabled donations among higher proportions of both young donors and those with lower incomes. "It feels like I'm more a part of the system," the Seattle resident Gina Owens, who used two of her vouchers on a city council candidate, told a reporter for *The Seattle Times* in 2017. "People like me can contribute in ways that we never have before. We can participate in ways that Big Money always has."

Public financing also gets different candidates into races—those who don't have wealthy networks. "By making realistic amounts of public financing available, the reforms have made it possible for a wider range of candidates—including, so far, waitresses, teachers, and a convenience-store clerk—to run for office and win," wrote the Georgetown professor David Cole in *The Atlantic*.

In America, money talks. Putting people-powered money into

voters' hands will help humanize our politics and provide legislators with the real ability to make decisions on behalf of constituents.

And if they don't, ideally they would actually be subject to the will of the people when they seek reelection.

COMPETITIVE DISTRICTS

As we learned in part 2, more than 80 percent of congressional districts are considered "safe" seats; they are either clearly Republican or clearly Democratic. This is one reason the incumbent reelection rate is so high. It is also one reason why many of our representatives tend toward extremes: they are more worried about being challenged in the primaries than in the general election.

Some of this is natural. No matter how you draw the district lines in a state like Alabama, which Trump won by 25 points, districts are likely to be safely Republican. But some of this is by design. For example, in 2011 the Wisconsin legislature redrew district lines to increase the likelihood of gaining additional seats for Republicans in subsequent elections.

Voters should be choosing their representatives rather than representatives choosing their voters.

The Supreme Court affirmed in 1995 that gerrymandering along racial lines is a violation of constitutional rights. However, the Court in a 2019 case, *Rucho v. Common Cause,* said in a 5–4 divided ruling that gerrymandering is a political question to be resolved by Congress or the states. Translation: "We don't want to touch this."

Nicholas Stephanopoulos, while at the University of Chicago, and the political scientist Eric McGhee developed a measurement—the "efficiency gap"—to determine how fair or unfair district lines are based upon how many votes are "wasted" for either Democrats or Republicans, meaning how many voters cast ballots for losing candidates relative to what you'd expect if lines were drawn fairly.

If Republicans dominate in Ohio because that reflects voter preference, that's fine. But if district lines are drawn in Ohio in a way that
consistently wastes many more Democratic votes than Republican,
then there's something wrong.

Ideally, the Supreme Court and Congress would take a firm
stance against gerrymandering by either party as a violation of constitutional rights. Given the current makeup of the Court, this
seems unlikely. As Justice Elena Kagan said in her dissent in the
Rucho case, "Of all times to abandon the Court's duty to declare the
law, this was not the one. The practices challenged in these cases
imperil our system of government."

However, a number of states—California, Michigan, Idaho, Arizona, Colorado, Washington—have appointed independent non-
partisan or bipartisan commissions to examine district lines and
ensure fairness. These should be standard in every state to try to
make it so that voters are choosing legislators and not the other way
around.

FINAL-FIVE OPEN PRIMARIES

The next challenge is the way that parties control the primary system for congressional candidates. Our current primary system has a
number of drawbacks. It rewards extremity and polarization rather
than effective policy or principled action. It disproportionately em-
powers partisan gatekeepers. And it does a poor job of reflecting
the true preferences of the voters in a district. By the time the primaries are over, in most districts the candidate who will go on to
win the general election is a foregone conclusion, and 80 percent
of voters haven't had any meaningful input.

William "Boss" Tweed, who ran the Democratic Party machine
in New York in the nineteenth century, famously declared, "I don't
care who does the electing, as long as I get to do the nominating."
That is the situation many Americans find ourselves in today: we

don't truly have much of a choice when we show up for Election Day.

How do we change the two-party primary system in a way that both gives voters a say and broadens the field? Katherine Gehl and Michael Porter propose a system where party primaries are replaced by a top-five primary that is open to all voters. Candidates could identify themselves with a party or not. The top-five finishers would then go on to the general election.

California and Washington have already implemented top-two open primaries, in which the top-two finishers advance to the general election regardless of party affiliation. In some districts that means the top-two candidates from the same party—generally Democrats—run against each other in the general. California made this change in 2012, and the results have been compelling. The number of races deemed competitive immediately doubled. Legislators seemed to notice and became more responsive. The approval rating of California's legislature shot up from 10 percent in 2010 to 50 percent in 2016.

Gehl and Porter argue that five candidates in the general election is better than two in providing a level of choice and innovation for voters. It also would encourage more people to run, allowing for different points of view and openness. I agree.

The relative losers of this shift would be incumbents and political party insiders who right now control the process very tightly. The winners would be the voters and the public.

RANKED-CHOICE VOTING

"Now," you might say after reading the passage above, "what if you have two Democrats and one Republican among the top five in the general? Couldn't the Democrats then split the vote and have the Republican win, or vice versa?"

This would be true in our current plurality voting system, where whoever gets the most votes wins. But the general election for each congressional seat, and virtually all of our elections moving forward, should be conducted via ranked-choice voting.

Ranked-choice voting is simple: you rank the candidates in order of preference, 1 through 5. You do not have to rank them all: if you like only two candidates, you can just make a first and a second choice. If a candidate gets more than 50 percent as voters' first choice, that candidate wins. That makes sense; anyone who gets more than 50 percent would win under any system. If no one breaks 50 percent, then the least popular candidate—the one who got the fewest 1s—is discarded, and that candidate's voters get reassigned to their second choice. You continue this process until a candidate gets over 50 percent, and that candidate is the winner.

Here's a real-life example: Paul LePage became governor of Maine with less than 40 percent of the vote in 2010 and won re-election with less than 50 percent in 2014. After LePage made national headlines for numerous unflattering reasons, such as calling a journalist a "cocksucker" in a voice mail, voters in Maine had seen enough and adopted ranked-choice voting in 2016 via referendum.

Let's see how ranked-choice voting applied to the Maine 2018 congressional race.

In 2018, there were four candidates in the Second Congressional District in the general election. The incumbent, the Republican Bruce Poliquin, received the highest proportion of votes—46.2 percent to the Democrat Jared Golden's 45.5 percent. The two independents, Tiffany Bond and Will Hoar, received 5.7 percent and 2.4 percent, respectively. In a standard election, Poliquin would have been the winner. But because no one reached 50 percent, they reallocated Will Hoar's voters to their second choice. Still no one was at 50 percent, so they did the same with the third-place finisher Tiffany Bond's voters. At this point Jared Golden cleared 50 percent of the vote and was declared the winner. Ranked-choice voting ensures that more than 50 percent of voters express a preference for their representative.

The benefits of ranked-choice voting are profound. You don't need to worry about any candidate being a spoiler. You can vote however you'd like without worrying about "wasting" a vote. It expresses voter preferences better. The winner has to get 50 percent—something that doesn't always happen with plurality voting if you have more than two candidates (for example, Governor LePage in Maine in 2014, Bill Clinton in 1992). It diminishes the incentives to campaign negatively, because you're running against multiple opponents and people will notice if you start trashing your opponents. And it favors coalition building and reaching out to different types of constituents.

Ranked-choice voting has been adopted in more than a dozen cities across the country in the last several years, most notably New York City, Minneapolis, and San Francisco. In addition to Maine, it was adopted statewide in Alaska in 2020. A study of seven cities using ranked-choice voting for municipal elections found that candidates focused more on issues than on attacking each other. It creates incentives where you're trying to win over more people than your opponents rather than tear anyone down.

It is completely up to the states how to conduct their elections. When people realize what ranked-choice voting means, they love it. I have no doubt that it will sweep the country as soon as voters realize that we can upgrade from the current system. In twenty-four states, it can be enacted via ballot initiative, which allows one to get a proposition in front of voters by gathering signatures—more on this later.

TERM LIMITS

So, you've been elected to Congress. You're eager to do whatever you think is going to be good for your constituents. But you run into a room of people who have been there for twenty-five years.

Do you sometimes get the sense that Congress lags behind the rest of us—that they are playing catch-up on issues like social media, data collection, and basically any trend that has occurred in the last few decades? I sure do. And it seems I'm not alone. In one poll, 82 percent of voters agreed with the statement "Members of Congress stay in office too long." By one measure, 74 percent of registered voters support term limits for members of Congress.

In the 1990s there was a drive to initiate term limits at the state level. Voters in eight states in 1994, including Massachusetts, Colorado, Nevada, and Maine, approved term limits for their members of Congress by wide margins, and an additional sixteen states were considering doing the same. Then, in 1995, the Supreme Court ruled 5–4 in *U.S. Term Limits Inc. v. Thornton* that states could not impose term limits on their own members of Congress. The dissenting justices wrote, "Nothing in the Constitution deprives the people of each State of the power to prescribe eligibility requirements for the candidates who seek to represent them in Congress. The Constitution is simply silent on this question. And where the Constitution is silent, it raises no bar to action by the States or the people."

At the same time this ruling was made, the House of Representatives passed a bill 227–204 to impose term limits of twelve years—six terms—in the House and twelve years in the Senate. This fell short of the two-thirds they needed to pass a constitutional amendment, and the effort stalled thereafter, though dozens of members of Congress continue to support similar bills on both sides.

Here are some of the arguments commonly made for term limits:

- Lawmakers would be more motivated to pass successful policy if they knew that their time in D.C. was limited.
- They would become less beholden to the ways of Washington and to trying to climb the ladder within their own party.

- There would be a period of time when they did not worry about fundraising or reelection and could do what they knew to be right without any fear or concern.
- It would ensure a sense of rejuvenation as new leaders with new ideas regularly rotated into Washington without being there for literally decades. It would mean a likely end to the gerontocracy.

The counterarguments are these:

- Voters should get to keep legislators around forever if they want.
- Lawmakers wouldn't develop the same degree of expertise over time. Good lawmakers would be rotated out alongside the bad ones.
- Special interests and bureaucrats would have more power because newbie lawmakers would be showing up all the time who wouldn't understand what to do.

To me, the counterarguments are unpersuasive, particularly if what is proposed is eighteen-year terms each in the House and the Senate. If someone is phenomenal from a particular state, they could have up to thirty-six years representing their constituents. There is no learning curve that takes more than ten years; surgeons get trained in less time. Eighteen years is plenty of time to organize and form relationships. And one could argue that the power of legislators would go up, not down, in an environment where action and dynamism are more the norm.

Literally three-quarters of Americans support this; we know something is wrong with sending people to Washington to govern for decades on end. It changes people in a way that disconnects them from the rest of us. If you're tired of Washington, D.C., seeming behind the curve and out of touch, this is a great way to change it.

I have a plan too for how we can implement it: allow term limits to exempt current lawmakers. "Every member of Congress who gets seated after this date is subject to term limits of eighteen years in either House." This way the current members wouldn't even be affected by it. But eventually they would migrate out and be replaced by a different generation of legislators with a different sense of priorities and urgency.

Beto O'Rourke wrote in praise of George Washington, who ended his tenure as an elected official to set a norm that leadership sometimes means stepping aside. Beto co-chaired a bipartisan group of dozens of congressmen who support term limits, and he wrote about their findings in a piece on Medium:

> We see that the longer you serve in Congress, the less connected, the less responsive, the less accountable you can become to the people you represent . . . If we truly have faith in those we serve . . . then let's help clear the way for new leaders to step up and bring their unique experiences, expertise, and energy to bear on the problems and opportunities before us.

PASSING LAWS

Our legislators serve for a long time but then tend to accomplish little in the way of actual legislating. It was never easy to pass a law, but it's gotten even harder recently. The rules and practices of Congress have become increasingly partisan; often the minority party won't be meaningfully consulted and will only find out what's in a law when it's too late to do anything but vote. When the majority changes hands, the new leadership will threaten in turn to repeal the laws passed by the previous Congress, and the pendulum swings back and forth instead of moving us anywhere.

In a piece for *The Atlantic,* Representative Mike Gallagher of Wisconsin wrote, "Until we fix the processes and structures of power within Congress, we should expect more of the same—polarization, vitriol, and demagoguery. Every two years candidates will inveigh against the status quo in the swamp, and then promptly get swallowed by it."

The Constitution is essentially silent—beyond six brief paragraphs—on how the House and the Senate should work, but the House and Senate rule books run hundreds of pages each. Traditions have built up lives of their own.

Perhaps the most brutal example is the filibuster in the Senate. It arose because of the removal of an arcane rule in 1806 that prevented senators from stopping the previous speaker from talking. That evolved over time into an effective veto by the minority because you weren't allowed to bring something to a vote if someone wanted to block you from speaking. The Senate eventually changed the rules in 1975 to their present form so that you can break the filibuster with sixty votes. There is nothing in the Constitution saying you need sixty votes to do anything; everyone agrees that if fifty-one senators decided to do away with the filibuster and change the rules, they could do so. The Senate has voluntarily reduced its ability to pass legislation because of the equivalent of a typo more than two hundred years ago.

Katherine Gehl and Michael Porter suggest a bilateral legislative machinery innovation commission that reexamines everything from the dining rooms to the structure of committees. They acknowledge that substantially changing practices will likely take years and a turnover of many of the current legislators.

However, three immediate suggestions that would make an enormous difference would be restoring earmarks, establishing measures of legislative success, and abolishing the filibuster.

Earmarks are spending allocations for a particular district—for anything from a bridge to a museum to a school renovation. They got a bad rap in the middle of the first decade of the twenty-first century and were banned by House Republicans in 2011. Now many experts believe that killing off the practice of earmarks has drastically increased the difficulty of getting legislation passed.

This is common sense. Prior to 2011, individual members might be offered something specifically for their district in order to get on board with a law they were on the fence about. Perhaps the law isn't even relevant to my community; it pertains to coastal areas, and I represent a landlocked state. Without earmarks, there is less to offer and less to negotiate. Earmarks were something of a lubricant.

Representatives in both the House and the Senate are there to represent and serve their local constituencies. Having something concrete to work toward makes legislation more practical and less abstract. Those who have constituents less affected by a given piece of legislation are often faced with a binary yes-no decision. Earmarks allow another level of negotiation in the governing process; those representatives can generate benefits for their area that might offset the negative impacts their constituents would face in an otherwise nationally desirable piece of legislation.

Money spent within districts is a small price to pay for a functional legislature. Providing lawmakers with incentives to cooperate again would pay massive dividends.

How do we tell if a law is any good? Congress should adopt a series of measurements and goals—let's call it the American Scorecard—that can be modified and reexamined over time. Each member of Congress could select a set number of goals they believe in from a menu of options. Examples could include poverty rate, life expectancy, rates of business formation, overdose deaths, government efficiency, income growth and affordability, environmental sustainability, highway fatalities, recidivism rates, clean drinking water—basically a dashboard of things that we should use to evaluate how we are doing as a country.

Members of Congress should select from these measures based on what they believe their constituents would care about and then suggest how the laws that they are passing will improve them. A dashboard could be installed in the halls of Congress to show how we are performing, and members' websites could include the measures that they have chosen to prioritize.

We can tell right now that reelection rates have nothing to do with legislative quality. Incentives right now are to avoid any tough vote that could be used in an attack ad against you. Instead, there need to be some incentives to adopt policies that will improve our way of life.

Last, the Senate should get rid of the filibuster. Much has been written about this subject, and I don't need to dwell on it here. Simply put, it's hard enough to get a law passed without requiring something close to a supermajority. Why would a body abandon its ability to actually pass laws when we need our government to modernize? There's nothing in the Constitution about a filibuster; it's just a rule that the Senate unilaterally adopted and then modified. It can be modified again to allow the Senate to fulfill its role.

CIVIC JURIES

In theory, as representatives of the people, members of Congress should pay attention to polls—that is, data about what their constituents think. But in many cases the majority of the country can be for something—say, cash payments to people during a pandemic— and legislators ignore "the will of the people." It's also the case that media organizations tend to move on from polls quite quickly, and polls reflect voters' opinions based on limited information.

The Harvard Law professor Lawrence Lessig has advocated for a more robust system of civic juries utilizing "deliberative polling," a system first developed by the Stanford professor James Fishkin. What might this look like in practice? The first step would be to gather together a representative sample of the public. Then this "civic jury" would weigh various courses of action on policy questions with the help of briefing materials provided by interest groups on all sides of an issue. The group would report its viewpoints both at the beginning and at the end of the deliberation process, and the shifts in their thinking would be taken as a direction for policy makers. The idea is not so different from a big company whose leaders decide to establish a diverse working group of employees from across its ranks to research and advise the company on a particular problem. Because the company was transparent about meaningfully seeking the counsel of the working group, the rest of the employees are more likely to get on board with the eventual decisions that are made.

One enormous advantage of this system is that media organizations would have a field day on the findings and would likely interview participants to determine what they found most convincing and compelling. Countries as diverse as Iceland, Mongolia, and Ireland have adopted versions of these gatherings to suggest constitutional amendments.

Unlike prospective civic juries, Congress does not much look like a representative set of Americans on any of a host of dimensions: age, gender, wealth, education, race, and so on. But it's entirely feasible to simply convene a group of truly representative Americans and determine what they think about an issue. The natural authority of this group could steer legislation and the national conversation in important directions.

BAN ON LOBBYING

For 42 percent of the retiring members of Congress between 2009 and 2015, the next stop in their career was joining a lobbying firm. An additional 25 percent took a position at a company involved in lobbying. Almost half of registered lobbyists are some type of former government official, either regulators or congressional staffers.

A friend of mine from college used to work on Capitol Hill as a senior staffer for two senators. He's a good guy. When he got there, he said to me, "I'm never going to become a lobbyist." Years later, what is he? A highly paid lobbyist making much more than he ever made on the Hill. I don't blame him one bit; he'd spent years accruing relationships and institutional knowledge that are immensely valuable in one sector. If he left D.C., all that value currently directed to getting things done on the Hill would go to waste.

Government jobs don't pay as well as high-level private sector jobs, which leads to a revolving door between government and industry. Often, industry will pay a government employee many times their salary after they leave office. This makes it very natural for regulators and lawmakers to go easy on the companies that might employ them later.

There is something naturally corruptive about being a successful politician that makes you want more money. Here's the dynamic: You're prominent and highly visible. You're around rich people—your donors—who defer to you and whom you grow to consider friends. You're plied by highly paid lobbyists every waking hour. You naturally start to compare yourself with these other people and think, "I deserve at least as much as they have. I'm the center of attention in all of this. I'm just as smart and important as they are." And people want to do you favors that involve money, including you in investment opportunities and the like.

We need to immunize those in charge of government from this kind of influence by compensating them at higher levels and then making it so they don't feel they have to head to industry right afterward.

Here's a proposal: ban members of Congress from becoming lobbyists after their service but give them a stipend of $100,000 a year for ten years if they work for a nonprofit or academic institution afterward.

I'm in favor of giving members of Congress a raise, too. Although $174,000 is a very high salary by normal standards, it's small potatoes relative to the value of a genuinely independent legislature and the amount of money that industry is going to throw at many of these people for lobbying-type activities. Paying legislators enough to free them from influence and the need to take a high-paying job afterward would likely reduce corruption and be the best investment we ever made.

Taken together, all of these reforms would dramatically improve the nature of our legislators and their ability to pass laws on our behalf. At the end of the day, these lawmakers should work for us.

However, most of these ideas have been on people's lists for a while and have run aground of the system. Campaign finance reform requires Congress to act and perhaps a constitutional amendment. Term limits or a ban on lobbying would similarly require an act of Congress. How do you get an institution to reform itself?

The main lever that we can access without Congress is to get ranked-choice voting and open primaries in states across the country. As I've said, this, to me, is the skeleton key that could unlock our government from stasis and engender meaningful reform. You don't need Congress; you just need motivated people in states around the country to activate this process change that would strengthen and enliven our democracy.

CHAPTER 21

THE RATIONAL PUBLIC

O ne night in December 2019, I was campaigning in Iowa on perhaps my eighteenth trip to the state. I did four or five events of different types throughout the day, eating meals in the rental car. By then I was well staffed with a dozen people in several vehicles and an advance team that staged events so that they looked good and were well attended. The goal was always to maximize the local impact of my time. After a long day we got into the hotel around 10:00 p.m., and I turned on the TV to relax while I got dressed for bed. I halfheartedly flipped through channels and landed on C-SPAN. And on TV I saw myself.

I was kind of surprised. It was a town hall I'd held earlier that day at a high school in Cedar Rapids on climate change. C-SPAN was rebroadcasting the event a few hours later. I watched myself answer questions from the students in attendance. There was no commentary. Toward the end of the event, after the moderator closed the program, I stuck around to take pictures and answer individual questions from attendees. To my surprise, C-SPAN had filmed that too; every exchange was audible and presented as I smiled for photos and the line gradually dwindled. I was glad these exchanges were nondescript; occasionally I said something a little off-color when it was one-on-one. Again, the camera just silently recorded these exchanges with no interpretation or commentary. Afterward, the network cut to another recorded event. This night stuck with me because the treatment was in such stark contrast to the vast majority of my broadcast media appearances, almost all of which included some kind of content moderation or back-and-forth with a journalist.

How many people were watching that replay on C-SPAN? Probably not many; you have likely flipped past C-SPAN myriad times while looking for something else to watch. Its ratings are something of a guess, because C-SPAN's viewership is not measured by Nielsen and it doesn't sell advertising. Repeat: it doesn't sell advertising. C-SPAN stands for Cable-Satellite Public Affairs Network; it's a nonprofit network that started back in 1979. The network's founder, Brian Lamb, called it "anti-commercial" television. Its annual budget is about $73 million, paid for by a tiny cable license fee covered by the cable companies themselves. While we don't have the viewership numbers, surveys have shown that C-SPAN viewers are evenly divided politically; apparently, an equal number of viewers of different political leanings like unfiltered public affairs programming.

C-SPAN is a glimpse of what journalism would look like with no ratings or advertising pressure. It seems almost purposefully dull and personality-less; even the colors seem drab and muted. C-SPAN often simply broadcasts congressional hearings or floor discussions with no commentary, providing what it calls an "unfiltered view of government."

I have appeared on CNN dozens of times, and the production values are generally quite high. A few times the network has even sent a mobile studio to me so I could have a uniform backdrop and seem as if I were in the same place as other commentators. I suspect that C-SPAN does not own a mobile studio.

C-SPAN seems stuck in a time capsule from a kinder, gentler era. Lawrence Lessig, a Harvard legal scholar, writes of a time when Americans all watched the same thing on broadcast television and it brought us together. Throughout the 1970s, networks would compete for sixty to seventy million viewers on any given night; that's more than the number of Americans who watch the Super

Bowl today when adjusted for population. Every night was Super Bowl Sunday. The scholars Benjamin Page and Robert Shapiro called this period the "rational public" era, which stretched from about 1940 to 1990, when public attitudes were driven by relatively uniform information. Not everyone agreed, but everyone had a basic agreement on what the news was. It was presented as an objective reality—like a congressional hearing with a minimum of commentary.

I'm old enough to remember when we had but three TV networks: ABC, CBS, and NBC. There were essentially three news broadcasts that covered world events in strikingly similar fashion. When I was growing up, the anchors were ABC's Peter Jennings, NBC's Tom Brokaw, and CBS's Dan Rather, who each delivered the news in serious, somber tones. I'd watch the nightly news with my parents some nights; they were partial to Connie Chung. (I remember too when Fox got started as the fourth network in 1986; *Married . . . with Children, The Simpsons* [when they were still shorts], and *21 Jump Street* made an impression on my twelve-year-old mind.)

From the 1980s on, the dominance of the three major networks plummeted. In 1980, more than 90 percent of television viewers watched one of the three major networks in prime time. By 2005, that number was down to 32 percent. Cable networks proliferated during this stretch, with Fox News and MSNBC both hitting cable boxes in 1996—CNN got started back in 1980—and dozens of other cable channels competing for the public's attention.

The internet began to fragment our media landscape starting in the late 1990s, creating the equivalent of thousands of news channels in the form of independent commenters and social media accounts. What was one shared reality in 1980 has today become thousands. When there is a major event, like the death of George Floyd or the subsequent protests, we beam into the smartphone camera of someone who is standing in downtown Minneapolis or

Portland or Chicago and watch a sixty-second video that we then interpret in different ways, as seen in the comment sections on our social media feeds.

This is the fundamental challenge of today's media: we still assume a news monoculture that hasn't existed in more than thirty years. We pretend that what Page and Shapiro called the "rational public" based on uniform information exists today, and then we are confused about why it doesn't seem to be acting rationally at all. Cable, the internet, and social media have splintered the public consciousness to the four winds.

The question is, what could we do about it, if we decided to try? It's impossible to revert to the media landscape of 1980; there is no time machine. Time flows in only one direction. And there are positives to our current reality that has enabled a proliferation of diverse voices and points of view. Still, if you are going to pin your hopes on a functioning representative democracy, I would argue that curbing some of the worst problems of our media landscape would be crucial.

The time is due for us to recognize that journalism is a vital public good for a democracy. We should fund it publicly as an investment in our own society. I know some people reading this just groaned. "Oh no. Journalism can't be publicly funded. Journalism is all about speaking 'truth to power.' If it's funded by the government, it will lead to Orwellian totalitarianism."

I get the objection. But we are in an era where we are going to need our government to address some fundamental needs. The choice is to tackle this together or just give up. Nonprofits and volunteers are not going to replace $20 billion in lost annual revenue among local news providers. Either we find a way to provide local journalism publicly or it dies.

Consider that publicly funded journalism exists in other countries and it works well. The British Broadcasting Corporation—BBC—is funded primarily through a license fee charged to every household that owns a television set. It maintains rigorous journalistic standards and seems to successfully irritate politicians of every variety.

We have our own templates to follow as well—NPR and PBS. National Public Radio and the Public Broadcasting Service were established by Congress with the Public Broadcasting Act of 1967. Wherever I went around the country, people love NPR and its affiliates. People find it soothing. I've done many interviews with NPR, and it was one of the few needle movers on the campaign. NPR is both a nonprofit media organization and a membership organization that licenses to different radio stations across the country; hence your local NPR station. It was mainly funded by the federal government during the 1970s, but that has shifted to less than 4 percent of its support today. Today, NPR generates more than $200 million in annual revenue from station dues, corporate sponsorships, individual contributions, and distributions from its endowment. It has an endowment of $258 million, largely due to a $235 million gift in 2003 from Joan Kroc of the McDonald's fortune.

PBS, the television equivalent to NPR, receives $445 million a year from the federal budget for the Corporation for Public Broadcasting (CPB). Half of this money goes directly to support local public television stations—the local PBS stations you know and love. The other funds go to support its original programs like *Frontline, PBS NewsHour,* and PBS Kids.

Evelyn and I love PBS Kids for our sons; the programming is very wholesome. The majority of parents agree: 66 percent of parents named PBS Kids as the most educational media brand in one poll, with Disney a distant second at 8 percent.

NPR and PBS consistently rank among the most trusted news outlets. A 2017 survey found that they ranked number one and number two in the number of people who said they are "not biased at all." The CPB has zero editorial input to the hundreds of local PBS and NPR stations in terms of their programming. It's possible to provide public financing to local news organizations from afar and let them manage programming independently.

In the last decade, another trend in the media has emerged. Big legacy media organizations have been getting gobbled up by tech billionaires. Jeff Bezos owns *The Washington Post*. Marc Benioff owns *Time* magazine. Laurene Powell Jobs effectively owns *The Atlantic* through her foundation. Major legacy publications have become trophy acquisitions for technology titans who don't like sports. Media ownership is changing whether the public likes it or not; it is better to understand and address it than to pretend that nothing has changed. It's also noteworthy that local publications don't hold the same appeal to this next generation of owners, probably because of both more limited reach and less appealing economics.

FIXING LOCAL NEWS

A friend of mine, Steve Waldman, is the co-founder and president of a nonprofit, Report for America, that recruits journalists to work in local newsrooms that are under-resourced. The organization has placed three hundred reporters in more than two hundred newsrooms from Wichita to Albuquerque. We met when I invested in an online obituary start-up called LifePosts that he founded (yes, we both thought that was a good idea). We've been thinking for years about the void that local news would leave.

Steve says, "Local journalism is a must to increase civic engagement and decrease polarization. Newspaper revenues have shrunk by $23 billion over the past twelve years, and the number of reporters has plummeted by 60 percent since 2000. We have to acknowledge that philanthropy and public support will need to sustain local journalism."

Steve and his partners at the National Newspaper Association, the American Journalism Project, the National Federation of Community Broadcasters, and half a dozen or so other journalism nonprofits have proposed a plan to invest $3 to $5 billion in local journalism and help organizations convert to nonprofits. The Rebuild Local News plan includes a $250 refundable tax credit for each person to pay for a subscription or donation to a local news source, a credit of up to $5,000 for any small business to buy local advertising, and a $300 million fund that would match three to one any donations to a journalism nonprofit. They also recommend that the IRS define public service journalism as a viable tax-deductible nonprofit activity and allow newspaper chains to divest local newspapers into locally owned nonprofits or public benefit corporations in return for enhanced tax benefits. Federal advertising budgets would be spent on local media organizations, and tax credits would be provided for maintaining journalists and staffers. Five thousand local reporters would be sent to local newsrooms through national service programs.

The Local Journalism Sustainability Act, which includes some of these measures, has attracted fifty co-sponsors in Congress as of this writing, from both parties. You can see the whole plan at RebuildLocalNews.org.

One thing that could be helpful to this plan would be for Congress to create a new type of tax classification—a J Corp—that conveys nonprofit status to any organization whose primary purpose is original local journalism. This would qualify an organization for matching tax credits, favorable treatment if a local newspaper is transferred to the entity, and other benefits that give the organization a better chance at sustainability. The great thing is it's pretty easy to see whether an organization is acting like a J Corp; just go to the website and see if it is covering local affairs through original reporting.

Investing in local news in this way would be extraordinarily helpful. It begins with a recognition that local journalism is no longer viable as a for-profit business in most communities and its survival requires a hastened evolution to a combination of public support, philanthropy, and community support. I believe we should adopt Steve's plan as quickly as possible, while there are still local newspapers that can be restored and salvaged.

You can imagine an even more revved-up version of this plan, where instead of a tax credit consumers got "Local Journalism Credits" that they could allocate to their favorite local news source. A few billion dollars is a pittance compared with the need for a functioning democracy at the local level; there are more than 500,000 elected officials throughout the country at the state and local levels.

CABLE NEWS

How do we depolarize cable news? It won't be easy. As we established in previous chapters, cable news business models mean the networks are incentivized to keep their coverage polarizing and dramatic. But the idea of regulating the media to ensure balance is actually woven into broadcasting history. Between 1949 and 1987 the Federal Communications Commission (FCC) had a rule—the fairness doctrine—that said broadcasters must present controversial issues of public importance in a way that was honest, equitable, and balanced. In practice, this meant that broadcasters who aired commentary on one side of an issue would then make sure that the other point of view was also represented. Though there was no rule that equal time must be afforded, if you presented one side, you had to at least make space for opposing perspectives.

This rule was repealed in 1987 by the Reagan administration, which tried to deregulate just about everything under the sun. There has recently been some interest in reviving it because people believe—correctly—that the end of the fairness doctrine led to a more polarized media landscape and population.

Restoring the fairness doctrine would dramatically change the tenor of the coverage on Fox and MSNBC in particular, because they would be forced to introduce more balanced points of view on any issue of public importance or face FCC fines. Would this be a bad thing? I doubt it.

The FCC could also more rigorously require that segments be labeled either "News" or "Opinion" and require that what is presented as news be objective and free from commentary. Right now the commingling of news and entertainment has led to a blurry news universe that prizes conflict and tribal appeals over information.

One major element is the way the news gets delivered. As I've learned, cable news segments have a certain rhythm. They are typically five to ten minutes long and comprise two to four blocks of interviews interspersed with advertising blocks of approximately four minutes. Each segment has some graphics or video footage included to make it punchier and more visually stimulating.

Ratings pressures drive the format. Ezra Klein wrote in his book *Why We're Polarized* about how ratings warp people's psyches in cable newsrooms: "I used to regularly guest host on cable news, and the emotional rhythm of that workday crested around four p.m., when the Nielsen numbers came out, and everyone stopped to compare how their show did against the competition. If you beat your competitors . . . you could rest easy. If you didn't, you had to worry. And if you lost a few times in a row, you'd start getting calls from upstairs. Maybe your programming should stick closer to the news of the day. Maybe you needed shorter intros, or longer intros, or more guests, or more heat." The bite-sized format drives engagement, which keeps viewers from changing the channel.

This is in sharp contrast with a podcast, where you have a guest sit and simply confer with a host or journalist for a thirty- or sixty-minute block. Imagine a cable news program with no advertisements where an expert and journalist simply confer on a particular subject. This would be a very different way for a viewer to get information. The problem is that it doesn't have advertisements.

It could be possible for the government to introduce incentives for different formats. Perhaps a network gets a tax credit for forgoing advertising for a longer block if the subject matter can be deemed in the public interest. I know plenty of journalists and producers who would love to be free from ratings and format pressures for a proportion of their schedule. And I believe plenty of viewers would be thrilled to hear something longer than five minutes from someone with something meaty to share. It's harder to feel outraged after seeing two people sit together and have a nuanced conversation that's more similar to how human beings interact in real life.

SOCIAL MEDIA

Social media seems to be the most intractable problem of all. These platforms actually have a few interrelated problems: market incentives that maximize engagement and addiction, misinformation and deepfakes, and data-enabled targeted advertising.

There is a big rule when it comes to social media platforms you might have heard of, thanks to Donald Trump: section 230 of the Communications Decency Act (CDA). Section 230 says that "no provider or user of an interactive computer service shall be treated as the publisher or speaker of any information provided by another information content provider." It has been interpreted to mean that platforms that publish content provided by someone else—say, a user of a forum—don't have any legal responsibility for the published content.

The importance of this law cannot be overstated. It's been referred to by commentators as "the twenty-six words that created the Internet." Keep in mind that the CDA was written in 1996 before the modern internet existed. Facebook wasn't even founded until 2004; the drafters of the law could not have envisioned the internet we experience today. Still, this rule has allowed the growth of some of the most powerful companies in history. And it's one reason you'll constantly hear Facebook argue that it's a "platform, not a publisher." Being a publisher would bring with it the civic responsibilities and legal liabilities that any newspaper or television network bears every day.

In 2020 major politicians on both sides of the aisle began either calling to or threatening to "repeal section 230." This has been due to dissatisfaction with Facebook's and Twitter's treatment of various types of content. Conservatives complain that conservative-facing content—most recently, QAnon-related posts, calls by Trump that suggested violence, medical misinformation, and now Trump himself—has been singled out for censorship or redaction. Progressives on the other hand argue that hateful and racist language and ideologies have been allowed to spread unchecked on these platforms.

The latter concern led to a boycott of Facebook known as "Stop Hate for Profit" in July 2020 that included hundreds of companies like Pfizer, Ford, Unilever, and Verizon. In response, Facebook's CEO, Mark Zuckerberg, reportedly told people that these companies account for a tiny slice of Facebook's revenue and there was nothing to worry about: the top hundred advertisers on Facebook are less than 6 percent of the company's revenue. The Stop Hate for Profit campaign continued with celebrities like Rosario Dawson and Katy Perry taking a break from Instagram.

The reliance of companies on the safe harbor from civil liability afforded by section 230 indicates something incredibly important: the Communications Decency Act can easily be amended to hold social media companies more responsible for the content they publish and to force them to share their data with the public so we know what they know. Right now, we are sadly reliant upon limited third-party data and bland corporate communications about the extent of various problems while the social media companies themselves have unfathomably large data troves.

There has also been some fundamental confusion about Facebook's interaction with freedom of speech and the First Amendment, in part because Zuckerberg himself argues in these terms when defending Facebook's hands-off policies. The First Amendment says that Congress will pass no law that circumscribes freedom of speech or freedom of the press. However, nowhere in the Constitution does it say that a private company must necessarily give you the opportunity to share your thoughts with others. If I had a restaurant with a community bulletin board and someone posted something there that the folks who frequent the restaurant found bothersome and offensive, I'd take it down, and no one would think anything of it.

This has come to a head with the banning of Trump by major social media platforms in the wake of the Capitol Hill riots. Social media companies are being asked to make decisions on what kind of speech is acceptable as private companies that control de facto public commons, and their boundaries are unclear.

There is a distinction between allowing something to be posted on a social media platform and then amplifying it by, for example, algorithmically planting it into the news feed of thousands of viewers. The first decision is that of the individual. The second one is a commercial decision by a near-trillion-dollar company designed to maximize advertising that benefits Facebook. There is no reason to protect a company from the consequences of an affirmative decision it makes to maximize its own profitability, as distinct from allowing the initial post.

At present, Facebook has been arguing for itself as something of a public commons that should be left to its own devices and allowed to self-moderate while having all of the for-profit benefits of a private company. Mark Zuckerberg is worth $100 billion running a social network that reaches billions but still pretends to be the town bulletin board.

Amending section 230 is thus immensely powerful and a historic opportunity. Instead of saying "Platforms are not responsible for the content they publish that is created by someone else," we could change the standard to "Social media platforms are responsible for any content they amplify." We could also include standards such as "All data relevant to misinformation, usage patterns, use by minors, and the health and integrity of the public shall be made freely available in real time to the public for research, commentary, and examination." If you want the franchise and a liability shield, you're going to have to both take responsibility for any content that you amplify and are profiting from and then open up.

We are allowing billion- and trillion-dollar social media platforms to operate as black boxes because of a twenty-five-year-old provision in a law that was written before the modern internet existed. It's patently ridiculous. Meaningful amendment affords us an enormous opportunity to curb some of the worst abuses.

We could push social platforms to immediately adopt a number of practices that would help. Social media sites should provide tools to help users monitor use and prevent excesses. Users should have a way to verify their identity as a real-life human being, and those who use real names and faces could be marked as verified. Obvious or likely bots should be identified as such or expunged. Real news sources could be certified, with consistent abuses leading to decertification. Social media networks should establish partnerships with smartphone and video camera companies to be able to verify that a video is real based on device-specific watermarks. There could be a designated eight-hour period when social media services aren't easily accessible for minors—say, midnight to 8:00 a.m. Everything should be on the table.

Twitter's CEO, Jack Dorsey, and others have expressed a desire to get tech companies, media companies, nonprofits, and the government together to work through some of these issues. This is an area that requires genuine leadership and vision from the public sector, not a sensationalized hearing and browbeating.

Another path to reform involves changing the business models of these companies. Social media companies are wired to maximize user engagement. The way to change this is to change their incentives, which right now are based on maximizing advertising revenue.

Jaron Lanier, the futurist and internet pioneer, said in an interview, "We were all hippies, and we were trying to figure out a way to make this all free. And the best thing we could think of was to use advertising to pay for everything. And it turns out that was a massive mistake that had enormous implications." Having advertising pay for everything online has had a massive cost, and the bill is coming due.

The Google founders, Larry Page and Sergey Brin, in the early days of their company, wrote that "advertising funded search engines will be inherently biased towards the advertisers and away from the needs of the consumers." They were right and could easily have written the same about social media companies.

There is a pretty straightforward fix for this: ask each site to provide an advertising-free version for users, and then provide users with the funds to make this election if they so choose.

Facebook—which includes Instagram—reported advertising revenues in the United States of about $34 billion a year in 2019. Here are the user bases and advertising revenues of the top social media companies in the United States:

Platform	Number of users	Annual ad revenue in billions	Annual ad revenue per user	Monthly ad revenue per user
Facebook / Instagram	183 million	$34	$186	$16
YouTube	205 million	$4.4	$21.50	$1.80
Twitter	68.7 million	$1.94	$28.23	$2.35
Snapchat	80 million	$1.1	$13.75	$1.14
TikTok	100 million	$1.2 (est.)	—	$1 (est.)
			Total:	$22.29

Note that most people use a few of these platforms but not all of them. We could give every American about $20 a month that they can redeem to buy ad-free access to their favorite social media sites and get rid of advertising on social media for the average American. Imagine showing up to Facebook one day and having a pop-up that says, "Would you like to switch to advertisement-free Facebook?" The total cost would depend on how you structure the plan, but complete eradication of ads for the average user buying ad-free versions of all major social media sites would cost about $40 billion a year, or about 1 percent of the federal budget.

This sort of model has been demonstrated to be successful with Hulu; it has a "free" ad-supported subscription and a paid ad-free version. We could simply graduate most Americans to the ad-free versions of these platforms.

Think about how this would transform the incentives and operations of the social media companies. No more harassing ads, no more need to track every bit of data to resell to advertisers, no more serving us up disinformation, less competition to maximize your time spent, fewer rabbit holes. They would modify their approach so that more casual users actually enjoy the service and don't get annoyed. As long as you're happy enough to not discontinue your subscription, they're satisfied. And their incentives to fight commonsense measures to ameliorate abuses would go down overnight.

Americans would love this: use your services for free and get rid of advertisers, who would then turn to local media and other means to reach you. Who loses?

This is the kind of change we need to make if we are truly going to recover our minds and democracy from social media.

CHAPTER 22

THE RETURN OF FACTS

I ran for president on a platform of eradicating poverty. In order to compete, I became a character that was at first marginalized and has now been normalized.

There have been times when I've felt like the *Black Mirror* character in the episode "Fifteen Million Merits," where the protagonist played by Daniel Kaluuya rages against the system and is then given a weekly TV show, plugging into the system again in a different way.

At the beginning of my presidential campaign, way back in October 2018, I spoke at an Iowa Democratic event, the Johnson County Democrats' BBQ fundraiser. It was billed as a gathering of potential presidential candidates, though I was the only candidate who had actually declared: the speakers were Tulsi Gabbard, the Oregon senator Jeff Merkley, Governor Jay Inslee of Washington, and me.

I spoke directly after Jeff Merkley. His speech had a series of applause lines invoking health care, drug companies, Betsy DeVos, Brett Kavanaugh, separating children from families at the border, internment camps, climate change, voter suppression, corruption, Democratic majorities, and blue-collar working families, among other topics.

My introduction was not great: the county supervisor said to the crowd, "Keep an open mind; there may be twenty-five candidates running; it's our job to start weeding them out. This man has some very interesting ideas." Not exactly a ringing endorsement. I delivered my usual remarks about automation, a transforming economy, and universal basic income. My speech cited several facts about Iowa and job loss: the state had already lost forty thousand manufacturing jobs and twelve thousand retail jobs. The country's largest truck stop—Iowa 80—was in Walcott, Iowa. What happens when the trucks drive themselves? I got very limited applause; my main applause lines were when I referenced health care and the value of parents.

I walked offstage thinking, "Huh, did I not do a great job? Am I not a fit for this state?" In most cases politicians are communicating with their most active partisans in the most activating language possible. They are throwing out a red-meat list of issues they know will elicit a fiery response.

A year later I would give a similar speech in Iowa at the Liberty and Justice Dinner at the Wells Fargo Arena in Des Moines for about fourteen thousand people. By then, attendees were able to shout answers to my questions.

"One state has had something like universal basic income since 1982," I proclaimed. "And what state is that?"

"Alaska!"

"And how do they pay for it?"

"Oil!"

"And what is the oil of the twenty-first century?"

"Technology!"

Eventually, my facts had become symbols that brought with them their own responses. I had managed to introduce a new language and new applause lines to the people of Iowa. It had taken a year.

I've had thousands of conversations with Americans of all political backgrounds. If you sit down with the average person and ask a question like "Hey, do you think prescription drug prices are too high?" or "Do you think you should have health care even if you lose your job?" most people will agree with you regardless of their political affiliation. But if you use loaded terms like "Do you think we should have socialized medicine?" that have been coded as negative, many people will dislike it intensely.

Michael Grunwald wrote in *Politico* in 2020, "There is a line of thinking that America has entered a kind of postmodern political era where the appearance of governing is just as politically powerful as actual governing, because most Americans now live in partisan spin bubbles that insulate them from facts on the ground." Passing laws, solving problems, and measuring impacts don't matter anymore. You can simply argue for your version of reality and aligned media outlets will trumpet and reinforce that narrative to your people. Value statements and virtue signaling have assumed the role of laws and policy for many in the day-to-day back-and-forth of cable news.

Instead of achieving results, our leaders are asked to demonstrate the correct moral approach by evincing sadness or anger, invoking certain words and issues, and inveighing against the excesses of the other side. Speaking to a group is now an enormous expression of alignment or allegiance. Neither side can pass laws, so we are reduced to warring languages and symbols.

The former Michigan congressman Justin Amash observed of fellow members of Congress in 2020 that there is now a "performative aspect" to their activities and "the sad truth is that the majority of them prefer this system . . . If they bend the knee to leadership, say we'll go along with whatever show you're doing, you're putting on the Democrat Show, you're putting on the Republican Show . . . As long as they play along and do the performance, they are taken care of, they're babied."

In his book *The Righteous Mind* the social psychologist Jonathan Haidt tried to answer a fundamental question: Why is it that well-meaning people can disagree so violently when it comes to politics? He argues that there are six fundamental human values that cross all cultures and constitute our universal sense of morality: caring, fairness, liberty, loyalty, authority, and sanctity. Haidt posits and observes that people on the progressive side of politics naturally use arguments that emphasize the values of caring and fairness: "Every child deserves a quality public education" or "Women should have equal rights." Conservatives acknowledge caring and fairness but are much more likely to make appeals to loyalty, authority, and sanctity: "Protect our troops," "Respect law enforcement," or "Preserve American families and values."

You can see this dynamic play out in issue after issue. When it comes to separating children from their parents at the southern border, progressives are outraged at the shocking mistreatment of families. Conservatives are more likely to question why immigrants are breaking the law by entering the country illegally. The first point of view is about caring and empathy. The second is about authority.

Haidt argues that conservatives' ability to use and appeal to all six values gives them a broader moral palette that gives them an advantage in political communication. They can hit more varied notes that ring true to different types of people.

Case in point: I remember sitting in the waiting room before one Fox News appearance watching the programming before I was to be interviewed. The hosts were showing images of the remains of soldiers arriving back in the States on a flight from Afghanistan after being killed by an explosive device. The MSNBC stories while I was waiting in their greenroom were generally about Trump officials' malfeasance or families separated at the border. There is a specific symbolic language that works for people on each side. Fox News ratings are typically about 60 percent higher than MSNBC's or CNN's; more Americans self-identify as conservatives and enjoy appeals to loyalty, authority, and sanctity than caring and fairness.

Our media organizations relentlessly push us into tribes with our own applause lines and sources of outrage. Our leaders are transformed into characters to either cheer or boo, to catalog their steps or missteps. We are degenerating into a set of characters in a play, with the media mapping our relative rise and fall while our communities at home fall apart. As the author Philip Howard put it, we are playing games of "You lose, I lose," passing the ball back and forth while the people lose no matter what.

While campaigning for president, I met many people who voted for Donald Trump; this group includes some family members of mine. The vast majority of them struck me as good people. Many seemed open to supporting me or at least listening to me because I adopted a language that was neutral in their view; it wasn't coded either positively or negatively. It was for the most part just numbers and economic trends. Later, a January 2020 survey of my supporters indicated that 42 percent of them weren't planning on supporting the Democratic nominee if I didn't win the nomination. I was using a different terminology and moral language and thus reached people who weren't traditionally Democratic or, in many cases, even political.

I awakened a significant group of people who were not politically engaged. In the book *Open Versus Closed,* the political psychologists Christopher Johnston, Howard Lavine, and Christopher Federico tested responsiveness to various political opinions among those who did not follow politics. They found that disengaged citizens had less of a fixed political identity based upon their psychological profile. They were more pragmatic and practical when presented with a question. They reacted to a policy by trying to answer "What will this policy *do for* me?" They heard "$1,000 a month" and did the math.

Meanwhile, those who are more politically attentive were more likely to try to answer "What will supporting this policy *say about* me?" They are joining a group.

This indicates something very important—that political engagement ends up forming an allegiance based on perceived values and identity as opposed to perceived advantage or disadvantage of a policy. If you watch a lot of Fox or MSNBC or listen to conservative radio, you actually get pushed into tribes that are completely distinct from how you might be affected by, say, a tax cut. It's one reason why some voters seem to "vote against their own interests"; they define their interests based on what their vote says about them rather than what they think their vote will do for them.

My appeal—which struck many partisans as ridiculous initially—was to say we should give everyone enough money to get by. The politically disengaged heard this and responded, "Hey, that would help me a *lot*." This appeal was initially dismissed because it didn't fall into an existing group narrative or language structure. But eventually this idea made headway among the more engaged as well.

POLITICAL STRESS IS at an all-time high. We are at pre–Civil War levels of animosity, according to Peter Turchin, an evolutionary anthropologist at the University of Connecticut, and Jack Goldstone, a sociologist at George Mason University, who study sources of unrest and political conflict. They developed a statistic—the political stress index—that incorporates income and wealth inequality, wage stagnation, national debt, competition between elites, distrust in government, social mobility, tax rates, urban density, demographics, and other factors that lead to instability and conflict. Goldstone's prior work with the Political Instability Task Force predicted civil wars and democratic collapses in developing countries with about 80 percent accuracy over two-year periods. They both believe that the United States is now ripe for political violence on a scale not seen since what Turchin calls the first Civil War.

Some Americans would have doubted the above argument prior to the Capitol Hill insurrection in January 2021 that demonstrated just how big a threat political violence has become. The foiled plot to kidnap Michigan's governor, Gretchen Whitmer, by right-wing extremists and the protests stemming from George Floyd's murder in 2020 are other examples of how polarized we are. To make things dramatically worse, we are the most heavily armed society in the history of the world, with approximately 300 million firearms, almost one for every man, woman, and child. Disintegration and polarization are unlikely to be gentle when the country is an arsenal.

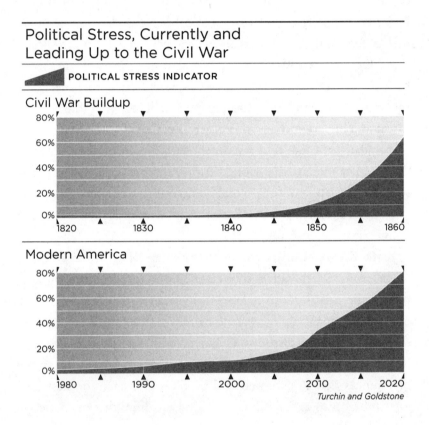

Turchin and Goldstone

How do we reverse this? Jonathan Haidt made a couple of other observations about political orientation. He found that there is a strong correlation between one's politics and several biological attributes: attraction to novelty, disgust reflex, and threat sensitivity. If you like novelty—that is, eating new foods and experiencing new environments—then you are more likely to be liberal and progressive. If you have an active disgust reflex—if you are shown a disgusting image of a decomposing body or vomit or other disturbing image and you have a very strong and visceral negative reaction—you are more likely to be conservative. Similarly, if you have a high sensitivity to threats or contagion, you are more likely to be conservative.

Haidt's findings have been affirmed by others. The political psychologists Christopher Johnston, Howard Lavine, and Christopher Federico similarly found that political leanings line up with the measured quality "openness to experience." Their data indicated that "Democrats and Republicans are now sharply distinguished by a set of basic psychological dispositions related to experiential openness—a general dimension of personality tapping tolerance for threat and uncertainty in one's environment."

Similarly, the political scientists Marc Hetherington and Jonathan Weiler identified a strong relationship between one's perception of how dangerous the world is and one's political views. If your makeup is geared toward seeing threats, you're likely to be more conservative.

Ezra Klein summarized the research in *Why We're Polarized:* "The common thread is that openness to experience—and the basic optimism that drives it—is associated with liberalism, while conscientiousness, a preference for order and tradition that breeds a skepticism toward disruptive change, connects to conservatism." Klein emphasizes that these are not positives or negatives but simply preferences tied to psychological profiles. Conscientiousness leads one to be organized, faithful, and loyal, qualities that many people value deeply.

I worked in the Midwest for a number of years when I was with Venture for America. A woman in Ohio said something to me that has stuck with me ever since: "Around here, 'change' is a four-letter word." That mindset was somewhat new to me, but in her context it made sense. For her, change meant the plant closing, jobs disappearing, and her kids looking for greener pastures.

Here's something I don't believe we acknowledge enough: attraction to novelty, disgust reflex, openness to experience, and threat sensitivity are psychological qualities that are at least somewhat genetic, according to Haidt. They are as much nature as nurture.

I have two sons, eight and five. I was raised to try to treat your kids the same: if my parents did something for me, they did the same for my brother. We had a lot of matching clothing; it was great for our self-esteem. Evelyn and I love both our boys dearly and also buy them a lot of the same clothes for convenience.

Our older son ignores people and social graces. If you walked into the room, he wouldn't notice. He likes to get lost in his own world. He has a hard time controlling his body. He asks the same questions over and over again. He also likes to eat the same thing every day.

Our younger son is a ham. He likes people and is a charmer. He will hold your hand and lead you places. He exclaims his love for his mom multiple times a day. He's more adventurous and is always skinning his knee or bumping his head.

Ask any parent and they will tell you that our children are born with certain tendencies that have nothing to do with our treatment or parenting of them. We are all born with qualities and psychological makeups that lead us in directions that now, in our highly polarized environment in particular, tend to land us in one political camp or another. How much? According to Haidt's research, genetics determines between one-third and one-half of political differences in a group, more than the politics of the household we are raised in. In a country where there are only two major choices, we are essentially born either Democratic leaning or Republican leaning.

One rule I try to live by is not to judge someone for something that is not in their control, including most circumstances of their birth. No one chooses their parents or race or gender or sexual orientation or hometown or the faith of their parents and the environment they are brought up in.

If one's psychological makeup helps determine our political

views, then I should not hold your politics against you, because there's a substantial chance you were born with a disposition toward the candidates and party you support. If you have a conscientious personality and inherited a high disgust reflex or threat sensitivity— and perhaps have parents with similar traits or grew up in a rural environment—you probably became a conservative. I shouldn't be mad at that even if I'm on the other side of the spectrum. And of course the reverse is true for those who have a high appetite for novelty and parents who encouraged it—perhaps by immigrating to a new country.

This also means that I'm unlikely to persuade you to switch sides by making you aware of a particular piece of information. Indeed, Ezra Klein points out that exposure to news from the other point of view actually tends to increase, not decrease, one's polarization. It's not an information issue when you are trying to persuade someone from one side or the other.

It turns out there is a weak relationship between how much a person identifies as a conservative or liberal and how conservative or liberal their views actually are; in both cases it's about a 0.25 correlation, which is a lot lower than the perfect correlation many of us imagine. One reason policy is not the true driver of political disagreement is most people don't have very strong views about policy unless they have been pushed to do so. We are operating in groups, not in policy white papers.

This strikes me as a real blind spot for many progressives. Many liberals would not dream of berating someone for the circumstances of their birth or what they'd consider immutable parts of their identity—like race and gender. But they might not feel the same about someone who voted for Trump or approved of a particular Supreme Court nominee. "Partisan animosity is one of the few forms of discrimination that contemporary American society not only permits but actively encourages," writes Klein. This blind spot dramatically fuels division, because many conservatives feel that they are constantly being dismissed as uneducated rubes and their moral language is deemed not worthy of consideration.

If you're curious, I personally have a high attraction to novelty, a moderate disgust reflex, and low threat sensitivity. I also enjoy pro wrestling and mixed martial arts, so go figure.

We're all human. Again, I have family members who voted for Trump. Heck, seventy-four million Americans voted for him! When seventy-four million people do something, you need to try to understand it.

I have a general enthusiasm for positive change. But change is not an absolute good. There are times when conscientiousness and a preservation of preexisting norms, relationships, and loyalties are just what you need. Right now many Americans are being buffeted by economic changes and institutional failures that are not benign; that's the reality. Openness and risk tolerance are likely being reduced dramatically by the coronavirus and an increasingly punitive economy. A lot of people's actions are going to be increasingly driven by a sense of threat to their way of life. This is not going to be a time for a lot of new generosity and openness.

The question is, how do we dampen polarization and generate a new political language that people of both sides would find unifying or at least interesting? Is it possible to improve our political discourse, keep our media from inflaming mini-controversies of the day, and reward action and policy rather than symbolic gestures that separate us into tribes?

Beginning in the 1990s, there has been a movement toward something called evidence-based medicine; that is, a doctor's recommendations should be based on what the data says would be the course of treatment with the best patient outcome. When I first heard about this, I had the same reaction you might have—what the heck else could you refer to? But the practice of medicine has been developed over decades during which doctors did not have tons of clinical information to rely on. Instead, it was based on practices that had become customary through training and the constantly evolving body of knowledge of various conditions. Dr. David Eddy, who originated evidence-based medicine and was a mathematician as well as a physician, described his approach as "tying the policy to evidence instead of standard-of-care practices or the beliefs of experts."

One possible antidote to the inchoate political discussion is to adopt an approach of fact-based governing—that is, advocate policies based on their ability to deliver an improvement to some attribute or measurement of societal progress or health.

Earlier, I suggested an American Scorecard to determine how we are doing. I also detailed how the United States has plummeted to twenty-seventh or lower along a variety of dimensions, including such basic measures as life expectancy, clean water, and infant mortality. One could ask, how could the richest country in the history of the world allow itself to decline in such fundamental ways?

When I ran for president, I made a case for adjustments based on the transformation of the economy due to advancing technologies. During interviews I would often cite various facts and figures—like that we had lost five million manufacturing jobs across various states primarily to automation or that labor force participation rates and business formation rates had already plummeted to multi-decade lows. I was stunned at how infrequently either journalists or lawmakers engaged with the substance of what I was saying. It truly was as if I were speaking a different language.

This is what we have to change: we have to give rise to the use of evidence, facts, and results and have legislator accountability based on whether they can demonstrate that they've helped move us in a better direction. In practice this would mean that in addition to the controversies of the day there would be periodic reports on how we have been doing along various dimensions for the press to amplify. Imagine if major outlets discussed how our kids are faring or our mental health or air quality in the same way they currently do GDP or a big company's quarterly stock performance. It would at least provide some concrete grounding for a set of stories that would bring people back to reality. And it would make us and our quality of life the point.

Some of the measurements I argued for on the trail were life expectancy, average income and affordability, childhood success rates, mental health, freedom from substance abuse/deaths of despair, environmental sustainability, quality of infrastructure, social mobility, incarceration and rehabilitation rates, public trust, arts and culture, and civic engagement. Virtually all of these have been trending negatively for years. Reversing these declines should be the point of public service and the purpose of politics, policy, and government.

If one fears that these goals wouldn't work for people of different political alignments, there are measurements that conservatives would be likely to embrace, including GDP growth, rates of entrepreneurship and small business starts, labor force participation rate, efficiency of public resources, military readiness, global perception of the United States, crime rates, marriage rates and proportion of children in a two-parent household, volunteerism, and philanthropy. I'm a fan of many of these measurements too.

While campaigning for president, I pledged to use a PowerPoint deck during my State of the Union to report how we are doing instead of the strange theater performance we are currently subject to. Imagine the head of a business walking in to update his or her people without any numbers or baselines to measure improvements or declines.

Again, you make what you measure. If we measure the right things, we may have a chance to pull people together.

This should become the future of politics. The main point is to shift from trying to win arguments to winning the future. Governing based on facts—and having those facts recognized by all parties—might just bring us back.

CHAPTER 23

THE TAX MANDALORIAN

W hen I ran for president, some voters seemed attracted to me because I had run businesses and been a CEO. Many Americans have an instinctual belief that businesses are efficient and high functioning while government is bureaucratic and wasteful.

I was never someone who said, "I'm going to run government like a business." That would appeal to a subset of voters who enjoy oversimplification. Running a government and running a private business are different activities and leadership roles. When you are the CEO of a company, you are the boss. You're paying everyone and can hire, fire, and give bonuses or raises at will. You can tell everyone to do something or set a policy, and people pretty much have to do what you say. Whether you are doing a good job is determined in large part by the numbers. If the company is performing well financially and you avoid scandal, you're likely to be judged a good CEO. If the company has a board of directors or public shareholders, as long as the profit margins are good and there is a sense that you are working to "maximize shareholder value," then you're generally left alone.

I've been the CEO of a private company and still marvel at how direct the lines of accountability were. If I wanted to make a change, I could meet with the people involved and the change would be rolled out within a matter of days or even hours. There was almost no bureaucracy.

I had a very different experience when I started and ran an entrepreneurship nonprofit—Venture for America—for six years starting in 2011. I was nominally the founder and CEO, but I had myriad stakeholders whom I was beholden to: staff, donors, volunteers, the young aspiring entrepreneurs who had put their careers in our hands, companies who were employing our fellows, our board of directors, foundations, corporate partners, and on and on. So many people were working or donating because they believed in the mission of the organization, and my job was to continually present a vision that would galvanize people. They don't work for you so much as you work for them.

That's closer to government leadership; you have to continuously build consensus among supporters and stakeholders. You set a vision and hope others will build toward it. You should be establishing trust and communicating as much as possible. You do not have the ability to fire legislators or judges or journalists or those who disagree with you, and their interests could be in direct opposition to yours. Instead of commanding, often you have to pick your opportunities and try to get done as much as you can within a preexisting framework.

They are different animals. That said, there are a few things that, in my opinion, governments could adopt from business practices.

What do I mean? Imagine if you were a company that got hundreds of billions in revenue on one day every year. How would you feel that day? You might celebrate that day. You might even thank your customers.

That's tax day, which is a day that virtually all Americans dislike. No one looks forward to April 15, even though some of us might even get a refund. It's hard for the federal government to build trust with Americans when the most direct interaction we have is something we like to ignore until the very last minute.

MAKING PAYING TAXES SIMPLE

Most of us dread paying taxes. None of us has time to figure out where the receipts are, what we donated, and what we owe, and we're constantly stressed that we're screwing things up or leaving money on the table. We feel like other people are taking advantage of rules that we are not. In the aggregate all of this time and energy has a massive social cost: we Americans spend 1.7 billion hours and $31 billion a year filing our taxes. Turning us into a nation of tax experts is a ridiculous waste of citizen time and energy.

Paying taxes is a slog. Let's make it a celebration.

The IRS should be able to tell us how much we owe and automatically file our taxes for us. Every time we do something that we think is tax relevant, we should have the option of simply sending the information or documents to an IRS email address or upload it to an online portal and the data point gets added to our tax profile. The IRS would have almost all the information they need to calculate our taxes within a high degree of accuracy. They could do this automatically, guaranteeing that we hold on to more of our money throughout the year and never need to spend money on tax-preparation services or audit-protection insurance. Other advanced countries have already taken the step of having many people's taxes automatically filled out. Taxes are a perfect candidate for automation and artificial intelligence because there are clear rules to follow. We can use technology to simplify all of our lives and focus on more important things.

When you run a business, you make it easy, not hard, for people to pay you.

You also try to make them feel good about it. I'd reframe tax day as "Revenue Day" and make it a federal holiday where we celebrate everything the federal government does for its citizens. You could invite families from around the country to the White House to celebrate another great year and thank them for supporting our way of life. Make it a party. We would give everyone the day off to spend with our families.

Most important, we would thank everyone for paying their taxes and not take it for granted. People like to know where their money is going. I'd give each taxpayer the ability to direct 1 percent of their taxes to a specific department, be it Veterans Affairs or the Forest Service or the National Endowment for the Arts, and then have a thank-you video from employees who work at that department expressing their gratitude. They could describe what they are working on for the following year so you get a sense of progress.

Some of these ideas might fall flat. But would it make you feel at least marginally better about both paying taxes and your government? At least it would show that the government treats you more like an owner or stakeholder than like a supplicant to be ignored.

Why does this seem so far from the world we live in? One reason is that Intuit—the maker of TurboTax software—has successfully limited our ability to auto-file our taxes and furiously lobbied anyone who tries to simplify filing for the American people. They are protecting a business that generates more than $1.5 billion in profits for their shareholders each year.

Intuit's co-opting of the IRS is indicative; it has managed to convince everyone that government couldn't possibly provide a service as well as industry, even for something as relatively simple as automatic tax filing, a practice that has already been adopted in other countries.

The $31 billion and 1.7 billion hours Americans spend every year trying to file taxes may pale in comparison to the lost revenue from intentional evasion and unintentional errors of $458 billion per year—$406 billion after the IRS pursues late payments and enforcement actions, according to a 2019 report from the Government Accountability Office. Eighty-five percent of Americans say it's never okay to cheat on one's taxes, but it's definitely happening.

If you were to run the government a little more like a business, you would want to reduce the $406 billion in lost revenue a year, which is more than half of what we spend on the defense budget. The IRS, with a budget of $11.8 billion, generates immediate value of about $52 billion a year just getting revenue from people who underpaid, and there's another $406 billion on the table.

Sometimes individual tax evaders can account for a significant figure. In October 2020, Robert T. Brockman, the CEO of a Texas software company, was charged in a $2 billion tax evasion case, the largest-ever tax charge in the United States. The indictment stated that Brockman engaged in wire fraud, money laundering, and other crimes over nearly twenty years to conceal around $2 billion in income from the Internal Revenue Service and defraud investors in his company's debt securities. Allegations against Brockman included operating a web of foreign companies and bank accounts, using unreported income to buy a yacht called *Turmoil,* creating an encrypted email system to communicate with employees using code names such as Bonefish and Snapper, asking a money manager to attend a "money laundering conference" under an assumed identity, and persuading that manager to destroy evidence using shredders and hammers.

Imagine recapturing $2 billion in tax revenue from one case; that's almost 20 percent of the budget of the entire IRS for a year. While Brockman is somewhat unique, you know there are thousands of smaller cases that would be measured in the millions or tens of millions.

So why not invest more? You could dramatically increase revenue and compliance pretty quickly. The obvious thing to do is increase the resources available to the IRS, though that's strangely a tough sell even for theoretically deficit-concerned legislators. Ro Khanna has championed a bill in Congress to dramatically increase both the resources of the IRS and the proportion of wealthy companies and individuals who get audited. I'm for this bill, but it will be difficult to pass even though it would generate hundreds of billions in new revenue for the American people simply by enforcing tax laws as they are already written.

If you can't hire a new army of IRS auditors, you could allow private firms to finance or even assist with IRS audits and enforcement actions against some of the bad actors. Imagine if the IRS were to say that private investors get 25 percent of any settlement. That would be a $100 billion pot, one of the biggest opportunities in all of industry. You would have a new army of talented auditors and forensic accountants tracking down fraud for a piece of the action along with investors willing to bankroll the whole thing. A friend of mine in the legal industry said to me, "You already have lawsuit investors. Investors would throw money and people at this immediately; the financial upside would be enormous."

This would employ the market's own dynamics against tax evaders. I half jokingly called this plan "the Tax Mandalorian," where you have bounty hunters chasing down evaders who owe millions of dollars. When I said this to a friend who works in television, he exclaimed, "I love it! We should make a television show out of it!"

I guarantee that there are many businesspeople reading this who both recognize the merits of the above plan and would absolutely hate it; we are used to our government being slow and cumbersome and to people taking advantage of those traits. The government actually performing its functions at a high level would foreclose many business opportunities, just as with Intuit and tax reporting. Companies regularly decamp to Washington and lobby frantically against making a change that would destroy jobs, even when preserving these inefficiencies serves as a hidden tax on society.

Would I actually authorize private-sector-assisted tax collection if I had the power to do so? I would, at a minimum, signal to people that we were looking at implementing it two years from now and declare a tax holiday the next year so that people could check their books. I have the feeling even this would spur billions in extra revenue and maybe make people more receptive to increasing the resources of the IRS.

If our government were a private company, we would have switched vendors out of frustration years ago. The bigger issue than any of the technical hurdles is a lack of incentives for the federal government to treat us like users who have any choice or agency. Who is individually responsible for making sure that you get government benefits promptly or that you get the right info? No one knows. The author Philip Howard calls it the "rule of nobody." There is no accountability because everyone relies upon a faceless bureaucracy to administer services, and the responsiveness is uneven and hard to measure.

While traveling the country during my presidential campaigning, I could tell how fed up many Americans are. I talked to a veteran in Iowa, Marshall, who had served in Afghanistan and had waited six months to receive hip surgery through the Veterans Administration. He was still waiting. He was hobbling around on a cane and was angry. "They have me on a waiting list, and I have no idea where I am on that list. I served the country and came home with shrapnel in my body. I've written letters—nothing."

MAKING THE MACHINE WORK BETTER

I've talked at length in the previous chapters about how the machinery of government is outdated and broken. So how do we improve our federal agencies and bureaucracy so that they work better?

One example of how we can do things better stems from the botched rollout of HealthCare.gov. Remember Mikey Dickerson, the Google manager who came to D.C. to help turn it around? After his work on HealthCare.gov wound down, Mikey stayed to head the brand-new U.S. Digital Service (USDS), a group intended to help the government more effectively utilize the internet that was formed in part because of the HealthCare.gov debacle. What he found was overwhelming demand for the new agency's services, citing more than five dozen proposed projects within the first year.

Dickerson got hooked on doing good, calling his new vocation "more important and meaningful than anything I could have accomplished in a lifetime working at my old job." He also said that when they tried to hire ten new people for the USDS, they received more than a thousand applications, which suggests that his desire for greater purpose and meaning in work among technologists is a widespread feeling.

I personally know hundreds of techies who would love to help solve big problems. The problem is that the last thing most of them want to do is get embedded in a massive bureaucracy that will tie them up in knots. "I could never really figure out how to get hired into the government as someone who is a digital services expert," said Jonathan Sullivan, who had worked in tech on the East Coast for years before joining the USDS.

Today the U.S. Digital Service still exists, but employs only around 180 people in a federal government that employs more than 2 million people (not counting postal workers). The agency is headquartered on two floors of an 1870s town house blocks away from the White House that was once briefly the residence of Theodore Roosevelt. It doesn't look like a typical government office. It is adorned with crab-themed decorations of the agency's unofficial mascot, Mollie the Crab, presidential Pez dispensers, and cleverly hidden White House Easter eggs. The "Oval Office" where they have meetings is a storage room in the basement that doubles as a server farm. The USDS members wear jeans and T-shirts, with a button-down qualifying as being dressed up.

"We have a much faster hiring process than most federal agencies. The standard process in the federal government takes about nine months. I'm not going to sit around waiting nine months for a job when I can get hired in two weeks in Silicon Valley," Sam Gensburg, a software engineer at USDS, told a reporter for the *Federal Times*. On any given day the majority of USDS employees are based at other agencies trying to shepherd projects forward. USDS members are typically signed up for terms of only a few months or a year, so it operates more like a consulting arm attached to the government than a traditional agency. Still, according to one analysis the USDS is on track to save the federal government $600 million and redirect approximately fifteen hundred labor-years over a five-year period. That's a phenomenal return on 180 employees.

I've seen how excited people are to help make things work better. In May, while the pandemic was raging and our government struggled to give millions of Americans money, I tweeted, "We could use a citizenship portal where we could access benefits, see tax info, renew licenses, connect a bank account, fill out a census, register to vote and get updates. It's 2020. Right now this would be indispensable and ease this pandemic for millions."

My tweet was retweeted 10,500 times and seen more than 4 million times. More remarkably, hundreds of designers and technologists volunteered to build a citizen portal. We then created a Google Doc, and dozens of people signed up. My friend Eric Starr, who brought the idea to my attention, volunteered to manage the project. By the fall we had a working beta of "citizen.us" that would enable people to receive information and money from anywhere in the country.

When I did a Zoom call with these volunteers, I was blown away. There was a user interface designer from Los Angeles, a developer from Washington, D.C., a cloud architect from Connecticut, a software engineer from Paris, and on and on. They were all doing this without any compensation. For them, the prospect that they could solve a meaningful problem was excitement enough. Their work was top-notch.

Why is citizen.us not real? There are a few major barriers to overcome, the largest being data privacy, security, and interoperability of government data sets. State unemployment benefits are run out of state agencies that don't interface with the federal government. The IRS, CDC, Census Bureau, and Small Business Administration don't pool data with each other. And there would be concerns among some that the site would not be secure and would be subject to hacks. Our volunteer team was using blockchain technologies to better synchronize online government platforms and ensure site security.

Of course these kinds of volunteer efforts aren't a fit for every problem. Much of the time, the best thing you can do is identify dedicated people within a bureaucracy and empower them to do their jobs. But there are lessons to be learned that will strike most people as common sense. If you have a clear goal, accountable leadership, and a lightweight non-bureaucratic process, you can get expert people to take on important work and projects almost independent of the money involved. You want experts in the work, not experts in the government procurement process. One of the wonders of entrepreneurship is seeing small, nimble teams execute large, daunting tasks at a higher level than some might believe possible.

Mikey Dickerson was an altruistic site reliability manager at Google. If you had a big, high-stakes technology project and had to choose either the Centers for Medicare and Medicaid Services spending $1 billion on it, as they did with HealthCare.gov, or Dickerson and his 180-person team taking it on, who would you choose?

I once spoke to Ben Bernanke, the former head of the Federal Reserve, about ways we could make the government work better for us. We talked about his nickname, Helicopter Ben, after his statement years ago that money could always be distributed to prevent deflation. He commented to me, "Well, if we wanted to give everyone money during a crisis, we could give every citizen a Fed account. Then we could give everyone the money in about five minutes."

In that version of the United States of America, people would begin to think that great things are possible at the hands of their government. There is no reason we can't get there.

CHAPTER 24

GRACE AND TOLERANCE: HUMANITY IN ACTION

In September 2020, my sons were attending school via Zoom like so many children around the country. As I've mentioned, my older son, who is eight years old and in third grade, is autistic. He is very gifted in some ways, but his self-control and interpersonal awareness are limited.

One morning, I came to the kitchen and saw that Christopher had wandered into the living room and was playing games. I heard the teacher from the laptop in the kitchen saying his name, "Christopher? Christopher?" plaintively and realized that he had simply wandered off, leaving his teacher hanging.

It frustrated me on behalf of the teacher. Irritated, I strode into the living room and said, "Christopher! Go back to class now! Go! Do not leave people waiting for you!" At the same time, I grabbed his arm and moved him toward his laptop. He stumbled a bit as he tried to take his seat.

Evelyn, who had just entered the room, looked at me disapprovingly. The teacher had overheard my outburst and was trying to soothe Christopher and welcome him back. I felt self-conscious and retreated from the screen, in part so the teacher couldn't see me.

Some parents reading this can relate to it—a moment as a parent that you're not proud of, when you react poorly to stress or irritation. If someone were to replay those five seconds, I'm sure that I would seem like a jerk, or worse.

I consider myself pretty even-keeled. But I had similar reactions on the campaign trail. When you are on the road 24/7 for weeks at a time and someone drops a ball or forgets something, you're not always going to have a constructive response.

There have been any number of times when I've been a highly flawed father. And husband. And boss. And friend.

Being a parent has taught me a lot. My son Christopher sometimes does very inappropriate things. He occasionally makes very obnoxious comments to strangers.

"Why are you here? You shouldn't be here."

"You look old. Why do you have so many wrinkles?"

"You have no hair."

"This place looks bad. Why does it look so bad?" To a restaurant proprietor.

You're reading this and thinking, "That's kind of cute or funny," because he's eight. But he also doesn't have a sense of physical boundaries. He will press his body against other people's, including occasionally people he doesn't know. He is prone to pulling his shirt up or reaching into his pants. His behaviors are the kinds that are problematic but forgivable when a boy is eight but could be grounds for expulsion or legal action when he's eighteen. His lack of awareness would translate into something much worse if you attribute bad intentions to him and a sense of agency. I live in fear of his reaching puberty and having a whole new set of impulses with limited self-control.

Why am I sharing these things? If you were to show a minute-long highlight reel of someone's worst moments on their worst days, most of us would look pretty awful. Even irredeemably terrible. This is particularly true when we are younger and ill-formed and don't have a full sense of the impact or importance of our actions, or when our actions are taken from a digital remove hundreds of miles away against someone else's digital avatar.

Issues of race are particularly sensitive. I grew up one of the only

Asian kids in my town in upstate New York in the 1980s. I had skipped a grade and so was extra small and scrawny for most of my childhood. Among the reminders I got of my identity were these:

"Hey, Yang, you hungry? You want a gook-ie?"

"You see that?" Demonstrates a blank face. "That's the way the gook laughs."

"Hey, Yang, I see where you're looking. No interracial dating."

"Hey, Yang, what's it like having such a small dick? Everyone knows Chinese guys have small dicks. Do you need tweezers to masturbate?"

When I was young, these taunts from my peers evoked confusion and shame. The ridicule burned. It gnawed at me, producing a sinking sense in my gut of alienation and anxiety. I wanted to hide from it. I felt like a perpetual outsider. As I got older, my shame turned to anger. I would sometimes take my anger out on other people. I would accost kids who were even more alienated than I was and somehow lower on the totem pole. I might shove or punch someone who wouldn't fight back, or decide to fight if someone provoked me. I wrestled—poorly—for a year in junior high in part because I felt as if my masculinity were always in question.

One of my first jobs was as a busboy at the Imperial Wok in my town as a teenager. I wasn't a waiter, because my written Chinese was too weak to translate orders for the cooks to understand. On the other hand, the customers of the restaurant were a bit taken aback by my casual perfect English or the fact that I went to school with their kids as I poured them water or took their plate away.

When I was seventeen, I started going to the gym twenty minutes away with a friend. I felt daunted by it and out of place at first. The feeling of benching one plate on each side—the litmus test of manhood—after weeks of effort was a breakthrough. I became addicted for a while to protein shakes, adding weight, and maxing out.

For a long time, I felt smaller than everyone around me. I might have literally been smaller. And I wanted to catch up.

Every month or so when I was growing up, someone would ask

me, "Do you know karate?" I eventually thought it was time to be able to say yes. I studied martial arts in college and competed to limited success. I had seen someone break a board in a movie with a technique called a ridge hand—kind of a reverse karate chop with the top of your hand instead of the bottom—and asked to break with that technique when I tested for a blue belt. The master looked at me, squinted, and nodded. I shouted and hit the board with my hand, leading with the top knuckle and pivoting my hips. The board broke, people clapped, but I felt my hand start to swell up immediately. I yelled to my master, "Sir, permission to ice my hand, sir!" He waved me off in disgust.

I felt a desire throughout my twenties to prove myself to be as good as anyone else. When my first start-up failed, it shook me to the core. I was often sad, angry, lonely, and alienated as I tried to get my feet under me. I wasn't making much money relative to my peers. My dating life was pretty poor.

Eventually I mellowed—largely when I met Evelyn. The anger abandons you somewhat when you get married and have kids. The protein shakes get replaced with vanilla milkshakes that actually taste good. But I was still fired up enough to run for president as I rolled into my forties. I asked myself before I started, "Am I still angry?" I am, but about different things.

I've had someone say, "Go back where you came from," or make singsongy Asian sounds while passing me probably once every couple years, most recently yelled by a teenager out of a truck window in New Hampshire when I was out with my boys for ice cream. Now this kind of thing bounces off me—what hurt and confused and shamed me as a child now seems to be more about the speaker than me—even as anti-Asian sentiment and even violence have surged with COVID.

Of course, my place in American life is very different now than it was when I was twelve or thirteen, the first generation born here and struggling to fit in. Now this country is more welcoming to me than it likely is to that teenager in New Hampshire.

When the coronavirus hit, Asians became more visible, but as objects of contempt and hostility. It was a different feeling.

One aspect of my interpretation of Asian-ness that I hadn't realized until recently is that I thought I could blend in quite easily. No one is really focused on the Asian guy. We barely merit eye contact. We are stoics ourselves. We have invisibility cloaks that we can turn on on command.

Or so I thought. I'm no longer invisible. I've written earlier about how shocked I was when I was recognized on the street for the first time in 2019. I thought it was a fluke until it recurred. I continue to be surprised. I'll be wearing jeans, a hoodie, and a mask, and someone will still say to me, "Hey, you look familiar. Are you Andrew Yang?" I would never imagine that my face with a mask could be so recognizable.

People I didn't know had opinions about me. When I was still running for president, the comedian Shane Gillis came under fire for, among other things, calling me a "Jew chink." I thought, "Who the hell is this guy?" Evelyn was angry. The two of us sat down together to watch some clips of his comedy. Upon watching his work, we both concluded that Shane was a comedian who was still finding his feet and did not seem malignant or evil. I publicly commented that I didn't think he should lose his upcoming job at *SNL*. I figured, as the actual individual slurred, I should make a point.

Some people disagreed with my stance, particularly on social media. I was interrogated about it for several days. I said that I think we've become unduly punitive in American life, and we should exercise forgiveness more often.

NBC didn't listen and rescinded his offer. I wasn't surprised. Its investment in Shane at that point was negligible, and it's not like he was a huge revenue generator. Why risk bad PR for someone who hadn't even been on air yet? Shane called me a couple of days later. We had a nice conversation about his words and intent and what sort of person he was. It made me feel more confident that I had taken the right direction.

We are all filled with dysfunction and pain. We make mistakes. My worst moments would make me plainly unlikable, or worse. We should try to treat people with the kind of grace and understanding we would want for ourselves or our children.

Of course, the above makes for bad politics, bad media, and particularly bad social media. We currently thrive on conflict, on characters, on casting someone else as wrong, immoral, racist, or closed-minded and ourselves as clear-eyed and fighting for what is right.

In October 2020, I attended an online fundraiser for Pam Keith, a congressional candidate in Florida. Pam is phenomenal. She served in the U.S. Navy as a JAG Corps lawyer for years and was running on an ambitious platform that included cash relief during the pandemic. She is also a woman of faith.

Pam's team had trouble making Facebook Live work, so they adjusted by posting a Zoom link and we moved over there. The drawback was that the Zoom link was public. "We will keep an eye out for trolls," Pam's staffer added ominously.

Pam and I began our discussion, which involved universal basic income and her congressional campaign. Things were fine for the first few minutes as Pam discussed her background and why she was running. I began talking about why I was so excited for her campaign. Then I saw in the chat box the words "Ching Chong Ching Chong" pop up. I paused mid-sentence and then resumed while Pam's staffer tried to identify and remove the person.

Seconds later, in all caps a racial epithet directed at Pam—who is African American—appeared in the chat box over and over again, dozens of times. I studiously ignored it, making eye contact with Pam's Zoom avatar and keeping my gaze locked. I wondered if Pam could see it or perhaps had mercifully muted the chat window.

Occasionally, a new Zoom window would open with someone at the top of the screen. Sometimes it was a confused person in a darkened room. At least once it was a graphic digital image of an animated phallus thrusting back and forth. I did my best to ignore it, unsure if others could see it. This went on for minutes. There was an absurdity to the whole exercise, like a perverse *SNL* skit gone wrong in the Zoom era. Here were two aspiring political figures talking about a positive vision for Pam's district and the country while numerous people Zoombombed the proceedings with hate speech, obscenities, and terrible images.

I soldiered through, still unsure if others had seen what I'd seen, and also what I had managed to avoid seeing.

After the event ended, I related the experience to Evelyn and realized that this Zoom event reminded me of our current approach to politics. We have a conversation among ourselves with a veneer of civilization and a thousand shared assumptions: about goodwill, education, shared purpose, the ability of government to actually adjust and change, the fact that voting for someone like Pam could make a difference, and on and on.

Just to the sides of our field of vision lies human failure and frailty and venom and anger and obscenity. It's a world of friends dying of drug overdoses in a Walgreens parking lot or in a shed in Connecticut. The world outside our shrinking conversation is growing more visceral and hateful with the trappings of civilization falling away. We pretend we can't see it, but we can. None of us acknowledges it. It's growing stronger all the time. It's in us too, clawing to get out or submerged by years of acculturation and training and responsibility.

Much of this book has been about systemic problems and structural fixes. Yet the most important thing we can do to improve our future is the most personal: to extend a sense of grace and tolerance toward the people who disagree with us or who are different from us in some way—even those who attack us. This sense of forgiveness starts with each of us.

We're only human. The goal should not be to tear each other down but to make each other whole. It starts with forgiving ourselves.

CHAPTER 25

CHOICES, CHOICES

E velyn and I arrived in Georgia to campaign for Jon Ossoff and Reverend Raphael Warnock in November 2020. Control of the U.S. Senate hinged on the runoffs, which would occur on January 5.

One big issue facing candidates was how they should conduct their campaigns amid increasing cases of COVID in late 2020. Initially, both the Democratic Senatorial Campaign Committee and the campaigns were not sure if they were going to canvass or knock on doors. To me, this was obvious—of course they had to. The Biden campaign had made the same decision in October despite focusing very strongly on Trump's mishandling of the coronavirus. There were ways to canvass responsibly and safely by wearing a mask and standing far away from people outdoors. If you're in an all-hands-on-deck situation, you take any opportunity to reach people. But it wasn't until the week of Thanksgiving that the campaigns conveyed a clear message that they wanted volunteers to knock on doors. By then, a number of people who had considered coming to help had gotten the impression that they should stay at home.

Along the same lines, there were concerns about prominent Democrats coming to Georgia and "nationalizing" the Senate races. This struck me as odd; Senators Marco Rubio and Rick Scott of Florida had come to town immediately for Republicans, and Donald Trump came to headline a rally not long thereafter. This was clearly a national race, with the Republicans sending in a thousand operatives and spending $32 million immediately. Having major Democrats participate who could raise money and awareness and get out the vote struck me as a very natural step. Democrats had just won the state in November, albeit narrowly, and there was an opportunity to register some new voters by December 7.

I was scheduled to appear at a fundraiser for both candidates with John Legend, Ken Jeong, and others. Republicans started attacking Ossoff as "Hollywood Jon" in advertisements; in response the organizers changed the event so that it was just me interviewing the candidates. I thought this was a miscalculation: Who cares if celebrities wanted to do stuff for you? The goal was just to get out all of the voters who came out in November. You'd already proven that if every voter comes out, the state was winnable. It seemed like Democrats were trying to shy away from certain segments of their support.

Calls came out in the press advising Joe to move his transition office to Atlanta in order to convey how serious the Georgia races were. I agreed with that sentiment. What happened in Georgia would determine your ability to govern more than anything else.

Happily, as the days went on, the energy in the state amped up. Everyone agreed that it was a national race—after all, the outcome would fundamentally affect Biden's ability to pass legislation—and the resistance faded. I co-founded an online campaign—Win Both Seats—that raised more than $2.5 million for organizations that were registering and activating voters on the ground in Georgia.

Campaigning in Georgia was tremendous. I knocked on doors with Martin Luther King III in Atlanta; everyone recognized Martin wherever we went. He and I had met when I was campaigning for president; he loved that I had embraced his father's message of a guaranteed minimum income. Martin and his wife took Evelyn and me to both his father's childhood home and the Ebenezer Baptist Church, which his father had led for years. Reverend Warnock was the current pastor and a direct successor to Dr. King's legacy.

Campaigning with Martin Luther King III in Atlanta

I gave a speech in Columbus, Georgia, to a rally of volunteers who were getting out the vote. "Some people are talking about checks and balances. You know what will happen if Mitch McConnell still controls the Senate? Absolutely nothing. He will aim the car of government at a ditch and we will just spin our wheels going nowhere. That is the last thing you want during a crisis."

Dozens of volunteers from my campaign around the country arrived in Georgia to help get out the vote. One group rented a house they cheekily called the MATH Mansion—it was a pretty modest house—for volunteers to live in near Columbus for weeks while they knocked on doors. I held a rally with Reverend Warnock for Asian Americans at a goat farm in Atlanta. I spoke on how I had visited Reverend Warnock's food pantry and how he was exactly whom we needed fighting for the people in the Senate. Asian Americans were 4.7 percent of the vote in Georgia—the swing vote in the swing state—and we had to show up in force.

While I was in Georgia, I was also thinking about what was next for me. I interviewed with the Biden transition team for the secretary of labor role. They asked me to present a vision for the department. I said that we are in the midst of a crisis. We are down more than ten million jobs, and 42 percent of the jobs that have been lost will not return. Half of restaurants and hundreds of thousands of small businesses may close. Artificial intelligence could displace five

The family campaigning in Georgia

million workers in driving and call centers alone. Millions are leaving the workforce, giving rise to higher levels of desperation and deprivation that would lead to domestic violence, suicides, drug addiction, homelessness, and deaths of despair surging to record levels. I said that we needed a modern, activist, and impact-driven Department of Labor, given the rate of transformation in the economy. The Department of Labor has a $40 billion budget and is the hub of trying to connect people to the workforce.

I wrote a seven-page memo about what I would do as secretary. It started with the basics of a higher minimum wage, paid family leave, and rights to organize. I proposed a "race for 1,000,000 jobs" that would fund companies and organizations that were investing in upskilling and apprenticeships as well as a massive expansion of vocational and technical education. I envisioned a "Future Corps" to help young people start their careers in green jobs, infrastructure, elder and adult care, forest care, helping veterans, government, and public service. We need to modernize our labor statistics to include the gig economy, caregiving, and underemployment. Benefits should be portable and accompany workers from job to job, and workers should have any move for work subsidized. We should encourage some companies to pilot a four-day workweek. I had a lot of ideas.

One of the interviewers asked me, "You've got a high public profile. How do we get more attention to the activities of the department?"

I responded,

Look, a lot of Americans don't know what the Department of Labor is. But Americans are turning on their television sets every week to exploitation; if you address that, you can change the narrative. What do I mean? Professional wrestling shows are among the highest-rated shows on cable every week. Vince McMahon has been falsely labeling them independent contractors for years while controlling every aspect of their behavior, including whether they use Twitch or Cameo, and firing any employee who breathes the word "union." It's a similar situation for UFC fighters who are labeled independent contractors even while their lives and schedules and attire are controlled. NCAA athletes are being pushed to play sports in the time of COVID because schools have too much on the line financially for them not to play, and the athletes don't have a say. If you start addressing problems that people see in everyday life, they may realize that the Department of Labor is fighting for workers and could help them too.

I was told that the interview went "terrific." A former secretary of labor as well as a former secretary of commerce told me that if I wanted the job, I should lobby everyone associated with the transition for that role and have my connected and influential friends do the same. Some members of Congress were pushing me for secretary of commerce. I had also proposed a new secretary of technology and innovation role to the transition team that would consolidate the USDS and the Office of Science and Technology Policy in the White House into an expanded role.

AROUND THE SAME time I was discussing potential jobs in the Biden administration, my team commissioned a poll to see how I would perform if I decided to run for mayor of New York City. The results came back that I would start as the front-runner thanks to high name recognition and high favorability. I knew, though, that this just gave us a chance: everyone looks good before they start running.

Although, in the past, many people erroneously concluded I lived in California due to the vague sense of me as a "technology entrepreneur," I have lived in New York City for most of my adult life; I moved into Manhattan when I was twenty-one years old. I remember driving in with my parents' Honda Accord full of belongings for my first apartment I was sharing with a roommate. I was in Madison Square Garden for Larry Johnson's four-point play. I came of age, fell in love, and eventually became an entrepreneur and a father in New York City. My boys are in school here, though it's been Zoom classes lately.

I watched the towers fall on 9/11 and walked north away from the smoke. My older son was born during Hurricane Sandy, with blackouts blocks away. I have had a career that I never would have imagined possible when I was growing up because of this city.

New York made me who I am. Now I was seeing my home face its darkest time in a generation. The thought that I might be able to contribute to the city's revival was both an incredible responsibility and an incredible opportunity.

I knew it would be an extraordinarily difficult job. But I also thought I could do an immense amount of good. I wanted to pursue the path of having the most positive impact possible, and it felt like my city needed me.

I wrestled with the decision—go all out for a cabinet role, or dive headfirst into this new campaign for the city I love. My team asked me if they should start calling everyone with a connection to the administration about a cabinet role. But I wasn't sure if this was what I truly wanted. Did I think I was going to be able to meaningfully address the problems I saw in the amount of time we had? What was the honest approach?

There was also something about the cabinet-selection process that made me uncomfortable; it seemed like everyone was jockeying for roles in the administration. Frankly, if Joe had called me and said, "Andrew, we need you to do this," it would have generated a lot more interest on my part. But I was confident I could get a lot done whether as part of the administration or not.

During this time, my team and I were furiously lobbying Congress to include cash relief as part of the pandemic aid bill coming out of Congress. Humanity Forward had converted into a lobbying organization for cash relief. I jokingly called us "the people's lobbyist" after an *Onion* headline: "American People Hire High-Powered Lobbyist to Push Interests in Congress." I spoke to sixty-seven members of Congress, including Bernie Sanders and the eventual co-sponsors of our cash relief bill in the House, Lisa Blunt Rochester of Delaware and David McKinley of West Virginia. I found that almost every member of Congress I spoke to was receptive, particularly when they heard that 80 percent of Americans, including a majority of both parties, were for cash relief. They had seen the suffering among their constituents.

Anytime a member of Congress appeared on my schedule, I was pumped. I thought, "There's a chance that this meeting could unlock hundreds of billions of dollars for the American people." I spoke to several members a day. Whenever I spoke to a Democratic senator, I would say, "I'm here in Georgia trying to get you some new colleagues you'll like," and they would laugh and cheer me on. Still, despite the positive feedback, I wasn't sure if these conversations were going to bear fruit.

This was particularly the case when the news came out in the first week of December that a bipartisan group of senators had converged on a $900 billion deal that centered on funds for unemployment insurance, small business relief, coronavirus countermeasures, and aid to state and local governments. There were no stimulus checks in the proposal. Senators Bernie Sanders and Josh Hawley both stated that they wanted stimulus checks in the deal, but they didn't immediately kick off a chorus of senators. Meanwhile, Lisa Blunt Rochester and David McKinley put forward our bipartisan cash relief bill in the House, which quickly drew dozens of cosponsors from both sides of the aisle.

The following week, the Senate could not agree on $160 billion worth of aid to city and state governments that was resisted by Republican senators who were advocating for a corporate liability shield that Democrats disliked. That left room in the $900 billion for stimulus checks. At that point, a critical mass of both representatives and senators had expressed support for cash relief to leadership, and the legislative language had already been written in the House bill.

I thought that Senate Republicans' seeking a cap on relief spending was the wrong approach: when the house is on fire, you get the fire hoses out and don't worry about how much water you're using. I wanted to do more. But when I worked with legislators, the two goals were to make sure more money went out and increase the proportion that went directly to people.

I got a call from Liam deClive-Lowe, Humanity Forward's point person on our lobbying efforts, on Wednesday, December 16. He said to me, "I can hardly believe it, but I think our efforts have paid off. It looks like stimulus checks will be in the final bill." I just about jumped for joy. The relief bill announced on December 18 would include $600 for every adult and child in the country.

I ran to find Evelyn to tell her: "This is the greatest accomplishment of my career. I think we helped get $160 billion in cash relief out to tens of millions of families during the toughest winter in

American history." I couldn't get over the number. You could work for a million lifetimes and never make that much money or have that kind of impact. Given what we had spent on our lobbying efforts, it was a return of 100,000,000 percent for those who had donated to Humanity Forward. It meant a single mom with a couple kids would get $1,800 in January. It also meant that stimulus checks were more likely to be a part of relief efforts moving forward.

Despite the win, I dearly wished that the amount could have been higher and recurring. I tweeted, "I think sending everyone $600 will make it clear that we could also have sent everyone a significantly higher amount." But we had normalized cash relief and helped millions of people.

I had a Zoom call with our donors that night, and I thanked them all. "This was not us; this was you. This was the culmination of a movement that you built up over the past several years. When some of you supported my presidential campaign, you thought you were helping bring new ideas to the American people. Well, you helped us mainstream the idea of universal basic income just as this crisis descended on the country. You gave us a platform that enabled me to attract millions and get an audience with lawmakers. And you gave us a chance to unlock hundreds of billions of dollars for the American people in their time of need. This victory is yours."

On January 5 the results in Georgia came in. Down the stretch I was pushing as hard as I could, including releasing conversations with both candidates on my podcast and driving last-minute voters. The first huge news came that evening: Reverend Warnock had defeated Kelly Loeffler. This was not entirely surprising to me, though I was pumped. Driving around Georgia, you would see David Perdue signs as well as Warnock and Ossoff signs. Kelly Loeffler signs, however, were a rarity. She had been appointed the year prior and did not have an organic connection to voters.

David Perdue, on the other hand, had a long-term legacy in Georgia, with the Perdue name carrying a lot of weight. His race with Jon Ossoff was neck and neck, with Perdue holding a narrow lead throughout the night but Democratic areas around Atlanta yet to report. Late in the night, it became clear that Jon was going to pull it out. He eventually won by 54,944 votes out of almost 4.5 million votes cast.

I literally jumped up and down for joy celebrating with Evelyn when it became clear that Jon would join Reverend Warnock in the Senate. I texted both candidates, "Congratulations, you did it!!" as well as my co-founders at Win Both Seats, who were just as elated. With these victories, our government could function and our country would have a chance to respond to the pandemic. It had come down to a relative handful of voters in Georgia.

The celebration didn't last long. The very next day thousands of Americans overran the Capitol Hill police in an attempt to overturn the election of Joe Biden. I watched with horror along with the rest of the country as the mob marched up the Capitol steps and smashed into the building past the officers trying to hold them back. The images and videos were unimaginable.

I texted friends of mine in Congress out of concern. I heard back from one with just one word—"Terrifying." Many were on lockdown in various offices with staff. It would become clear in the hours afterward just how fortunate we were that no lawmakers were hurt or killed in this attack, in part due to the heroism of Capitol Police officers like Eugene Goodman. Our country had narrowly avoided total catastrophe.

I was stunned at the speed of it all. Things were even worse than I had believed; millions of Americans have been radicalized to the point that thousands were willing to march on our own seat of government. Polarization is metastasizing into violence. Reversing this process would take a mammoth effort on a scale that we have not seen in generations, if such is even possible today.

Our institutions are hanging by a thread. The challenge is to rebuild them as quickly as possible to address the true needs of our time. If we actually want to rise to this challenge, we have no time to waste.

CHAPTER 26

THE FORWARD PARTY

I n the previous chapters I have presented a series of problems. Our democracy is failing. Legislative incentives spur polarization and a lack of accountability. Media institutions and social media companies profit more by presenting reinforcing narratives and turning us against each other. Our economy is rewarding increasing automation as our way of life declines. We have degenerated into a group of people talking about problems and behaviors without real hope for solutions, so we simply police behaviors and argue while the problems get worse.

What is the way forward?

We have an abundance of structural problems with our government. Often in a book like this one, the author presents a series of reforms with a light touch and some very evenhanded language like "Here are some improvements to consider." Many of the necessary changes, however, would require significant political reform. In part 3, I've suggested measures that would only be possible with great difficulty.

This is part of the disease of constructive institutionalism, the condition I described in chapter 18. Many smart people are equipped to diagnose structural problems. But when it comes to remedies, they hold back. Suggesting what would actually be necessary to remedy the rot in question would seem dramatic, political, revolutionary, and possibly inflammatory. We are generally conditioned not to go there.

This is one thing that distinguished my presidential campaign. A number of people who came before me had tried to sound the alarm about the ongoing automation of jobs. But no one was dumb or foolhardy or extreme enough to run for president.

Similarly, a lot of people who pointed out the problem stopped short of arguing for the obvious solution—universal basic income. But there is no practical way to meaningfully assist the millions of Americans who work in retail, hospitality, trucking, call centers, food preparation and delivery, manufacturing, cleaning, accounting, and other highly automatable or threatened industries that doesn't require putting money into their hands quickly and directly. During the pandemic this has become obvious.

When I ran for president actually proposing universal basic income, I was dismissed as a fringe, unserious candidate by many until my campaign was embraced by hundreds of thousands of Americans, we raised $40 million, and we outcompeted half a dozen political brand names on the way to contention.

I learned a lot. I used to think that the problem was that Americans did not know about universal basic income. Today, in large part thanks to a coronavirus-induced recession and a global pandemic, 55 percent of Americans support universal basic income, and more than 80 percent of Americans support cash relief during the pandemic.

Still, despite building a popular consensus, our halting relief efforts centered on plowing money into various institutional pipes and bailing out big companies. The CARES Act had a headline cost of $2.2 trillion; that's enough to give every American $1,000 a month for six months. We got a small fraction of that. I was staggered by the fact that Congress could not muster a new relief bill from April through December 2020 even as more than ten million Americans lost their jobs.

The dysfunction is going to kill us. Worse, there's no reason to think that it will change. The two sides will be trapped in a war that

both sides win—they will still be hovering in one of the most afflu-
ent areas in the country trading power—but the people will lose.

This is not a knock on all of the people who head to Washington, D.C., to do great work. I know some of them. Many of them
are good, noble, well-intentioned public servants who are chosen
by their communities because they are exceptional. But Ezra Klein,
who spent fifteen years in Washington, D.C., reporting on politics,
described what happens with many of these people in a way that
has stuck with me: "Toxic systems compromise good individuals
with ease."

He is right. We have a plumbing problem, and we need to clean
the pipes. We must stop pretending that if we embed a few good
people in a corruptive system, the individuals will somehow become a cleansing agent. At the risk of mixing metaphors, they are
more likely to become flies stuck in amber reduced to dialing for
dollars and talking themselves into biding time. We have to free
them to actually do the work that motivated them to run for office
in the first place. We have to tackle the problem of structural incentives.

At this point a majority of Americans recognize aspects of this
problem and agree that our politics needs a new dynamic. The solution is the emergence of a viable third party. More than 60 percent of Americans say that both political parties are out of touch,
while 57 percent say there is a need for a major third party. But the
structural forces make it nearly impossible. You can't win races. You
don't have a capital structure financing you. The media will mar-
ginalize, attack, or ignore you. Partisans will say that you are em-
powering their opponents—whom they will characterize as a toxic
threat—to win. You will lose friends who occupy every position of
power in the nation.

It is nearly impossible to start a viable third party in the United
States.

You would need a candidate with a national following who

could raise tens of millions of dollars and reach people independently.

You would need a crisis that woke up millions to the fact that our government is not working for us.

You would need a set of unifying ideas and principles that Americans of every alignment could get excited about.

More than that, you would need millions of us getting together and saying, "Enough is enough. Things aren't working very well, and I want them to work better."

We can do all of the above.

Energy and passion won't accomplish anything if all efforts are pitted in opposition to each other and the political system is designed to reward inertia. It's the system itself that needs to be amended.

It's not left or right; it's Forward.

If you want to solve these problems, welcome to the Forward Party.

The Forward Party has six key principles:

- Ranked-Choice Voting and Open Primaries. Party primaries disenfranchise the majority of voters. In 80 percent of cases the general election is essentially a foreordained conclusion. Non-major-party candidates are regarded as a "waste" of a vote and can never compete. Candidates spend millions trashing their lone opponent, making us all more cynical. Ranked-choice voting better captures voters' true preferences and enables a more dynamic and truly representative democracy while addressing all of these problems. It is the key to unlocking real reform.
- Fact-Based Governance. Politicians today compete in messaging and news cycles. They should compete on results. The only way to know how you are doing is if you agree on facts and if all parties can agree on one version of reality. We should be very concerned about political leaders who don't accept

that measurements of social and economic health have weight and that science is real. Spin must have its limits. Parties can differ on what goals they would most like to pursue, but we need to share a baseline of where we are and how we are doing.

- Human-Centered Capitalism. We measure our economic health based on GDP, stock market prices, and headline unemployment rates. Meanwhile, life expectancy is declining, deaths of despair are surging, and millions of Americans are getting pushed aside. Our economic system should be geared to benefit us, with life expectancy, average income and affordability, childhood success rates, mental health, clean air and water, and other measurements of our well-being front and center. We must humanize our economy to work for us instead of continuing to see ourselves as inputs into a system.

- Effective and Modern Government. Americans have lost faith in our government at multiple levels because it often seems hopelessly bureaucratic and behind the times. Interacting with our government should be easy and painless—even elevating—instead of something to dread. In many ways, the best way for us to restore faith in our ability to accomplish big things is to adopt higher standards for what we are doing right now. Imagine if a trip to the DMV or interaction with the IRS were as easy and seamless as online banking. You might become more optimistic about our solving big problems. Most important, our government should treat us as human beings and owners.

- Universal Basic Income. In a period of unprecedented economic change and technological disruption, we should acknowledge that millions of Americans will need a new way to meet their basic needs and a pathway to stand on. We all have intrinsic value. The majority of Americans are now for universal basic income. Putting money into people's hands will shore up our economy, create jobs, and improve physical health, mental health, the ability of children to learn, public trust, optimism, and rates of business formation. It is the biggest step we could take toward a human-centered economy.

- Grace and Tolerance. Most parties need an enemy. Our enemy is those who would cast our fellow Americans as enemies and an existential threat, and the forces of inertia that make our government out of touch with the people. We all come to the table with different experiences and qualities. We are all human and fallible. We are polarized and tribal. We will give the benefit of the doubt to ourselves and each other and avoid engaging in the politics of personal attack or destruction. If my family member disagrees with me on politics, they remain my family and I love them as much as ever.

I hope you consider joining this movement. And here's the great thing: if you subscribe to these principles and ideas, you can consider yourself part of the Forward Party while keeping your current party affiliation. There will be Forward Democrats and progressives, Forward Republicans and conservatives, Forward independents and unaligned, and so on. This movement is inclusive; it's about giving our democracy and government a real chance to function in a way that benefits us.

There are approximately forty-nine million registered Democrats and forty-four million registered Republicans in the United States. I'd estimate that if we get to twenty million Forward Party members, we will transform American politics. More than a million Americans supported my campaign and are on my mailing list. My social media following is more than three million across platforms. Independents currently outnumber Republicans or Democrats in surveys. And Democrats and Republicans who are frustrated with our current politics can join while keeping their current party affiliation.

This is the real fix we've been waiting for—an unclogging of the pipes. If you'd like to join the Forward Party, go to ForwardParty .com. The first major initiative will be getting ranked-choice voting in states around the country. Anyone who wants a more dynamic and truly representative democracy will be for it, so it should be all of us.

As I've said, two states—Maine and Alaska—have already adopted ranked-choice voting, as have New York City, Minneapolis, San Francisco, and other cities around the country. Ranked-choice voting does not require legislation in two dozen states that have ballot initiatives at the state level. That means motivated citizens could adopt ranked-choice voting in Arizona, Arkansas, California, Colorado, Florida, Idaho, Illinois, Massachusetts, Michigan, Mississippi, Missouri, Montana, Nebraska, Nevada, North Dakota, Ohio, Oklahoma, Oregon, South Dakota, Utah, Washington, and Wyoming with a simple up-or-down vote on a ballot initiative enabled by a petition of thousands of signatures. A motivated group can gather signatures. In the other states, lobby your state legislators and let them know you want a real choice and a more vital democracy.

Let's solve the real problems together. No one else is coming. There is no cavalry; it's only us. Let's move this country of ours— the one we love and will leave to our children—Forward.

wrote this book while I was deciding to run for mayor of New
York City. It was both an easy and a hard decision.

Seeing New York City hollowed out by the COVID-19 pandemic was heartbreaking. Thousands of restaurants and small
businesses closed, Fifth Avenue was partially boarded up, and
Broadway's lights went out. More than 30,000 New Yorkers died
from COVID-19, and, according to one estimate, more than
200,000 left the city's metro area in 2020. The coronavirus devas-
tated New York and made living among millions of other people
a drawback instead of a strength.

Running for mayor offered me the chance to apply the principles of governance I have been fighting to bring to the country to
our biggest city, my hometown, with its population of 8.3 million,
a budget of $90 billion, and an economic output of more than
$1.6 trillion a year. We could invest in universal basic income, a
human-centered economy, local journalism, fact-based governance,
smart policing, ranked-choice voting, technology in service of
people, human dignity, grace, and tolerance. We could make the
city I call home the antipoverty city.

We launched the campaign on January 13, 2021, my forty-sixth
birthday, to great fanfare. The city was still mostly shut down, but I
started campaigning in person immediately. I knew that reopening
the city would be a top priority and that essential workers had been
out there the whole time. I thought that the mayor should be out

there too. I began visiting neighborhoods throughout the city, meeting with small business owners, activists, and community leaders. I took appropriate precautions of wearing a mask, socially distancing, and getting tested regularly.

I contracted COVID about a month into the campaign. It knocked me out for a couple of weeks. I felt like a prisoner, as Evelyn slid my food across the floor of the bedroom every mealtime for a number of days. I would occasionally get on a Zoom to keep the campaign running before returning to bed, and felt an immense amount of relief when my symptoms subsided fully about four weeks later.

So many of the things I've written about in the previous pages were manifest in the mayoral race. Whereas on the presidential trail I was always trying to get attention, in running for mayor I was a contender from the beginning. As a result, both the attention paid to me and the scrutiny were high. The media had narratives in mind that it worked to reinforce, portraying me as either unserious or corrupt. Other campaigns made it a point to attack any perceived misstatement, often using surrogates on social media to amplify manufactured controversies.

As I met with labor unions and interest groups to court their support, I was often told, "Well, we've had relationships with one of your opponents forever." The elected officials who did step forward to support me reported receiving dozens of phone calls and text messages from various officials exhorting them not to do so, which made me appreciate their support all the more. Still, many remained excited by my candidacy. We had more individual donors to a New York mayoral campaign than any other campaign in history.

Bureaucratic dysfunction was evident. One day on the trail, I remarked that New York City's public schools had been closed for longer than they should have been—my younger son had barely been in a classroom all year—and this comment then became politicized. As I saw it, officials were endlessly talking about what was necessary to reopen schools—a textbook display of constructive institutionalism—while many schools remained empty.

By April, the city had begun to reopen as more people were being vaccinated. I got the vaccine as soon as it was available, in hopes that others would follow suit. Then, as the city opened up, crime and shootings surged. I attended a vigil for a ten-year-old boy who had been shot in his own home in Queens. Crime became the number one issue for the majority of voters. This favored Eric Adams, who had built his campaign around his experience as a police officer.

In the final week of the campaign, I made a choice to campaign alongside Kathryn Garcia, the former head of the Department of Sanitation. I liked Kathryn and regarded her as an honest public servant free of undue influence. I chose to campaign with her because I wanted to make sure that New York City got the best possible mayor, whether it was me or not, and told my supporters to rank Kathryn second on their ballots.

On primary night I received about 12 percent of the first-choice vote, which wasn't enough to win, and I decided to announce the end of my campaign even as votes continued to be counted. The Board of Elections declared a vote count days later and then retracted it, saying that 135,000 dummy votes had been mistakenly included.

Despite the slow vote count and the headlines provoked by the Board of Elections' incompetence, it quickly became clear that ranked-choice voting was having exactly the kind of impact its supporters had intended. While Kathryn Garcia trailed significantly in the initial round of first-choice votes on election night, a critical mass of voters ranked her as their second or third choice, which brought her to within about eight thousand votes of the lead. Ranked-choice voting had enabled people to express their preferences more accurately; according to an exit poll conducted by Edison Research, 77 percent of New York voters said they wanted to keep using ranked-choice voting in future elections and 95 percent found their ballot simple to complete.

Still, even with a modest increase in turnout and the advent of ranked-choice voting, only about 11 percent of New Yorkers turned up for the primary and voted to select the person who would almost certainly be the next mayor. This is due in large part to the closed primary system, which requires registered voters to re-register as Democrats more than four months prior to the primary. Much work remains to be done.

Our systems won't amend themselves. The need for real change is clear.

But change won't come easily. If we are going to have a chance, we are going to need to fight for it. The time for patient belief is ending. The time to build anew is now.

ACKNOWLEDGMENTS

I owe so many people so much.

Thank you to my editor, Paul Whitlatch, for believing in me and my ideas and for making this book better at every stage. You are the greatest collaborator an author could ask for and phenomenal at bringing out the best in people. I wouldn't want to write a book with anyone else.

Thanks to my agent, David Larabell, and the team at CAA and to Byrd Leavell at UTA for making me an author in the first place.

Thank you to Zach Graumann, Carly Reilly, Muhan Zhang, Andrew Frawley, Shelby Summerfield, Ericka McLeod, Ethan Dunn, Lacey Delayne, Jon Lou, Michael Chad Hoeppner, Edward Chapman, Conrad Taylor, Luke Hansen, Katie Dolan, Patricia Nelson, Erick Sanchez, Randy Jones, Madalin Sammons, Justina Sullivan, Ally Letsky, Eli Susser, Jon Herzog, Eric Ming, Katie Bloom, Simon Tam, Zach Fang, Wes Leung, Liam deClive-Lowe, Don Sun, Steve Marchand, Khrystina Snell, Al Womble, Jermaine Johnson, Wendy Hamilton, Heidi Johnson, Aarika Rhodes, Heidi Day, Brian Yang, MC Jin, Matt Skidmore, Cam Kasky, Dave and Elaine Chappelle, and everyone else who believed in me enough to give our vision for humanity a chance to reach hundreds of millions of people. This list could go on for dozens of pages. I feel so indebted and grateful to all who drove our campaign, and I hope you enjoy seeing some of our story in these pages.

Thank you to the entire #YangGang. You built this movement

by believing in our power to make things better. I hope I've made you proud.

Thank you to Ovidia Stanoi and Conrad Taylor for tracking down data for the book when I couldn't find it. Thank you, Matt Shinners, not just for the research but for informing several chapters and making them better.

Thank you to the team at Crown, including David Drake, Gillian Blake, Annsley Rosner, Todd Berman, Dyana Messina, Julie Cepler, Stacey Stein, and Chris Brand. Special thanks to editorial assistant Katie Berry for all the legwork with the images, diagrams, and other production details.

I owe a massive intellectual debt in this book to Ezra Klein, Katherine Gehl, Michael Porter, and Lawrence Lessig, whose work I reference heavily.

Thank you to Roger McNamee, Tristan Harris, Jim Steyer, Jaron Lanier, Enoch Liang, Mark Mao, Shoshana Zuboff, and Alastair Mactaggart for being voices of conscience in technology and data and steering my thinking.

Thank you to Sam Altman, Rutger Bregman, Annie Lowrey, Andy Stern, Scott Santens, Gisele Huff, Michael Tubbs, and everyone else who has been leading us to universal basic income.

Thank you to everyone who has supported Humanity Forward and its vision of an economy that works for people, including Albert Wenger, Susan Danziger, Daniel Negreanu, J. J. Redick, and Jack Dorsey.

Thank you to the family of Jacob Blake for trusting me to help and to Sam Sinyangwe and Campaign Zero for lighting the way.

Thank you to Xander Schultz, Martin Luther King III, and all of the founders of Win Both Seats. We did it!

For everyone who has decided to follow me and learn alongside me on my podcast *Yang Speaks,* thank you. Let's continue to learn.

Thank you to the journalists and individuals who gave my presidential campaign an objective look early and used your independent judgment to bring our ideas to the public. This list could go on for a long time, but Sam Harris, Kevin Roose, Kara Swisher, Stephen Dubner, Ali Velshi, Dana Bash, Van Jones, Anderson Cooper, Erin Burnett, Margaret Hoover, Joe Rogan, Ethan and Hila Klein, Don Lemon, Chris Cuomo, Chris Hayes, Stephanie Ruhle, Bari Weiss, Karen Hunter, Charlemagne and the Breakfast Club, Krystal Ball, Saagar Enjeti, Neil Cavuto, and others stick out in my mind. You all give me hope.

Thank you to the folks at CNN who had me on and welcomed me as a colleague: Jeff Zucker, Rebecca Kutler, Ana Cabrera, Wolf Blitzer, Poppy Harlow, Jake Tapper, S. E. Cupp, Mark Preston, Chris Cilizza, John Avlon, Dan Merica, John King, David Axelrod, Lisa Ling, Gloria Borger, Scott Jennings, Bakari Sellers, Abdul El-Sayed, John Berman, Alisyn Camerota, Beth Marengo, and others.

Thank you to everyone who supported and built Venture for America. You made me believe in people and our capacity to change the world.

Thank you to Evelyn, for making our family whole and showing me love and support even when it hasn't been easy. You and our family inspire me to be a better person and make a positive difference. I love you and am grateful for your love and companionship every single day.

Christopher and Damian, Daddy is working on it.

INTRODUCTION: DEMOCRACY BY A THREAD

xiv **Today 55 percent of Americans** "Poll: Majority of Voters Now Say the Government Should Have a Universal Basic Income Program," *Hill,* Aug. 14, 2020.

xiv **Dozens of mayors** "About Us," Mayors for a Guaranteed Income.

xv **Trust is fading** "Confidence in Institutions," Gallup.

xv **Local news is dying** Alexis C. Madrigal, "Local News Is Dying, and Americans Have No Idea," *Atlantic,* March 26, 2019.

xv **those who believe that our politics** Katherine Gehl and Michael Porter, *The Politics Industry: How Political Innovation Can Break Partisan Gridlock and Save Our Democracy* (Boston: Harvard Business Review Press, 2020); Ezra Klein, *Why We're Polarized* (New York: Avid Reader, 2020).

xv **"We collapse systemic problems"** Klein, *Why We're Polarized,* 16.

xvi **Right now, members of Congress** "Reelection Rates over the Years," OpenSecrets.org.

xvi **Congress's approval rating** "Congress and the Public," Gallup.

xvi **Their incentives rest on** Thomas E. Patterson, "Voter Participation in Presidential Primaries and Caucuses," Harvard Kennedy School, 2009.

CHAPTER 1: A WINDING PATH TO CENTER STAGE

8 **I called out the fact** Economist/YouGov Poll, July 21–23, 2019.

13 **getting awards for it** "Champions of Change—Andrew Yang," White House; "National Advisory Council on Innovation and Entrepreneurship (NACIE) Board—Andrew Yang," U.S. Economic Development Administration.

CHAPTER 2: DECIDING TO DO THE UNREASONABLE THING

14   **The headline for the piece** Kevin Roose, "His 2020 Campaign Message: The Robots Are Coming," *New York Times,* Feb. 10, 2018.

15   **Vermin Supreme** "Supreme, Vermin Love," Federal Election Commission, accessed March 1, 2021, www.fec.gov/data/candidate/P000 12492/.

15   **Jo 753** "753, Jo," Federal Election Commission, accessed March 1, 2021, www.fec.gov/data/candidate/P00011569/.

15   **Kurios I** "I, Kurios," Federal Election Commission, accessed March 1, 2021, www.fec.gov/data/candidate/P00015891/.

15   **President Caesar** "Caesar, President Emperor," Federal Election Commission, accessed March 1, 2021, www.fec.gov/data/candidate /P80003221/.

15   **Sexy Vegan** "Vegan, Sexy," Federal Election Commission, accessed March 1, 2021, www.fec.gov/data/candidate/P00007286/?cycle=2020 &election_full=true.

15   **Black Label Empire (House of Lords) Darth Cyber Units** "Statement of Organization," Federal Election Commission, accessed March 1, 2021, docquery.fec.gov/cgi-bin/forms/C00693259/1302486/.

15   **Heart Doc Andrew Stops the Oligarchy** "Statement of Organization," Federal Election Commission, accessed March 1, 2021, docquery.fec.gov/cgi-bin/forms/C00589002/1305437/.

15   **the Committee to Put Backbone in the White House** "Statement of Organization," Federal Election Commission, accessed March 1, 2021, docquery.fec.gov/cgi-bin/forms/C00696898/1316255/.

17   **his administration published a study** "Artificial Intelligence, Automation, and the Economy," Executive Office of the President, Dec. 2016.

17   **Millions of retail jobs** Rex Nutting, "Amazon Is Going to Kill More American Jobs Than China Did," *MarketWatch,* March 15, 2017.

19   **I had first discovered universal basic income** Andy Stern, *Raising the Floor: How a Universal Basic Income Can Renew Our Economy and Rebuild the American Dream,* with Lee Kravitz (New York: PublicAffairs, 2016); Martin Ford, *Rise of the Robots: Technology and the Threat of a Jobless Future* (New York: Basic Books, 2016); Rutger Bregman, *Utopia for Realists: How We Can Build the Ideal World* (New York: Back Bay Books, 2018).

CHAPTER 3: THE WING DING IS STACKED AGAINST ME; OR, HOW WE LEARN ABOUT CANDIDATES

25   **And in Iowa only 171,517** "Presidential Election in Iowa, 2016," *Ballotpedia.*

25   **In the summer of 2018** Andrew Yang, "We Must Evolve to a New Form of Capitalism," 2018 Iowa Wing Ding, YouTube, uploaded Aug. 20, 2018, www.youtube.com/watch?v=qkH0xGUgR0c.

25   **heard me on the Sam Harris podcast** Sam Harris, "Universal Basic Income," *Making Sense with Sam Harris,* episode 130, June 18, 2018.

26   **For his part, John Delaney** "John K. Delaney," OpenSecrets.org.

28   **The next day the headlines** Mike Memoli and Vaughn Hillyard, "Avenatti's 'Swagger' Stirs Iowa Democrats," NBC News, Aug. 14, 2018,   www.nbcnews.com/politics/elections/avenatti-s-swagger-stirs –iowa-democrats-n900486; Brianne Pfannenstiel, "Avenatti at Iowa Wing Ding: Democrats Need to 'Fight Fire with Fire,'" *Des Moines Register,* Aug. 11, 2018.

31   **My work in Iowa paid off** CNN/Des Moines Register/Mediacom Iowa Poll, CNN, cdn.cnn.com/cnn/2018/images/12/15/rel1iademo crats.pdf.

CHAPTER 4: ADVENTURES IN ADVERTISING AND SOCIAL MEDIA

38   **"Back in the South"** Andrew Yang (@AndrewYang), Twitter, May 18, 2019, 8:36 a.m., twitter.com/andrewyang/status/11297274 12957319168.

39   **"Before we buy Greenland"** Andrew Yang (@AndrewYang), Twitter, Aug. 15, 2019, 11:20 p.m., twitter.com/andrewyang/status/11622 02563048923142?lang=en.

39   **"I'm literally trying to give"** Andrew Yang (@AndrewYang), Twitter, Nov. 15, 2019, 8:55 p.m., twitter.com/andrewyang/status/119552 0687286308864?lang=en.

39   **"Man I can't stand"** Andrew Yang (@AndrewYang), Twitter, Sept. 7, 2019, 5:07 p.m., twitter.com/andrewyang/status/1170443428 926242821?lang=en.

39   **"I'm sorry Ms. Jackson"** Andrew Yang (@AndrewYang), Twitter, Sept. 21, 2019, 1:16 p.m., twitter.com/andrewyang/status/117545888 9917247490?lang=en.

42   **When I went on Joe Rogan's** "Andrew Yang," *The Joe Rogan Experience,* episode 1245, YouTube, uploaded Feb. 12, 2019, www.youtube .com/watch?v=cTsEzmFamZ8.

CHAPTER 5: THE REALITY SHOW OF RUNNING FOR PRESIDENT

47   **CNBC covered it** Catherine Clifford, "Presidential Hopeful Andrew Yang Is Giving This New Hampshire Mom $1,000 a Month to Show Cash Handouts Work," CNBC Make It, Jan. 9, 2019.

47   **Jodi and Chuck became local celebrities** Alison King, " 'Speechless': NH Family Receives $1,000 a Month to Test Andrew Yang's

Plan," NBC Boston, July 1, 2019; Todd Bookman, "One Year on Andrew Yang's UBI: How a N.H. Family Spent Their $12,000," NHPR,
Jan. 7, 2020; Ray Duckler, "Proof of Concept: Goffstown Family
Shows How Far Candidate's $1,000-a-Month Proposal Can Go," *Con-
cord Monitor,* Feb. 24, 2019; Travis R. Morin, "Goffstown Family Taking Part in Presidential Candidate's Freedom Dividend Program," *New
Hampshire Union Leader,* Jan. 11, 2019, www.unionleader.com/news
/politics/goffstown-family-taking-part-in-presidential-candidate-s
-freedom-dividend/article_9a4f2fd4-b2ca-5083-8856-5139d151e6d3
.html.

47   *The Daily Show* "Yang Is Out, but Universal Basic Income Still Matters," *The Daily Show,* YouTube, uploaded Feb. 13, 2020, www.you
tube.com/watch?v=9cBlhuqnZRw.

47   **This move was excoriated** Ephrat Livni, "Andrew Yang's Money
Giveaway Gimmick Undermines Universal Basic Income," *Quartz,*
Sept. 12, 2019; Sharon Poczter, "Why Andrew Yang's $120,000 UBI
Gimmick Was the Best and Worst Thing to Come Out of the Last
Democratic Presidential Debate," *Inc.,* Sept. 17, 2019.

47   **Some asked whether it was legal** Lissandra Villa, "Andrew Yang
Plans to Give Out $1,000 a Month to 10 Families. That May Be a Vio-
lation of Election Law, Experts Say," *Time,* Sept. 12, 2019.

48   **"Hey, *New York* magazine"** Yelena Dzhanova, "A Yearbook of the
2020 Presidential Candidates," *New York,* April 2, 2019.

49   **In August 2019** "Campaign 2020—Gun Safety Forum," C-SPAN,
Aug. 10, 2019.

51   **more than 90 percent** "Number of Mass Shootings in the United
States Between 1982 and February 2020, by Shooter's Gender," Statista.

51   **noting that a majority** John Gramlich, "What the Data Says About
Gun Deaths in the U.S.," Pew Research Center, Aug. 16, 2019.

51   **"My beautiful four-year-old"** "Campaign 2020—Gun Safety Forum."

52   **"Yes. Hey, FYI the footage"** "Presidential Candidate Breaks Down
over Gun Violence," CNN, Aug. 10, 2019.

53   **CNN, *Rolling Stone,* the *HuffPost*** Caroline Kelly and Arlette Saenz,
"Andrew Yang Breaks Down in Tears at Gun Safety Town Hall: 'I
Have a Six- and Three-Year-Old Boy, and I Was Imagining . . . ,'"
CNN, Aug. 10, 2019; Peter Wade, "Andrew Yang Gets Visibly Emo-
tional During Gun Safety Town Hall," *Rolling Stone,* Aug. 11, 2019;
Hayley Miller, "Andrew Yang Brought to Tears by Mother's Question
on Gun Violence," *HuffPost,* Aug. 11, 2019.

55   **"Hey, Michael posted"** Michael Kruse (@michaelkruse), "Some-

thing that just happened here is @AndrewYang did Jazzercise," Twitter, Aug. 15, 2019, 7:24 p.m., twitter.com/michaelkruse/status/11621429 28954974209?lang=en.

55 **Chance the Rapper** Chance the Rapper (@chancetherapper), Twitter, Aug. 16, 2019, 3:20 a.m., twitter.com/chancetherapper/status/11 62262768801611777?lang=en.

58 **a video of mine went viral** "Watch Andrew Yang Crowd Surf with Supporters," *Washington Post,* Sept. 10, 2019; Buzz60, "Crowd-Surfing 2020 Candidate Andrew Yang Enjoys 'Wave of Support,'" *USA Today,* Sept. 12, 2019; "Watch Andrew Yang Crowd Surf During Event," CNN, Sept. 8, 2019.

CHAPTER 6: THE EYE OF SAURON

63 **My first big break** Sam Harris, "Universal Basic Income," *Making Sense with Sam Harris,* episode 130, June 18, 2018.

63 **Everything changed after** "Andrew Yang," *The Joe Rogan Experience,* episode 1245, YouTube, uploaded Feb. 12, 2019, www.youtube.com /watch?v=cTsEzmFamZ8.

63 **One of the data points** Andrew Yang (@AndrewYang), "Deaths now outnumber births among white people in more than half the states in the country. Much of this is low birth rates and white men dying from substance abuse and suicide. Our life expectancy has declined for 2 years. We need to do much more," Twitter, Feb. 15, 2019, 11:13 a.m., https:// twitter.com/AndrewYang/status/1096442292527874048.

64 **MSNBC and CNN regularly omitted me** Kimberly Yam, "MSNBC Misidentifies Andrew Yang as 'John Yang,'" *HuffPost,* Sept. 10, 2019.

64 **An MSNBC on-air graphic** Ibid.

66 **During the first Democratic primary debate** Emily Davies et al., "Who Talked Most During the June Democratic Debate," *Washington Post,* June 27, 2019.

66 **At the next debate** CNN Transcripts, "CNN Live Event/Special: Second Night of Democratic Debates," CNN, July 31, 2019.

67 **When I realized this** Andrew Yang (@AndrewYang), Twitter, July 26, 2019, 10:10 a.m., twitter.com/AndrewYang/status/11547 55760104103937.

67 **This persistent minimization occurred** "Read: Democratic Debate Transcript, November 20, 2019," NBC News, Nov. 21, 2019.

68 **My supporters were furious** Ros Krasny, "Yang Gets #BoycottMS-NBC Trending on Debate Snub: Campaign Update," Bloomberg, Nov. 23, 2019.

68 **I eventually ended** "Andrew Yang on All In with Christ Hayes (Full Interview)," YouTube, uploaded Dec. 28, 2019, www.youtube.com /watch?v=dcWnesIllRQ.

69 **The audiences for the biggest podcasts** "The Infinite Dial 2020," Edison Research and Triton Digital, accessed April 11, 2021, www .edisonresearch.com/wp-content/uploads/2020/03/The-Infinite-Dial -2020-U.S.-Edison-Research.pdf.

69 **his audience has an average age** "Audience Demographic Varia- tions Are Specific to Genre and Even Individual Podcasts," Media Monitors, April 11, 2021.

69 **Around the same time** Joe Concha, "Trump Dings CNN, 'Morning Joe' Ratings as Tucker Carlson Sets Record," *Hill,* July 1, 2020.

69 **average age of prime-time Fox viewers** Eric Schaal, "How Old Is the Average Fox News Viewer in America?," *Showbiz CheatSheet,* Jan. 11, 2019.

69 **"Reading or watching the news"** Bari Weiss, "Joe Rogan Is the New Mainstream Media," *New York Times,* May 25, 2020.

70 *Freakonomics* Stephen J. Dubner, "Why Is This Man Running for President?," *Freakonomics,* Jan. 9, 2019.

70 *The Breakfast Club* "Andrew Yang Talks Universal Basic Income, Ben- efitting from Tech, His Run for President + More," YouTube, up- loaded March 8, 2019, www.youtube.com/watch?v=87M2HwkZZ cw&t=1s.

70 **Ben Shapiro** "Andrew Yang," *The Ben Shapiro Show,* episode 45, You- Tube, uploaded April 7, 2019, www.youtube.com/watch?v=-DHuRT vzMFw.

70 **Kara Swisher** Eric Johnson, "Why 2020 Presidential Candidate An- drew Yang Doesn't Want to Break Up Google," *Vox/Recode with Kara Swisher,* July 19, 2019.

70 **Ezra Klein** "Is Our Economy Totally Screwed? Andrew Yang and I Debate," *The Ezra Klein Show,* 2019.

70 **David Axelrod** "Live Taping of 'The Axe Files' with Presidential Candidate Andrew Yang," YouTube, uploaded Jan. 8, 2020, www.you tube.com/watch?v=B8Y5p0S-UGE.

70 *Pod Save America* "Andrew Yang Full Interview," *Pod Save America,* YouTube, uploaded June 14, 2019, www.youtube.com/watch?v= _ONkNw1jbVg.

70 *The H3 Podcast* "Andrew Yang," *The H3 Podcast,* episode 132, You- Tube, uploaded Aug. 7, 2019.

71 **"Right or wrong"** Weiss, "Joe Rogan Is the New Mainstream Media."

CHAPTER 7: POWER SCREWS WITH YOUR MIND

76   *The Daily Show* "Democratic Presidential Candidate Andrew Yang's Campaign for Universal Basic Income," *The Daily Show,* YouTube, uploaded March 17, 2019, www.youtube.com/watch?v=OFvJ8J5pK4A.

76   *Patriot Act with Hasan Minhaj* "Hasan Puts #YangGang to the Test | Deep Cuts | Patriot Act with Hasan Minhaj | Netflix," YouTube, uploaded Dec. 12, 2019, www.youtube.com/watch?v=anU4Agy1Fbk.

76   *Real Time with Bill Maher* "Andrew Yang on Real Time with Bill Maher (Full Interview)," YouTube, uploaded Jan. 21, 2020, www.you tube.com/watch?v=oYpUYg19GcM.

76   *The Late Show with Stephen Colbert* "Andrew Yang's Plan to Give Everyone $1K per Month," YouTube, uploaded June 25, 2019, www .youtube.com/watch?v=Jx5j1X9njHs.

76   *The View* "Andrew Yang on The View (Full Interview)," YouTube, uploaded July 8, 2019, www.youtube.com/watch?v=y6NdhXGXpp0.

76   *Late Night with Seth Meyers* "Andrew Yang on Universal Basic Income and Measuring Our Economic Health," YouTube, uploaded Sept. 20, 2019, www.youtube.com/watch?v=xnUAlTPlMz0.

76   **Ellen DeGeneres** "Presidential Candidate Andrew Yang Drops In to Explain Himself to Ellen," YouTube, uploaded Dec. 18, 2019, www .youtube.com/watch?v=vOmggWtW7b8.

77   **Ted had recently accepted** "Andrew Yang and Sen. Ted Cruz May Face Off in One-on-One Basketball Battle in Houston," ABC13 Eyewitness News, Sept. 12, 2019.

77   **more than once—like** *The View* "Andrew & Evelyn Yang on The View (Full Interview)," YouTube, uploaded Jan. 8, 2020, www.you tube.com/watch?v=2xlfTVUqSRY.

77   **The first ad** "Andrew Yang—A New Way Forward," YouTube, uploaded Nov. 7, 2019, www.youtube.com/watch?v=EgQb2NNQ43w.

78   **"a sort of tumor"** Henry Adams, *The Education of Henry Adams: An Autobiography* (Boston: Houghton Mifflin, 1918), 147.

78   **Dacher Keltner** Dacher Keltner, "Don't Let Power Corrupt You," *Harvard Business Review,* Oct. 2016.

78   **Sukhvinder Obhi** Jerry Useem, "Power Causes Brain Damage," *Atlantic,* July/Aug. 2017, www.theatlantic.com/magazine/archive/2017 /07/power-causes-brain-damage/528711/.

78   **Lord David Owen and Jonathan Davidson** David Owen and Jonathan Davidson, "Hubris Syndrome: An Acquired Personality Disorder? A Study of US Presidents and UK Prime Ministers over the Last 100 Years," *Brain* 132, no. 5 (May 2009): 1396–406.

79   **Subjects in one study** Katherine R. Naish and Sukhvinder S. Obhi,

"Self-Selected Conscious Strategies Do Not Modulate Motor Cortical Output During Action Observation," *Journal of Neurophysiology* 114, no. 4 (Oct. 2015): 2278–84.

79 **Susan Fiske** Susan T. Fiske and Eric Depret, "Control, Interdependence, and Power: Understanding Social Cognition in Its Social Context," *European Review of Social Psychology* 7, no. 1 (1996): 31–61.

79 **One behavior that did help** Gennaro Bernile, Vineet Bhagwat, and P. Raghavendra Rau, "What Doesn't Kill You Will Only Make You More Risk-Loving: Early-Life Disasters and CEO Behavior," *Journal of Finance* 72, no. 1 (Feb. 2017): 167–206.

CHAPTER 8: THE END OF THE BEGINNING

80 **Then, in January 2020** "Evelyn Yang Reveals She Was Sexually Assaulted While Pregnant," YouTube, uploaded Jan. 16, 2020, www.youtube.com/watch?v=wMbIQgCRtjw.

81 **Dr. Hadden was later indicted** Ray Sanchez and Sonia Moghe, "New York Gynecologist Charged with Six Federal Sex Abuse Counts," CNN, Sept. 10, 2020.

83 **He and I did** "Dave Chappelle Wants You to Caucus for Andrew Yang on Feb. 3," YouTube, uploaded Jan. 21, 2020, www.youtube.com/watch?v=SWOqJMoYfMQ.

85 **On January 28, the week** "ELECTION RESULTS 2020 Iowa Youth Straw Poll," Iowa Secretary of State, accessed March 1, 2021, sos.iowa.gov/youth/poll/results.aspx.

86 **On the bus to the convention** "Iowa Caucus Results 2020," *New York Times,* February 4, 2020.

88 **I wasn't getting 10** "New Hampshire Democratic Primary Results," *USA Today,* February 27, 2020.

CHAPTER 9: SYSTEMS FAILURE

95 **"Hey, Anderson, can you"** "Andrew Yang Endorses Joe Biden, and Delivers Message to Bernie Sanders Supporters," YouTube, uploaded March 10, 2020, www.youtube.com/watch?v=4TqsbMsIKvo.

97 **We announced the effort** "Andrew Yang's New Organization to Distribute More Than $1 Million to Working Families in New York and Across the Country," Neighborhood Trust, March 26, 2020.

99 **Even the government of Togo** Yomi Kazeem, "One of Africa's Smallest Economies Is Plugging Social Welfare Gaps with Digital Cash Transfers," *Quartz,* June 11, 2020.

99 **Ninety percent of Americans** "Internet/Broadband Fact Sheet," Pew Research Center, June 12, 2019.

99 **which is a significantly higher proportion** Philip Stallworth and

Daniel Berger, "The TCJA Is Increasing the Share of Households Paying No Federal Income Tax," Tax Policy Center, Sept. 5, 2018.

CHAPTER 10: THE CENTERS FOR PASSING THE BUCK

101 **But the coronavirus tests** David Willman, "Contamination at CDC Lab Delayed Rollout of Coronavirus Tests," *Washington Post,* April 18, 2020.

102 **"It was just tragic"** Sheila Kaplan, "C.D.C. Labs Were Contaminated, Delaying Coronavirus Testing, Officials Say," *New York Times,* April 18, 2020.

102 **out of the nearly fifteen thousand** "What Is the CDC and What Does It Do?," *Atlanta Journal-Constitution.*

102 **He couldn't identify** Kaplan, "C.D.C. Labs Were Contaminated."

103 **Weeks later, the director** Abby Goodnough and Sheila Kaplan, "C.D.C.'s Dr. Robert Redfield Confronts Coronavirus, and Anger," *New York Times,* March 13, 2020.

103 **Dr. George Schmid** Eric Lipton et al., "The C.D.C. Waited 'Its Entire Existence for This Moment,'" *New York Times,* June 3, 2020.

103 **People at the CDC** Ibid.

103 **But the data it sent** Ibid.

103 **"It was insane"** Ibid.

103 **When asked what** Ibid.

103 **When the agency was provided** Ibid.

103 **"We're still actively"** Ibid.

104 **According to people** Ibid.

104 **"We got crappy data"** Ibid.

104 **"If a high schooler"** Ibid.

104 **The CDC's official response** Ibid.

104 **CDC's total budget runs** Centers for Disease Control and Prevention, FY 2021 President's Budget, CDC, accessed March 1, 2021, cdc .gov.

104 **"You've got to be"** Alexis C. Madrigal and Robinson Meyer, "'How Could the CDC Make That Mistake?,'" *Atlantic,* May 21, 2020.

106 **$684 million was spent** "'Obamacare' National Marketing Campaign to Cost Nearly $700 Million," CBS DC, July 24, 2013.

106 **the website had massive problems** ABC123, "The Failed Launch of www.HealthCare.gov," Technology and Operations Management, Harvard Business School, Nov. 18, 2016.

106 **Jon Stewart joked** Ibid.

107 **To fix HealthCare.gov** Ibid.

107   **the budget for the project** Ibid.

107   **The Standish Group** Patrick Thibodeau, "Healthcare.gov Website 'Didn't Have a Chance in Hell,'" *Computerworld,* Oct. 21, 2013.

108   **According to an account** Mark Rockwell, "Mikey Dickerson on Failures and Fixes," *Federal Computer Week,* March 27, 2015.

109   **The regulations for a company** Clay Johnson and Harper Reed, "Why the Government Never Gets Tech Right," *New York Times,* Oct. 24, 2013.

109   **Henry Chao** Henry Chao, *Success or Failure? The Untold Story of HealthCare.gov* (Charleston, S.C.: Advantage, 2018).

110   **"the decline of responsibility"** Philip K. Howard, *Try Common Sense: Replacing Failed Ideologies of Right and Left* (New York: W. W. Norton, 2019).

CHAPTER 11: THE INHUMAN ECONOMY

111   **While worker productivity has skyrocketed** "The Productivity-Pay Gap," Economic Policy Institute, updated July 2019.

111   **On the other hand** Lawrence Mishel and Jessica Schieder, "CEO Pay Remains High Relative to the Pay of Typical Workers and High-Wage Earners," Economic Policy Institute, July 20, 2017.

111   **The chances that an American** Raj Chetty et al., "The Fading American Dream: Trends in Absolute Income Mobility Since 1940," *Science,* April 27, 2017.

111   **Most Americans live** "Living Paycheck to Paycheck Is a Way of Life for Majority of U.S. Workers, According to New CareerBuilder Survey," CareerBuilder, Aug. 24, 2017.

112   **Cumulative Growth in Income (chart)** "The Distribution of Household Income, 2015," Congressional Budget Office, Nov. 2018.

113   **Indeed, more than half** Estelle Sommeiler and Mark Price, "The New Gilded Age," Economic Policy Institute, July 19, 2018.

113   **The bottom 80 percent of Americans** Danielle Kurtzleben, "While Trump Touts Stock Market, Many Americans Are Left Out of the Conversation," NPR, March 1, 2017.

113   **Wages have been stagnant** Jennifer Ma, Matea Pender, and CJ Libassi, "Trends in College Pricing and Student Aid 2020," College Board, Oct. 2020.

114   **Forty percent of Americans** Alex Durante and Lisa Chen, "Report on the Economic Well-Being of U.S. Households in 2018," Board of Governors of the Federal Reserve System, May 2019.

114   **Seventy-eight percent of Americans** "Living Paycheck to Paycheck."

114   **Thirty-seven percent of Americans** Stefan Lembo Stolba, "Credit

Card Debt in 2020: Balances Drop for the First Time in Eight Years," Experian, Nov. 30, 2020.

114   **College has gone up** Ma, Pender, and Libassi, "Trends in College Pricing."

114   **resulting in more than** Jaleesa Bustamante, "Student Loan Debt Statistics," EducationData.org, April 12, 2020.

114   **Prescription drug use** American Psychological Association, "Mental Health Issues Increased Significantly in Young Adults over Last Decade," *ScienceDaily,* March 15, 2019.

114   **Deaths of despair** Steven H. Woolf and Heidi Schoomaker, "Life Expectancy and Mortality Rates in the United States, 1959–2017," *JAMA,* Nov. 26, 2019.

114   **Health-care costs have** Julio C. Ramos et al., "Medical Bankruptcy: Still Common Despite the Affordable Care Act," *American Journal of Public Health* 109, no. 3 (March 2019): 431–33.

114   **Here are some of the indicators** Katherine Gehl and Michael Porter, *The Politics Industry: How Political Innovation Can Break Partisan Gridlock and Save Our Democracy* (Boston: Harvard Business Review Press, 2020), 81.

115   **Economists estimate that 42 percent** Jose Maria Barrero, Nicholas Bloom, and Steven J. Davis, "COVID-19 Is Also a Reallocation Shock," National Bureau of Economic Research, May 2020.

116   **One in six Americans** Megan Leonhardt, "1 in 10 Americans Are Struggling to Afford Enough Food amid the Pandemic," CNBC, Sept. 10, 2020; Claire Hansen, "1 in 5 Young Children Don't Have Enough to Eat During the Coronavirus Pandemic," *U.S. News & World Report,* May 6, 2020.

116   **Thirty percent of Americans missed** Igor Popov, Chris Salviati, and Rob Warnok, "Missed Payments Stabilize in June—at Alarming Levels," Apartment List, June 9, 2020.

116   **By the summer** "Stress in America 2020," American Psychological Association, May 2020.

116   **Thirty-three percent of Americans** Scott Keeter, "A Third of Americans Experienced High Levels of Psychological Distress During the Coronavirus Outbreak," Pew Research Center, May 7, 2020.

116   **Half of companies indicated** Susan Lund et al., "What 800 Executives Envision for the Postpandemic Workforce," McKinsey & Company, Sept. 23, 2020.

116   **News reports have cited** Frederic Lardinois, "Google Signs Up Verizon for Its AI-Powered Contact Center Services," *TechCrunch,* July 13, 2020; Alexis Benveniste, "Sam's Club Is Putting Robot Janitors in All of Its Stores During the Pandemic," CNN Business, Oct. 21, 2020;

Alicia Wallace, "Tyson and Other Meat Processors Are Reportedly Speeding Up Plans for Robot Butchers," CNN Business, July 10, 2020.

117 **People who are unemployed** Matthew O'Brien, "The Terrifying Reality of Long-Term Unemployment," *Atlantic,* April 13, 2013.

CHAPTER 12: HOW WE KNOW WHAT WE KNOW

119 **The newspaper was founded** "Sentinel Mural," Historical Society of Cheshire County.

119 **the exchange would eventually** "Editorial Board Interview with Andrew Yang," YouTube, uploaded Dec. 3, 2019, www.youtube.com /watch?v=QPHRm85Cx2w.

121 **accounting for around 80 percent** "Local Newsrooms Across the Country Are Closing. Here's Why That Matters," *PBS NewsHour,* Jan. 1, 2020.

121 **In the last fifteen years** Clara Hendrickson, "How the Gannett/ GateHouse Merger Could Deepen America's Local News Crisis," Brookings, Nov. 19, 2019.

121 **Thirteen hundred communities** Ibid.

121 **Thirty thousand reporters lost their jobs** Elizabeth Grieco, "U.S. Newspapers Have Shed Half of Their Newsroom Employees Since 2008," Pew Research Center, April 20, 2020.

122 **before Gannett itself** Marc Tracy, "Gannett, the Owner of USA Today, Is About to Get a Whole Lot Bigger," *New York Times,* Aug. 5, 2019.

122 **GateHouse is a holding** Ibid.

122 **as Derek Thompson wrote** Derek Thompson, "The Print Apocalypse and How to Survive It," *Atlantic,* Nov. 3, 2016.

123 **A decline in local journalism** Sarah Holder, "When Local Newsrooms Shrink, Fewer Candidates Run for Mayor," Bloomberg CityLab, April 11, 2019.

123 **Without local news** Joshua P. Darr, Johanna Dunaway, and Matthew P. Hitt, "Want to Reduce Political Polarization? Save Your Local Newspaper," Nieman Lab, Feb. 11, 2019.

123 **The cost of municipal bonds** Clara Hendrickson, "Local Journalism in Crisis: Why America Must Revive Its Local Newsrooms," Brookings, Nov. 12, 2019.

124 **Their combined revenues** "Cable News Fact Sheet," Pew Research Center, June 25, 2019.

124 **On average, cable providers** Jack Shafer, "Fox Doesn't Need to Fear Trump's Wrath," *Politico,* Nov. 24, 2020.

125 **The ratings rankings pre-pandemic** Amy Watson, "Leading Cable

News Networks in the United States in Q4 2020, by Number of Primetime Viewers," Statista, Feb. 5, 2021.

126 **Growth in Prime-Time Viewing (chart)** Benjamin Mullin, "Life at CNN: Skeleton Staff, Record Ratings, and Vanishing Ads," *Wall Street Journal,* April 15, 2020.

126 **decided to analyze the transcripts** Gregory J. Martin and Ali Yurukoglu, "Bias in Cable News: Persuasion and Polarization," *American Economic Review* 107, no. 9 (Sept. 2017): 2565–99.

127 **At Fox and MSNBC** Jonathan Berr, "Has CNN Discovered 'the Fountain of Youth' in Cable News?," *Forbes,* March 2, 2018.

128 **"The problem is the job"** Ariana Pekary, "Personal News: Why I'm Now Leaving MSNBC," *Ariana Noel Pekary,* Aug. 3, 2020.

129 **The public, too, has noticed** "Confidence in Institutions," Gallup.

129 **Only 13 percent trust the media** Megan Brenan, "Americans Remain Distrustful of Mass Media," Gallup, Sept. 30, 2020.

130 **"The brain fires off"** P. W. Singer and Emerson Brooking, *LikeWar: The Weaponization of Social Media* (New York: Houghton Mifflin Harcourt, 2018), 3.

130 **In 2018, Massachusetts Institute of Technology** Robinson Meyer, "The Grim Conclusions of the Largest-Ever Study of Fake News," *Atlantic,* March 8, 2018.

131 **In a TED talk** "JP Rangaswami: Information Is Food," YouTube, uploaded May 8, 2012, www.youtube.com/watch?v=3A1LvXRnpVg.

131 **Jaron Lanier, the technology** Jeremy Price, "The Father of Virtual Reality on How Facebook Is Messing with Your Mind," *Next Big Idea Club.*

131 **in the graph** Jean Twenge, "Six Facts About Screens and Teen Mental Health That a Recent New York Times Article Ignores," Institute for Family Studies, Jan. 22, 2020.

131 **"Social media seems to systematically"** Meyer, "Grim Conclusions of the Largest-Ever Study of Fake News."

132 **In 2018, Jordan Peele** "You Won't Believe What Obama Says in This Video! 😀," YouTube, uploaded April 17, 2018, www.youtube.com /watch?v=cQ54GDm1eL0.

132 **Victor Riparbelli** Nina Schick, *Deepfakes* (New York: Twelve, 2020), 48.

133 **In 2020, Oxford University researchers** Ibid., 85.

CHAPTER 13: OUR DATA, WHOSE DATA?

134 **ExxonMobil is valued** Google Finance, accessed March 1, 2021, www.google.com/finance/quote/XOM:NYSE.

134   **What is Facebook** Google Finance, accessed March 1, 2021, www
.google.com/finance/quote/FB:NASDAQ.

134   **Google?** Google Finance, accessed March 1, 2021, www.google.com
/finance/quote/GOOGL:NASDAQ.

135   **"The artificial intelligences of companies"** Roger McNamee,
Zucked: Waking Up to the Facebook Catastrophe (New York: Penguin
Press, 2020), 9, 85.

135   **Facebook's annual revenue** "Facebook Reports Fourth Quarter and
Full Year 2020 Results," Facebook Investor Relations, Jan. 27, 2021.

135   **Google, which has a similar portfolio** "Alphabet Announces
Fourth Quarter and Fiscal Year 2020 Results," Alphabet, Feb. 2, 2021.

135   **Our data is worth** Hanna Kozlowska, "How Much Is Your Data
Worth?," *Quartz,* July 8, 2019.

135   **Data tracking and selling** WebFX Team, "What Are Data Brokers—
and What Is Your Data Worth?," *WebFX* (blog), March 16, 2020.

136   **How much your data is worth** Ibid.

136   **As James Zou** Kozlowska, "How Much Is Your Data Worth?"

137   **In his book, Roger** McNamee, *Zucked,* 68.

138   **We are not the client or end user** Ibid.

138   **"Microtargeting transforms the public square"** Ibid., 238.

138   **Trump raised more than $170 million** Shane Goldmacher and
Maggie Haberman, "Trump Has Raised $170 Million Since Election
Day," *New York Times,* Dec. 1, 2020.

139   **But starting in 2018, studies** Alice G. Walton, "New Studies Show
Just How Bad Social Media Is for Mental Health," *Forbes,* Nov. 16,
2018.

139   **In one study, 140 undergraduates** Melissa G. Hunt et al., "No
More FOMO: Limiting Social Media Decreases Loneliness and Depression," *Journal of Social and Clinical Psychology* 37, no. 10 (Dec. 2018).

139   **obesity** Datis Khajeheian et al., "Effect of Social Media on Child
Obesity: Application of Structural Equation Modeling with the Tagu-
chi Method," *International Journal of Environmental Research and Public
Health* 15, no. 7 (July 2018): 1343.

139   **sleep deprivation** Holly Scott, Stephany M. Biello, and Heather Clel-
and Woods, "Social Media Use and Adolescent Sleep Patterns: Cross-
Sectional Findings from the UK Millennium Cohort Study," *BMJ Open*
9, no. 9 (Sept. 2019).

139   **posture issues** Deana Carpenter, "Checking Social Media Can Sometimes Be a Pain in the Neck—Literally," *Pittsburgh Post-Gazette,* Aug. 24,
2017.

139   **An unprecedented surge** Russell M. Viner et al., "Roles of Cyber-bullying, Sleep, and Physical Activity in Mediating the Effects of Social Media Use on Mental Health and Wellbeing Among Young People in England: A Secondary Analysis of Longitudinal Data," *Lancet,* Aug. 13, 2019.

140   **"A lot of the stuff"** Jeremy Price, "The Father of Virtual Reality on How Facebook Is Messing with Your Mind," *Next Big Idea Club.*

140   **California Consumer Privacy Act** Rachael Myrow, "California Rings In the New Year with a New Data Privacy Law," NPR, Dec. 30, 2019.

142   **California Consumer Privacy Act has already** "New State Bills Inspired by the California Consumer Privacy Act May Reappear Next Year," Ropes & Gray, Nov. 7, 2019.

142   **At the same time, we realized** Jonathan Stempel, "Yahoo Strikes $117.5 Million Data Breach Settlement After Earlier Accord Rejected," Reuters, April 9, 2019.

142   **Facebook had just lost** Robert Channick, "Nearly 1.6 Million Illinois Facebook Users to Get About $350 Each in Privacy Settlement," *Chicago Tribune,* Jan. 14, 2021.

CHAPTER 14: LOYALTY CUTS BOTH WAYS

145   **The data shouted the same thing** Mark E. Cziesler et al., "Mental Health, Substance Use, and Suicidal Ideation During the COVID-19 Pandemic—United States, June 24–30, 2020," CDC, Aug. 14, 2020.

145   **Racism against Asian Americans** "Covid-19 Fueling Anti-Asian Racism and Xenophobia Worldwide," Human Rights Watch, May 12, 2020.

146   **Asian Americans had historically voted** "The Changing Racial and Ethnic Composition of the U.S. Electorate," Pew Research Center, Sept. 23, 2020.

151   **The final tally** "Kentucky Results," NPR, accessed March 1, 2021, apps.npr.org/elections20-primaries/states/KY.html.

151   **It's unclear how many** Ibid.

151   **Amy would go on to lose** "Kentucky—Senate," Federal Election Commission, accessed March 1, 2021, www.fec.gov/data/elections /senate/KY/2020/.

CHAPTER 15: WATCHING THE WATCHMEN

154   **I spent the next couple days** "Andrew Yang Relays Message from Jacob Blake's Father: My Son Is a Human Being," YouTube, uploaded Aug. 27, 2020, www.youtube.com/watch?v=Cf9CSG4ov4g.

154 **Many states have ignored** Peter Eisler and Jason Szep, "Congress Presses DOJ to Improve Jail Reporting System After Reuters Report," Reuters, Oct. 21, 2020.

154 **The most commonly cited** "The Counted—People Killed by Police in the US," *Guardian,* accessed March 1, 2021, www.theguardian .com/us-news/ng-interactive/2015/jun/01/the-counted-police -killings-us-database.

154 **The FBI even started** Mark Tran, "FBI Chief: 'Unacceptable' That Guardian Has Better Data on Police Violence," *Guardian,* Oct. 8, 2015.

155 **similar reporting in** *The Washington Post* "Fatal Force," *Washington Post,* accessed March 1, 2021, www.washingtonpost.com/graphics/in vestigations/police-shootings-database/.

155 **From 2015 to 2019** "Counted," *Guardian;* "Fatal Force," *Washington Post.*

155 **Across the country cities are spending** "City Lawsuit Costs Report," Governing, accessed March 1, 2021, www.governing.com/ar chive/city-lawsuit-legal-costs-financial-data.html.

155 **Police brutality is incredibly expensive** Olga Khazan, "In One Year, 57,375 Years of Life Were Lost to Police Violence," *Atlantic,* May 8, 2018.

155 **costs have bankrupted communities** Liz Farmer, "Police Misconduct Is Increasingly a Financial Issue," Governing, June 20, 2018.

156 **According to the Supreme Court** Joanna C. Schwartz, "Suing Police for Abuse Is Nearly Impossible. The Supreme Court Can Fix That," *Washington Post,* June 3, 2020.

157 **Against this backdrop** "City Lawsuit Costs Report."

157 **In 2018 there were 686,665** "Table 74: Full-Time Law Enforcement Employees," FBI Uniform Crime Reporting, accessed March 1, 2021, ucr.fbi.gov/crime-in-the-u.s/2018/crime-in-the-u.s.-2018/tables /table-74.

157 **He has identified a number** Aylin Woodward and Michelle Mark, "Research Shows There Are at Least 6 Proven Ways to Reduce Police Brutality—and 2 Strategies That Don't Work," *Business Insider,* June 3, 2020.

158 **Campaign Zero estimates that adopting** DeRay McKesson et al., "Police Use of Force Policy Analysis," Campaign Zero, Sept. 20, 2016.

158 **One survey of 280** Woodward and Mark, "Research Shows There Are at Least 6 Proven Ways to Reduce Police Brutality."

158 **De-escalation is a set** Jeremy Romo, "The Art of De-escalation and Conflict Resolution," National Adult Protective Services Association.

158 **Prior complaints indicate** Woodward and Mark, "Research Shows There Are at Least 6 Proven Ways to Reduce Police Brutality."

158   **Researchers studied more than** Marie Ouellet et al., "Network Exposure and Excessive Use of Force," *Criminology and Public Policy* 18, no. 3 (Aug. 2019): 675–704.

158   **"How we pair and assign officers"** Woodward and Mark, "Research Shows There Are at Least 6 Proven Ways to Reduce Police Brutality."

159   **One investigation found** Kimbriell Kelly, Wesley Lowery, and Steven Rich, "Fired/Rehired: Police Chiefs Are Often Forced to Put Officers Fired for Misconduct Back on the Streets," *Washington Post,* Aug. 3, 2017.

159   **For example, Sergeant Brian Miller** Woodward and Mark, "Research Shows There Are at Least 6 Proven Ways to Reduce Police Brutality."

159   **According to the Treatment Advocacy Center** Doris A. Fuller et al., "Overlooked in the Undercounted: The Role of Mental Illness in Fatal Law Enforcement Encounters," Office of Research and Public Affairs, Treatment Advocacy Center, Dec. 2015.

159   **In Eugene, Oregon** Zusha Elinson, "When Mental-Health Experts, Not Police, Are the First Responders," *Wall Street Journal,* Nov. 24, 2018.

160   **Departments that went through** Rob Arthur, "Jeff Sessions Is Walking Away from the Best Way to Reduce Police Shootings," *Vice News,* Dec. 18, 2017.

160   **Since 1997, eight thousand police** "Provides Law Enforcement Activities Logistical Oversight and Support in the Procurement and Accountability of DoD Excess Property," Defense Logistics Agency, accessed March 1, 2021, www.dla.mil/DispositionServices/Offers /Reutilization/LawEnforcement.aspx.

160   **One study showed that** Casey Delehanty et al., "Militarization and Police Violence: The Case of the 1033 Program," *Research and Politics,* June 14, 2017.

160   **I appreciated what** Anderson Cooper 360° (@AC360), Twitter, May 29, 2020, 8:57 p.m., twitter.com/ac360/status/1266534277208031233 ?lang=en.

161   **West appeared on CNN** "'We are witnessing America as a failed social experiment'—Dr. Cornell West Full CNN Segment," YouTube, uploaded May 29, 2020, www.youtube.com/watch?v=90G_QdxqqJs.

CHAPTER 16: WHY NOT MUCH PASSES

163   **Since 1976, an average** Bridget Bowman, "House Retirements Already Outpace Average for Past Election Cycles," *Roll Call,* Jan. 2, 2020.

164   **Reelection Rates for House Members (chart)** Tom Murse, "Do

Members of Congress Ever Lose Re-election?," *ThoughtCo.*, Dec. 10, 2020.

165   **That rules out most** "Report on the Economic Well-Being of U.S. Households in 2018," Board of Governors of the Federal Reserve System, May 2019.

165   **The average successful** Aliya Frumin, "How Much Does It Cost to Win a Seat in Congress? If You Have to Ask . . . ," MSNBC, March 11, 2013.

165   **Amanda Litman of Run for Something** Bonnie Berkowitz and Chris Alcantara, "How to Run for Congress," *Washington Post,* Nov. 15, 2019.

166   **Only about 1 percent of American** "Donor Demographics," OpenSecrets.org, accessed March 1, 2021, www.opensecrets.org /elections-overview/donor-demographics.

166   **"If voters haven't done"** Zach Bernard, "Name Recognition Can Have Impact on Elections," WBOI, Nov. 4, 2016.

166   **Unfortunately, as we learned** Kristen Hare, "The Coronavirus Has Closed More Than 60 Local Newsrooms Across America. And Counting," Poynter, Feb. 16, 2021.

167   **Brynne Kennedy, a former tech CEO** Emma Hinchliffe, "Brynne Kennedy Could Be the First Female Tech Founder to Serve in Congress," *Fortune,* Aug. 24, 2020.

167   **Thanks partially to gerrymandering** Katherine Gehl and Michael Porter, *The Politics Industry: How Political Innovation Can Break Partisan Gridlock and Save Our Democracy* (Boston: Harvard Business Review Press, 2020), 22.

167   **Less than 20 percent** Drew Desilver, "Turnout in This Year's U.S. House Primaries Rose Sharply, Especially on the Democratic Side," Pew Research Center, Oct. 3, 2018.

168   **"Freshman members of Congress"** John K. Delaney, *The Right Answer: How We Can Unify Our Divided Nation* (New York: Henry Holt, 2018), 23.

169   **The average age of a member** Jennifer E. Manning, "Membership of the 116th Congress: A Profile," Congressional Research Service, Dec. 17, 2020.

169   **There are a lot of egos** Karl Evers-Hillstrom, "Majority of Lawmakers in 116th Congress Are Millionaires," OpenSecrets.org, April 23, 2020.

170   **Members of Congress spend** Lawrence Lessig, *They Don't Represent Us: Reclaiming Our Democracy* (New York: Dey Street Books, 2019), 57.

170   **$296 million** "Democratic Congressional Campaign Cmte," Open

Secrets.org, accessed March 1, 2021, www.opensecrets.org/parties /totals.php?cmte=DCCC&cycle=2018.

170 **$205 million** "National Republican Congressional Cmte," OpenSe-crets.org, accessed March 1, 2021, www.opensecrets.org/parties/totals .php?cmte=NRCC&cycle=2018.

170 **Approximately $6.4 billion** Gehl and Porter, *Politics Industry,* 62.

171 **Francis Fukuyama calls** Ezra Klein, "Francis Fukuyama: America Is in 'One of the Most Severe Political Crises I Have Experienced,'" *Vox,* Oct. 26, 2016.

171 **By 2016–2018** Gehl and Porter, *Politics Industry,* 62.

172 **Republican congressman Mike Gallagher** Ibid., 8.

173 **Of the Democrats who didn't** Marty Johnson, "The 14 Democrats Who Broke with Their Party on Coronavirus Relief Vote," *Hill,* May 16, 2020.

174 **"The United States distinguished"** Nicholas Kristof (@Nick Kristof), Twitter, Aug. 21, 2020, 10:18 p.m., twitter.com/NickKristof /status/1296995123788619777.

174 **How could Congress fail** Nathaniel Rakich, "Americans Over-whelmingly Want Congress to Approve Another Coronavirus Stimulus Package," *FiveThirtyEight,* Dec. 18, 2020.

175 **Congressional Job Approval (chart)** "Congress and the Public," Gallup, accessed March 1, 2021, news.gallup.com/poll/1600/congress -public.aspx.

CHAPTER 17: THE WAVE THAT WASN'T

177 **I tweeted, "I've got"** Andrew Yang (@AndrewYang), Twitter, Aug. 11, 2020, 11:43 a.m., twitter.com/AndrewYang/status/1293211 531551952897.

177 **I built my remarks around** "Stress in America 2020: Stress in the Time of COVID-19, Volume Two," American Psychological Associa-tion, June 2020.

178 **When the real thing happened** "Andrew Yang's Speech at the 2020 Democratic National Convention," YouTube, uploaded Sept. 3, 2020, www.youtube.com/watch?v=HO7Yjgj3fGg.

178 **Much to my surprise** "Blitzer Presses Pelosi on Why She Hasn't Taken Trump Stimulus Deal," CNN, Oct. 13, 2020.

180 **After Debbie's comments, Don Lemon** "Race for the White House Narrows as Votes Are Counted; Federal Judge Unhappy with USPS," CNN, Nov. 5, 2020, transcripts.cnn.com/TRANSCRIPTS /2011/05/se.08.html.

180 **But later that day** "Andrew Yang: Trumpism Is Here to Stay," You-

Tube, uploaded Nov. 5, 2020, www.youtube.com/watch?v=QyG7Wo AFiWw&feature=emb_logo.

182 **I tweeted out** Andrew Yang (@AndrewYang), Twitter, Nov. 7, 2020, 8:27 p.m., twitter.com/AndrewYang/status/1325248601568796673.

182 **House Democrats, who had expected** David Wasserman et al., "2020 National House Vote Tracker," *Cook Political Report,* Nov. 2020.

183 **Julie Oliver, a very impressive** "Julie Oliver," *Ballotpedia,* accessed March 1, 2021, ballotpedia.org/Julie_Oliver.

183 **The same thing happened** "Kara Eastman," *Ballotpedia,* accessed March 1, 2021, ballotpedia.org/Kara_Eastman/.

183 **Ohio in particular has** "QuickFacts: Ohio," U.S. Census Bureau, accessed March 1, 2021, www.census.gov/quickfacts/OH.

183 **similar to Michigan's** "QuickFacts: Michigan," U.S. Census Bureau, accessed March 1, 2021, www.census.gov/quickfacts/MI.

183 **In Iowa, suicide** Tom Snee, "Long After '80s Farm Crisis, Farm Workers Still Take Own Lives at High Rate," *IowaNow,* June 12, 2017.

184 **Ohio is more diverse** "QuickFacts: Ohio," U.S. Census Bureau.

184 **significantly above the national** "Quickfacts: United States," U.S. Census Bureau, accessed March 1, 2021, www.census.gov/quickfacts /fact/table/US/PST045219.

185 **"We have an election system"** Zack Stanton, "How 2020 Killed Off Democrats' Demographic Hopes," *Politico,* Nov. 12, 2020.

185 **A geographic imbalance** Ezra Klein, *Why We're Polarized* (New York: Avid Reader, 2020), 241–42.

186 **35 percent to 26 percent** Ibid., 231.

186 **If that isn't enough** Megan Brenan, "Democrats Favor More Moderate Party; GOP, More Conservative," Gallup, Dec. 12, 2018.

186 **One study showed that the number** Klein, *Why We're Polarized,* 171.

186 **"sharply split across racial"** Ibid., 135.

187 **In 2008, 54 percent of the country** Ibid., 105.

CHAPTER 18: CONSTRUCTIVE INSTITUTIONALISM; OR, THE PRIESTS OF THE DECLINE

188 **the largest nonprofit** Mark Hrywna, "NPT Top 100 (2019): An In-Depth Study of America's Largest Nonprofits," *NonProfit Times,* Nov. 4, 2019.

189 **But the data shows that** James Coleman, "Equality of Educational Opportunity," National Center for Educational Statistics (popularly known as the Coleman Report), files.eric.ed.gov/fulltext/ED012275 .pdf.

189 **PhDs keep getting produced** Trevor Griffey, "The Decline of Faculty Tenure," LAWCHA, Jan. 9, 2017.

193 **More than sixty thousand journalists** Elizabeth Grieco, "U.S. Newspapers Have Shed Half of Their Newsroom Employees Since 2008," Pew Research Center, April 20, 2020; Lauren Harris and Gabby Miller, "The 2020 Journalism Crisis: A Year in Review," *Columbia Journalism Review,* Dec. 16, 2020.

195 **The actual success of government-funded retraining** Jeffrey Selingo, "The False Promises of Worker Retraining," *Atlantic,* Jan. 8, 2018.

195 **The country has lost more than** Heather Long, "U.S. Has Lost 5 Million Manufacturing Jobs Since 2000," CNN Business, March 29, 2016.

195 **"I'm seeing all of these"** "Process Determines Outcome: Justin Amash on the Rules That Broke Congress. | Andrew Yang," YouTube, uploaded Oct. 19, 2020, www.youtube.com/watch?v=g5aRvUu2daM.

CHAPTER 19: THE HUMAN ECONOMY: MAKING WHAT WE MEASURE

202 **Jamie Dimon, the CEO** Nicole Sinclair, "Dimon: We Have a National Emergency," *Yahoo!Finance,* April 4, 2017.

202 **Ray Dalio, the influential founder** David Randall, "U.S. Income Inequality a 'National Emergency': Billionaire Ray Dalio," Reuters, April 4, 2019.

203 **Even the inventor of GDP** David Pilling, "Why GDP Is a Terrible Metric for Success and Wealth," *Time,* Jan. 25, 2018.

203 **Bobby Kennedy famously echoed** Robert F. Kennedy, "Remarks at the University of Kansas, March 18, 1968," John F. Kennedy Presidential Library and Museum.

203 **Suicides, drug overdoses** Sherry L. Murphy et al., "Deaths: Final Data for 2018," *National Vital Statistics Reports* 69, no. 13 (Jan. 2021).

204 **The cost of the opioid epidemic** Curtis Florence et al., "The Economic Burden of Prescription Opioid Overdose, Abuse, and Dependence in the United States, 2013," *Medical Care* 54, no. 10 (2016): 901–6.

204 **Mental health issues at work** "Report: State of the American Workplace," Gallup, Sept. 22, 2014.

204 **And climate change, by the year** Frank Ackerman and Elizabeth A. Stanton, "The Cost of Climate Change: What We'll Pay if Global Warming Continues Unchecked," NRDC, May 2008.

205 **A basic income would make us** "Research Posts," Basic Income Earth Network, accessed March 1, 2021, basicincome.org/research/.

205 **UBI would also be a boost** Michalis Nikiforos, Marshall Steinbaum, and Gennaro Zezza, "Modeling the Macroeconomic Effects of a Universal Basic Income," Roosevelt Institute, Aug. 29, 2017.

206 **From Los Angeles** "Meet the Mayors," Mayors for a Guaranteed Income, accessed March 1, 2021, www.mayorsforagi.org/who.

206 **We spend twice as much** Irene Papanicolas, Liana R. Woskie, and Ashish K. Jha, "Health Care Spending in the United States and Other High-Income Countries," *JAMA* 319, no. 10 (2018): 1024–39.

206 **Studies have found nearly** Andrew P. Wilper et al., "Health Insurance and Mortality in US Adults," *Research and Practice* 99, no. 12 (Dec. 2009).

206 **70 percent of children** Laura Santhanam, "Why Mental Health Care Deserts Persist for U.S. Children," *PBS NewsHour,* Nov. 6, 2019.

206 **teen suicide rates are up** Sally C. Curtin and Melonie Heron, "Death Rates due to Suicide and Homicide Among Persons Aged 10–24: United States, 2000–2017," *NCHS Data Brief,* no. 352, Oct. 2019.

207 **Consider that 66.5 percent** Lorie Konish, "This Is the Real Reason Most Americans File for Bankruptcy," CNBC, Feb. 11, 2019.

207 **Without a fundamental restructuring** "CMS Office of the Actuary Releases 2017–2026 Projections of National Health Expenditures," CMS.gov, Feb. 14, 2018.

208 **Take the example of Google's AI** Frederic Lardinois, "Google Signs Up Verizon for Its AI-Powered Contact Center Services," *TechCrunch,* July 13, 2020.

208 **Certainly much less than** King White, "How Big Is the U.S. Call Center Market Compared to India, Latin America, and the Philippines?," Site Selection Group, July 23, 2018.

208 **The same will be true** Jennifer Cheeseman Day and Andrew W. Hait, "Number of Truckers at All-Time High," U.S. Census Bureau, June 6, 2019.

208 **Amazon famously paid zero** Jesse Pound, "These 91 Companies Paid No Federal Taxes in 2018," CNBC, Dec. 16, 2019.

209 **a policy that's currently** "VAT," International Monetary Fund, accessed March 1, 2021, www.imf.org/external/np/fad/tpaf/pages/vat.htm.

210 **During the pandemic, unemployment** "Civilian Labor Force Participation Rate," U.S. Bureau of Labor Statistics, accessed March 1, 2021, www.bls.gov/charts/employment-situation/civilian-labor-force-participation-rate.htm.

210 **Our infrastructure is crumbling** Norma Jean Mattei, "2017 Infrastructure Report Card: A Comprehensive Assessment of America's Infrastructure," American Society of Civil Engineers, 2017.

210 **We can expand broadband access** John Busby and Julia Tanberk, "FCC Reports Broadband Unavailable to 21.3 Million Americans, BroadbandNow Study Indicates 42 Million Do Not Have Access," BroadbandNow, Feb. 3, 2020.

211 **We also have almost eight million** Stephen Campbell, "New Research: 7.8 Million Direct Care Jobs Will Need to Be Filled by 2026," Paraprofessional Healthcare Institute, Jan. 24, 2019.

211 **We needed an army** James Temple, "Why Contact Tracing May Be a Mess in America," *Technology Review,* May 16, 2020.

CHAPTER 20: REWIRING GOVERNMENT

212 **Now a majority of Americans** "Poll: Majority of Voters Now Say the Government Should Have a Universal Basic Income Program," *Hill,* Aug. 14, 2020.

213 **Less than 10 percent of Americans** Adam Hughes, "5 Facts About U.S. Political Donations," Pew Research Center, May 17, 2017.

213 **The percentage who give** "Donor Demographics," OpenSecrets .org, accessed March 1, 2021, www.opensecrets.org/elections-overview /donor-demographics.

213 **"If there is one thing"** Lawrence Lessig, *They Don't Represent Us: Reclaiming Our Democracy* (New York: Dey Street Books, 2019), 57.

213 **In 2016, election-related spending** "Cost of Election," OpenSecrets .org, accessed March 1, 2021, www.opensecrets.org/elections -overview/cost-of-election?cycle=2020&display=T&infl=N.

213 **"The currency of votes"** Katherine Gehl and Michael Porter, *The Politics Industry: How Political Innovation Can Break Partisan Gridlock and Save Our Democracy* (Boston: Harvard Business Review Press, 2020), 34.

215 **An analysis the following year** Jennifer Heerwig and Brian J. Mc-Cabe, "Expanding Participation in Municipal Elections: Assessing the Impact of Seattle's Democracy Voucher Program," University of Washington Center for Studies in Demography and Ecology, Feb. 16, 2018.

215 **"It feels like I'm more"** Gene Balk, "Do Seattle's Democracy Vouchers Work? New Analysis Says Yes," *Seattle Times,* Oct. 13, 2017.

215 **"By making realistic"** David Cole, "How to Reverse *Citizens United,*" *Atlantic,* April 2016.

216 **more than 80 percent of congressional** Gehl and Porter, *Politics Industry,* 22.

216 **For example, in 2011** Michael Wines, "Judges Find Wisconsin Redistricting Unfairly Favored Republicans," *New York Times,* Nov. 21, 2016.

216 **the "efficiency gap"** Alvin Chang, "How the Supreme Court Could

Limit Gerrymandering, Explained with a Simple Diagram," *Vox,* Oct. 9, 2017.

217 **However, a number of states** "Redistricting Commissions," *Ballotpedia,* accessed March 1, 2021, ballotpedia.org/Redistricting_commissions.

218 **Katherine Gehl and Michael Porter** Gehl and Porter, *Politics Industry,* 126.

218 **The number of races deemed competitive** Ibid., 129.

219 **In 2018, there were four** Steve Mistler and Domenico Montanaro, "Ranked-Choice Voting Delivers Democrats a House Seat," NPR, Nov. 15, 2018.

220 **Ranked-choice voting has been adopted** "Where Ranked Choice Voting Is Used," FairVote, accessed March 1, 2021, www.fairvote.org /where_is_ranked_choice_voting_used.

220 **A study of seven cities** "Data on Ranked Choice Voting," FairVote, accessed March 1, 2021, www.fairvote.org/data_on_rcv#research_rcv campaigncivility.

220 **In twenty-four states, it can** "States with Initiative or Referendum," *Ballotpedia,* accessed March 1, 2021, ballotpedia.org/States_with_ini tiative_or_referendum.

221 **In one poll, 82 percent** Steven Kull et al., "Voter Anger with Government and the 2016 Election," Voice of the People, Nov. 2016.

222 **Literally three-quarters of Americans** "More Voters Than Ever Want Term Limits for Congress," Rasmussen Reports, Oct. 26, 2016.

223 **"We see that the longer"** Beto O'Rourke, "Congress Needs Term Limits," Medium, May 10, 2018.

223 **In a piece for *The Atlantic*** Mike Gallagher, "How to Salvage Congress," *Atlantic,* Nov. 13, 2018.

224 **legislative machinery innovation commission** Gehl and Porter, *Politics Industry,* 141–45.

225 **many experts believe** Jonathan Allen, "The Case for Earmarks," *Vox,* June 30, 2015; Stacey Vanek Smith and Cardiff Garcia, "The Case for Earmarks," *Planet Money,* NPR, Jan. 16, 2018; James T. Walsh et al., "The Case for Restoring Earmarks," *Washington Post,* Jan. 23, 2018.

226 **The Harvard Law professor Lawrence Lessig** Lessig, *They Don't Represent Us,* 176–78.

226 **a system first developed** "What Is Deliberative Polling?," Stanford Center for Deliberative Democracy.

227 **Countries as diverse as** "A Deliberative Poll on the Icelandic Constitution," Stanford Center for Deliberative Democracy, Nov. 8, 2019; "Mongolia's First National Deliberative Poll on Constitutional Amendments," Stanford Center for Deliberative Democracy, April 29, 2017;

Jane Suiter, "Lessons from Ireland's Recent Referendums: How Deliberation Helps Inform Voters," LSE, Sept. 10, 2018.

227 **Congress does not much look like** Mark Mellman, "Mellman: How Well Does Congress Represent America?," *Hill,* April 23, 2019.

227 **For 42 percent of the retiring members** Gehl and Porter, *Politics Industry,* 26.

227 **Almost half of registered lobbyists** Ibid., 27.

CHAPTER 21: THE RATIONAL PUBLIC

230 **And on TV I saw myself** "Andrew Yang at Iowa Climate Crisis Student Forum," C-SPAN, Dec. 11, 2019.

231 **While we don't have the viewership** "2017 C-SPAN Audience Profile," C-SPAN, 2017.

231 **Lawrence Lessig, a Harvard** Lawrence Lessig, *They Don't Represent Us: Reclaiming Our Democracy* (New York: Dey Street Books, 2019), 72–78.

232 **The scholars Benjamin Page** Benjamin I. Page and Robert Y. Shapiro, *The Rational Public: Fifty Years of Trends in Americans' Policy Preferences* (Chicago: University of Chicago Press, 1992).

232 **From the 1980s on** Lessig, *They Don't Represent Us,* 79.

233 **$20 billion in lost annual** Clara Hendrickson, "Local Journalism in Crisis: Why America Must Revive Its Local Newsrooms," Brookings, Nov. 12, 2019.

234 **Today, NPR generates more than** "2019 Annual Report," NPR, 2019.

234 **PBS, the television equivalent** "Fiscal Year 2020 Operating Budget," Corporation for Public Broadcasting, accessed March 1, 2021, www.cpb.org/aboutcpb/financials/budget.

234 **The majority of parents** PBS Publicity, "For 17th Consecutive Year, Americans Name PBS and Member Stations as Most Trusted Institution," PBS, Feb. 10, 2020.

234 **NPR and PBS consistently rank** Joshua Benton, "Trump Wants to Kill Federal Funding for PBS and NPR (Again); It Won't Happen, but It's Still Damaging," Nieman Lab, March 11, 2019.

235 **Steve and his partners** "The Importance of Local News," Rebuild Local News, accessed March 1, 2021, www.rebuildlocalnews.org /issue-at-a-glance.

236 **The Rebuild Local News plan** "Rebuilding Local News," Rebuild Local News, accessed March 1, 2021, www.rebuildlocalnews.org/our -plan.

238 **Ezra Klein wrote in his book** Ezra Klein, *Why We're Polarized* (New York: Avid Reader, 2020), 150.

239 **It's been referred to by commentators** Jeff Kosseff, *The Twenty-Six Words That Created the Internet* (Ithaca, N.Y.: Cornell University Press, 2019).

240 **In 2020 major politicians on both sides** Bobby Allyn, "As Trump Targets Twitter's Legal Shield, Experts Have a Warning," NPR, May 30, 2020.

240 **the top hundred advertisers** Rishi Iyengar, "Here's How Big Facebook's Ad Business Really Is," CNN Business, July 1, 2020.

242 **Social media networks should establish** Nina Schick, *Deepfakes* (New York: Twelve, 2020), 197.

243 **"advertising funded search engines"** Sergey Brin and Lawrence Page, "The Anatomy of a Large-Scale Hypertextual Web Search Engine," Computer Science Department, Stanford University, 1998.

243 **Here are the user bases**
- Facebook: Mansoor Iqbal, "Facebook Revenue and Usage Statistics (2020)," *Business of Apps,* updated Oct. 30, 2020.
- Instagram: Mansoor Iqbal, "Instagram Revenue and Usage Statistics (2021)," *Business of Apps,* updated Jan. 28, 2021.
- YouTube: Mansoor Iqbal, "YouTube Revenue and Usage Statistics (2020)," *Business of Apps,* updated Nov. 17, 2020.
- Twitter: Mansoor Iqbal, "Twitter Revenue and Usage Statistics (2020)," *Business of Apps,* updated Dec. 5, 2021.
- Snapchat: Mansoor Iqbal, "Snapchat Revenue and Usage Statistics (2020)," *Business of Apps,* updated Feb. 12, 2021.
- TikTok: Mansoor Iqbal, "TikTok Revenue and Usage Statistics (2021)," *Business of Apps,* updated Feb. 10, 2021.

CHAPTER 22: THE RETURN OF FACTS

245 **At the beginning of my presidential campaign** "Democratic Fundraiser in Iowa," C-SPAN, Oct. 14, 2018.

246 **My speech cited several facts** "Available Customized Tables," U.S. Bureau of Labor Statistics, accessed Dec. 20, 2020, data.bls.gov/pdq /SurveyOutputServlet.

246 **A year later I would give** "Our Kids Are Not Alright | Andrew Yang in Iowa (Full Speech)," YouTube, uploaded Nov. 1, 2019, www .youtube.com/watch?v=R9OBK3ss5W4.

247 **Michael Grunwald wrote** Michael Grunwald, "The Relief Deal Blowup: What Are Pelosi and Trump Thinking?," *Politico,* Oct. 7, 2020.

247 **"the sad truth is that the majority"** "Process Determines Outcome: Justin Amash on the Rules That Broke Congress | Andrew Yang," YouTube, uploaded Oct. 19, 2020, www.youtube.com /watch?v=g5aRvUu2daM.

247 **In his book *The Righteous Mind*** Jonathan Haidt, *The Righteous Mind:*

Why Good People Are Divided by Politics and Religion (New York: Vintage Books, 2013), pt. 2.

248 **Haidt argues that** Ibid., 214.

248 **Fox News ratings are typically** Ted Johnson, "Cable News Networks See Big Gains in Viewership During Tumultuous 2020," *Deadline,* Dec. 24, 2020.

248 **more Americans self-identify** Lydia Saad, "Americans' Political Ideology Held Steady in 2020," Gallup, Jan. 11, 2021.

249 **As the author Philip Howard** Philip K. Howard, *Try Common Sense: Replacing the Failed Ideologies of Right and Left* (New York: W. W. Norton, 2019).

249 **Later, a January 2020 survey** "National 2020: Biden and Sanders Battle in Two-Way Race for Democratic Nomination," Emerson College Polling, Jan. 2020.

249 **In the book *Open Versus Closed*** Christopher D. Johnston, Howard G. Lavine, and Christopher M. Federico, *Open Versus Closed: Personality, Identity, and the Politics of Redistribution* (New York: Cambridge University Press, 2017).

250 **We are at pre–Civil War levels** Laura Spinney, "History as a Giant Data Set: How Analysing the Past Could Help Save the Future," *The Guardian,* Nov. 12, 2019.

250 **Goldstone's prior work** Jack A. Goldstone et al., "A Global Model for Forecasting Political Instability," *American Journal of Political Science* 54, no. 1 (Jan. 2010).

250 **To make things dramatically worse** Christopher Ingraham, "There Are More Guns Than People in the United States, According to a New Study of Global Firearm Ownership," *Washington Post,* June 19, 2018.

251 **Political Stress (chart)** Peter Aldhous, "This Scary Statistic Predicts Growing US Political Violence—Whatever Happens on Election Day," *BuzzFeed News,* Oct. 24, 2020.

251 **Jonathan Haidt made a couple** Haidt, *Righteous Mind,* 325–27.

252 **"Democrats and Republicans are now sharply"** Johnston, Lavine, and Federico, *Open Versus Closed.*

252 **Similarly, the political scientists** Marc Hetherington and Jonathan D. Weiler, *Authoritarianism and Polarization in American Politics* (New York: Cambridge University Press, 2009).

252 **Ezra Klein summarized the research** Ezra Klein, *Why We're Polarized* (New York: Avid Reader, 2020), 44.

253 **According to Haidt's research** Haidt, *Righteous Mind,* 324.

254 **Ezra Klein points out** Klein, *Why We're Polarized,* 160–61.

254 **there is a weak relationship** Ibid., 73–74.

254 **"Partisan animosity is one of the few"** Ibid., 77.

256 **Dr. David Eddy, who originated** David M. Eddy, *Assessing Health Practices and Designing Practice Policies: The Explicit Approach* (Philadelphia: American College of Physicians, 1992).

256 **like that we had lost five million** Heather Long, "U.S. Has Lost 5 Million Manufacturing Jobs Since 2000," CNN Business, March 29, 2016.

CHAPTER 23: THE TAX MANDALORIAN

260 **Americans spend 1.7 billion hours** Justin Elliott and Paul Kiel, "Inside TurboTax's 20-Year Fight to Stop Americans from Filing Their Taxes for Free," ProPublica, Oct. 17, 2019.

260 **Other advanced countries** "The Tax Policy Center's Briefing Book: How Could We Improve the Federal Tax System?," Tax Policy Center, updated May 2020.

261 **They are protecting a business** "Form 10-K, Intuit Inc.," U.S. Securities and Exchange Commission, accessed March 1, 2021, s23 .q4cdn.com/935127502/files/doc_financials/quarterly/2019 /q4/817655_007_Print_CLEAN.pdf.

261 **lost revenue from intentional evasion** Clark Merrefield, "Federal Tax Evasion: Why It Matters and Who Does It," Journalist's Resource, Jan. 14, 2020.

262 **In October 2020** Clare Duffy, "Software CEO Robert Brockman Charged in $2 Billion Tax Evasion Case," CNN Business, Oct. 17, 2020.

264 **The author Philip Howard** Philip K. Howard, *The Rule of Nobody: Saving America from Dead Laws and Broken Government* (New York: W. W. Norton, 2015).

264 **"more important and meaningful"** Mark Rockwell, "Mikey Dickerson on Failures and Fixes," *FCW,* March 27, 2015.

265 **"I could never really figure"** Jessie Bur, "Inside the Agency Where You Wish You Worked," *Federal Times,* July 25, 2018.

265 **"We have a much faster"** Ibid.

265 **Still, according to one analysis** Ibid.

266 **In May, while the pandemic** Andrew Yang (@AndrewYang), Twitter, May 17, 2020, 9:30 a.m., twitter.com/AndrewYang/status/126201 2732402028547.

CHAPTER 24: GRACE AND TOLERANCE: HUMANITY IN ACTION

272 **When I was still running** Luis J. Gomez and Zac Amico, "403: CDII. Aunt Tom (Shane Gillis & Mike Figs)," *Real Ass Podcast,* May 30, 2019.

272 **I publicly commented** Andrew Yang (@AndrewYang), "For the record, I do not think he should lose his job. We would benefit from being more forgiving rather than punitive. We are all human," Twitter, Sept. 14, 2019, 1:25 p.m., twitter.com/AndrewYang/status/1172924384 539029511.

272 **we've become unduly punitive** Andrew Yang (@AndrewYang), "I think we have, as a society, become excessively punitive and vindictive concerning people's statements and expressions we disagree with or find offensive. I don't think people should be losing jobs unless it's truly beyond the pale and egregious," Twitter, Sept. 15, 2019, 1:01 a.m.

CHAPTER 25: CHOICES, CHOICES

277 **We are down more than** Jose Maria Barrero, Nicholas Bloom, and Steven J. Davis, "COVID-19 Is Also a Reallocation Shock," National Bureau of Economic Research, May 2020.

277 **Half of restaurants** Joanna Fantozzi, " 'Free-Fall': 10,000 Restaurants Have Closed over the Past Three Months, According to the National Restaurant Association," *Nation's Restaurant News,* Dec. 7, 2020; Bernadette Hogan, Julia Marsh, and Aaron Feis, "Half of NYC Restaurants, Bars May Close for Good due to COVID-19: Audit," *New York Post,* Oct. 1, 2020.

277 **Artificial intelligence could displace** King White, "How Big Is the U.S. Call Center Market Compared to India, Latin America, and the Philippines?," Site Selection Group, July 23, 2018; Jennifer Cheeseman Day and Andrew W. Hait, "Number of Truckers at All-Time High," U.S. Census Bureau, June 6, 2019.

278 **giving rise to higher levels** Bruce Bower, " 'Deaths of Despair' Are Rising. It's Time to Define Despair," *Science News,* Nov. 2, 2020.

279 **"Vince McMahon has been falsely"** James Dator, "Zelina Vega Firing over Her Twitch Is Turning WWE Contracts into a National Labor Issue," *SB Nation,* Nov. 16, 2020.

279 **"It's a similar situation for UFC"** Paul Wachter, "Fists Up: The Most Important Fight in the UFC Is Happening Outside the Octagon," *Ringer,* Jan. 23, 2019.

279 **"NCAA athletes are being pushed"** Azmatullah Hussaini and Jules Lipoff, "Op-Ed: COVID-19 Is Making the NCAA's Exploitation of Student-Athletes Even More Obvious," *Los Angeles Times,* June 23, 2020.

281 **after an *Onion* headline** "American People Hire High-Powered Lobbyist to Push Interests in Congress," *Onion,* Oct. 6, 2010.

281 **I found that almost every member** "States of Play: Battleground Survey on COVID-19," Change Research, May 6, 2020.

283 **Despite the win** Andrew Yang (@AndrewYang), Twitter, Dec. 21, 2020, 9:11 a.m., twitter.com/AndrewYang/status/134102336625 8565121.

CHAPTER 26: THE FORWARD PARTY

286 **55 percent of Americans support** "Poll: Majority of Voters Now Say the Government Should Have a Universal Basic Income Program," *Hill,* Aug. 14, 2020.

286 **more than 80 percent of Americans** "States of Play: Battleground Survey on COVID-19," Change Research, May 6, 2020, changere search.com/post/states-of-play-battleground-wave-4/.

286 **I was staggered by the fact** Paul Davidson, "U.S. May Have Lost Jobs in December for First Time Since April amid COVID-19 Surges," *USA Today,* Jan. 7, 2021.

287 **"Toxic systems compromise"** Ezra Klein, *Why We're Polarized* (New York: Avid Reader, 2020), xv.

287 **More than 60 percent** Jeffrey M. Jones, "Support for Third U.S. Political Party at High Point," Gallup, Feb. 15, 2021.

290 **There are approximately** John Gramlich, "What the 2020 Electorate Looks Like by Party, Race and Ethnicity, Age, Education, and Religion," Pew Research Center, Oct. 26, 2020.

290 **Independents currently outnumber** "Party Affiliation," Gallup, accessed March 1, 2021, news.gallup.com/poll/15370/party-affiliation .aspx.

ABOUT THE AUTHOR

ANDREW YANG was a 2020 Democratic presidential candidate and ran for mayor of New York City in 2021. Named by President Barack Obama as a Presidential Ambassador of Global Entrepreneurship, he is the founder of Humanity Forward and Venture for America. Yang's *New York Times* bestselling book *The War on Normal People* helped introduce the idea of universal basic income into the political mainstream. Yang is a graduate of Brown University, where he earned degrees in economics and political science, and Columbia Law School, where he was an editor of the *Columbia Law Review*. He lives with his family in New York.

ABOUT THE TYPE

This book was set in Bembo, a typeface based on an old-style Roman face that was used for Cardinal Pietro Bembo's tract *De Aetna* in 1495. Bembo was cut by Francesco Griffo (1450–1518) in the early sixteenth century for Italian Renaissance printer and publisher Aldus Manutius (1449–1515). The Lanston Monotype Company of Philadelphia brought the well-proportioned letterforms of Bembo to the United States in the 1930s.